INTEGRITY, COMMUNITY AND INTERPRETATION

Integrity, Community and Interpretation

A Critical Analysis of Ronald Dworkin's Theory of Law

SIMON HONEYBALL
JAMES WALTER

Routledge
Taylor & Francis Group
LONDON AND NEW YORK

First published 1998 by Dartmouth and Ashgate Publishing

Reissued 2018 by Routledge
2 Park Square, Milton Park, Abingdon, Oxon, OX14 4RN
52 Vanderbilt Avenue, New York, NY 10017

Routledge is an imprint of the Taylor & Francis Group, an informa business

A Library of Congress record exists under LC control number:

ISBN 13: 978-1-138-36992-4 (hbk)
ISBN 13: 978-0-429-42834-0 (ebk)

Contents

Preface		**vii**
1	**Early Views and Critics**	**1**
	Legal Positivism	1
	Dworkin's Critique	3
2	**The Interpretive Theory**	**29**
	The Nature of Legal Disagreement	32
	Drawing the Semantic Sting	35
	A Threshold Objection	37
	One Right Answer?	39
	Different Methodology, Same Argument?	43
3	**Conventionalism, Pragmatism and Interpretation**	**47**
	Concepts and Conceptions	47
	Strict and Soft Conventionalism	51
	Fit and Justification	55
	Pragmatism	61
4	**Integrity and Interpretation**	**69**
	Integrity as a Virtue	69
	Integrity and the Chain of Law	75
	Interpretation and Intention	87
	Conclusion	91
5	**Integrity, Liberalism and Community**	**105**
	Integrity and the Moral Legitimacy of Law	105
	True Communities	106
	Liberal Community	113
	Ethical Priority	119
	Conclusion	125
6	**Wider Contexts**	**130**
	Liberalism and Communitarianism	130

Law and Hermeneutics 142
Conclusion 154

Bibliography **165**

Index **171**

Preface

There can be no doubt that Ronald Dworkin is the leading legal philosopher of our time, or that his book *Law's Empire* is the crowning achievement of his work. It is now ten years since that work was published, and its impact and influence has been so extensive that it seemed to us timely to undertake an in-depth analysis of both the book itself and the critical reaction to it. Even so, in a book of this size, much of interest has had to be omitted or treated in a somewhat cursory fashion. Such is the richness of Dworkin's work that it would take a volume several times the size of this one to do full justice to its subject, ranging as it does far beyond legal philosophy simpliciter to many other disciplines in philosophy, literature and law. Nevertheless we trust that the reader will find a survey of the literature on *Law's Empire* between two covers to be fruitful and a stimulus to further exploration of the ideas contained in this remarkable book.

Many people have been of assistance to us in the preparation of this volume, and it would be invidious to mention merely a few. Nevertheless reference to our deep gratitude to Penny Danher for her painstaking preparation of the copy cannot go unsaid. For all types of errors, however, responsibility must rest with us.

Simon Honeyball
James Walter

1 Early Views and Critics

Law's Empire is Dworkin's most important work in legal theory, and likely to remain the only full-length exposition of his views on the nature of law. It was the culmination of the development of his thinking over many years. *Taking Rights Seriously*, published in 1977, is a collection of essays mostly published separately some years previously but which covers much the same ground as the later work. Nevertheless, it would appear to have been Dworkin's intention in publishing these essays as a whole that they be read apiece as representing a coherent exposition of his views at that time. *Taking Rights Seriously* was important and it still is in the sense that it is not only interesting to trace the development of Dworkin's thought in the nine years between it and *Law's Empire* but by examining it we can better understand the later work. Dworkin has not attempted to show how far he has had to abandon some of his earlier positions, and it is indeed difficult at times to determine how much he has done so. This is because, although the thrust of the arguments remain much the same as they were, Dworkin has radically shifted ground in the book not only in the way that he approaches his task, and in the intellectual tools he takes up in order to perform it, but also in that he remoulds his targets of attack whilst retaining them. We shall therefore begin by taking a critical look at the earlier work, at the difficulties to which it gave rise and the criticisms it attracted in order to set out Dworkin's concerns, to paint the problems arising from his earlier views with which he had later to deal, to understand better his solutions and to examine their originality.

Legal Positivism

Dworkin's legal theory has evolved from his views on a theory known as the plain fact view of law or legal positivism. In his early, seminal essay 'The Model of Rules'[1], Dworkin attacks this theory, and specifically the version of it espoused by H L A Hart[2] (his predecessor in the chair of jurisprudence at Oxford) which is widely regarded as being the most influential Anglo-American statement of the positivist thesis. However, Dworkin focuses on various basic tenets that are present in most theories purporting to be positivist. Broadly stated, the position Dworkin wishes to challenge is that which holds that the law of a particular community, and legal obligations arising from it, are discovered by reference to criteria based on the pedigree of special rules used by the community directly or indirectly for the purpose of determining which behaviour will be punished or coerced by the public order. This view emphasises the manner in which rules are adopted rather than their content and that, when these rules run out, the officials in the system (normally judges) must reach beyond the law in order to exercise discretion.[3] The exercise of this discretion creates a new legal right provided it is exercised correctly so as to infer 'pedigree'. Positivism as a theory based on these plain facts thus offers an account of law consisting of imperial, descriptive propositions. It describes the law as it is, not as it ought to be.[4] This does not mean that it is not possible to make meaningful if uncommitted accounts of normative judgements, in that they too can be descriptive. For example, it is possible for a non-vegetarian to tell a vegetarian friend that he should not eat a particular dish if it contains meat, even though this obviously does not apply to himself.[5] The appeal of this version of positivism lies in the fact that it offers the virtues of clarity and simplicity and thus appeals to us as a means of constraining law's apparent complexity. It is also attractive in that it is probably a widely-held view, and one closest to the popular vision of law.

In *The Concept of Law* Hart draws an important distinction between two types of rules he labels primary and secondary rules. Primary rules are those that impose obligations or grant rights to members of the community, whereas secondary rules are those that deal with the application and enactment of the primary rules.[6] Hart draws a further distinction between rules and orders on the basis that rules possess normative force. One is under an obligation, not just obliged, to do as a rule provides, and thus its authority is not simply dependent upon the physical power of its author as in the case of a gunman staging a bank robbery. Instead Hart distinguishes between two ways in which a rule may gain authority. It may do so through its acceptance by the community or through its validity in being enacted in accordance with a secondary rule. Hart argues that there must be a fundamental secondary rule, which he calls the rule of recognition, that acts as a criterion of the validity of all rules in the system, both primary and secondary. Once this is established there exists a distinct set of legal rules and hence law itself. This fundamental rule will be the only rule in the system whose binding force will be dependent solely on its acceptance as it cannot derive its validity from other secondary rules in that it gives validity to them, and thus to determine its nature we must observe the behaviour of the relevant community citizens, and most importantly the practice of its officials.

By locating the determination of the nature of the rule of recognition in the practice of officials in a system Hart adopted a decidedly linguistic approach in consructing his concept of law. As the rule of recognition is defined by reference to the shared practice of officials, to determine if a particular standard is a law it is necessary to look to the shared meaning that the officials have of law. In cases in which there are no shared meanings, that is to say where it is difficult to say what the law is on any particular point, officials are forced to exercise their discretion. Central to Hart's theory then is the need to cure the perceived defect of uncertainty arising from the exercise of this discretion within the law. It is to this that Dworkin devotes his attack by arguing that Hart's resultant account of the law is too simplistic.

Dworkin's Critique

The Role of Principles in Legal Reasoning

Dworkin's thesis in 'The Model of Rules I' is that where lawyers reason or argue about legal obligations and rights, particularly in hard cases,[7] they have recourse to standards that do not function as rules but operate differently as principles, policies and other sorts of standards.[8] Positivism, as Dworkin pictures it here, is a system built on the contention that the law consists solely of rules. Dworkin's claim is that, once we recognise that this is not the case, positivism's central notion that there is a single criterion of legal validity is inadequate as an explanation of the operation of these non-rule standards. Dworkin's immediate objective is therefore to distinguish these standards, which he refers to generically as principles, from rules. In order to establish this, Dworkin highlights decisions in which the courts have applied legal principles in preference to rules. The main example used is that of *Riggs v. Palmer*,[9] in which the court had to decide whether a murderer could inherit under his victim's will. The court noted that the "statutes regulating the making, proof and effect of wills, and the devolution of property, if literally construed ... give this property to the murderer".[10] However it also noticed that all laws including contracts "may be controlled in their operation and effect by general, fundamental maxims of the common law".[11] The court then proceeded to apply the old maxim, or principle, that no man shall profit from his own wrong and thus the murderer did not receive his inheritence. Dworkin conducts a similar analysis of *Henningsen v. Bloomfield Motors Inc.*[12] in which, despite the plaintiff's inability to provide any authority for his argument, the court agreed with his case and made a number of references to general principles in order to justify its decision.[13]

The difference between rules and principles for Dworkin is a logical one, for whereas rules apply in an all or nothing fashion[14] principles state a reason that argues in one direction that does necessitate a particular decision either way. Rules can of course be subject to exceptions but, if the facts they stipulate exist, provided the rule is valid it will supply the answer to the case in doubt. If the rule is not pertinent to the facts it will contribute nothing to the outcome. This first distinction between rules and principles entails another. This is that principles, unlike rules, possess a dimension of weight. Where principles are in conflict the dispute is resolved by taking into account the relative weight of each, and this judgement will often be controversial. Rules lack this dimension, for where two rules are in conflict one of them must be invalid.

These differences are problematic for positivists. A difficulty is that, whilst after a case is decided we can say that it stands as authority for a particular rule, in cases such as *Riggs* and *Henningsen* the rule does not exist prior to the case, and the courts appear to cite principles as being the justification to adopt and imply new rules. Therefore, positivists must account for the role of principles in legal reasoning. There are two possible lines that might be taken, each reflecting a different conception of the position of legal principles.[15] Firstly, they could deny that principles can be binding in the way that legal rules are, and state that in cases such as *Riggs* and *Henningsen* the courts reach beyond the law to extra-legal principles they are free to apply if they so wish. Alternatively, they could treat legal principles in the same way as legal rules and say that accordingly they must be taken into account in cases involving legal obligation.[16] These two options may initially appear to be based simply on a linguistic distinction as to how we would define 'law'. However, this would be to miss an important point about the nature of legal standards. For if we were to adopt the second line of defence we would hold that the judge had acted incorrectly were he not to consider principles in a situation where they were relevant. This will not however be the case were we to adopt the first defence, and in cases such as *Riggs v. Palmer* we must assert that the decision was an act of judicial legislation applied *ex post facto*. Which view we take has implications of a profound and theoretical nature as to how we view the law and in particular the judicial function.

Judicial Discretion and the Two Defences

Before we examine Dworkin's discussion of the two defences in more detail, we must return briefly to examine his views of judicial discretion which informs it.

Dworkin's argument is based on the idea that we use the term 'discretion' in three different senses depending on context.[17] He argues that sometimes we use 'discretion', in a weak sense, which is to say when we mean that the standards that an official must apply require the use of judgement. This would be the case if, for example, an army sergeant were instructed to select his five most experienced men, it being unclear who these were. We also use 'discretion' in a different weak sense to mean that an official has final authority to make a decision and that this cannot be reviewed or reversed as with unappealable jurisdiction or final courts in a judicial hierarchy. Sometimes however we use 'discretion' in a third and stronger sense. Here we mean not that the official must exercise judgement, or that no-one will review that exercise or judgement, but that on some issue "he is simply not bound by the authority in question".[18] This would be the case were the sergeant to be told to select any five men he would like to. It is however important to realise that this third sense of discretion does not amount to licence, for decisions made under a strong discretion can be subjected to criticism on the basis of poor judgement.

The distinction between the first weak sense of discretion, or judgement, and the strong sense of discretion, attracted trenchant criticism. Much of this was due to Dworkin's characterisation of the difference between the two as arising on the basis of whether or not the standard on which the judgement is required has been furnished. The difficulty with drawing the distinction on this basis is that by arguing that strong discretion arises where the authority has not furnished a standard, strong discretion appears to arise simply because there is no pedigree test identifying the standards that the judge must apply. This would clearly bind us to the conclusion that positivists must adopt strong discretion in hard cases, or cases about which lawyers may reasonably disagree, and hence would leave Dworkin open to the charge of circularity. For this reason some critics have claimed that Dworkin cannot maintain his sharp distinction between the weak and strong sense of discretion. However this is to misrepresent Dworkin's argument. The argument of the critics here amounts to the claim that the existence of borderline cases negates the distinction, and this simply does not follow. The existence of borderline cases actually entails that there be a distinction in the first place, or otherwise no borderline could arise.[19]

Dworkin's problem here arises from an unfortunate use of language, for in referring to standards furnished by authorities it seems that he is thinking about a pedigree test. However it is clear from his own examples that not all cases of weak discretion entail that there is a standard furnished by authority. Whether a hovercraft is a boat or an aircraft need not be determined by any standard set by authority, which may be entirely silent on a point.[20]

Dworkin argues that positivists, at least on occasion, use 'discretion' in the strong sense of the word. Otherwise if they simply meant to apply the first sense of discretion requiring judgement we would be left with a tautology that where no clear rule covers a case judgement must be exercised. The positivists speak as if they their doctrine of discretion "is an insight rather than a tautology", and thus as if it has a bearing on the treatment of principles.[21] As an illustration Dworkin cites Hart as an example of a positivist who views principles as extra-legal standards and thus requires that judges possess a strong sense of discretion in order to apply these standards. We are therefore led to the first defence of the positivists which is premised on the claim that judges may exercise discretion in its stronger sense.[22]

Dworkin on the First Defence Dworkin's argument is this. Where a judge exercises strong discretion he is effectively acting as a legislator in that he is creating new law. He is as unconstrained in coming to his decision as the legislator is in passing legislation. In order to justify the application of principles as extra-legal standards in these cases positivists could claim that principles cannot be binding, and thus that the situation is not analogous to that of legislation. However, as Dworkin points out, there is nothing in the logical character of the principle that would lead us to this conclusion.[23] In cases such as *Henningsen* we expect the judges to take the relevant principles into account, and indeed regard it as their duty to do so. This clearly indicates that principles may be of a binding nature. Positivists could therefore argue that, although it is true that some principles are indeed binding in that they must be taken into account where relevant, they cannot *determine* a particular result. This does not seem to solve the positivists' dilemma however, for it merely reaffirms the distinction between rules and principles, as by their nature principles may only incline a decision one way (but which are binding in that the judges may be under an obligation to take them into account) and are not invalidated should they lose out.[24] Given this, positivists may reply that precisely because the weight and authority of principles is congenitally controversial, they cannot count as law. This judgement of weight is however a case of the exercise of weak, as opposed to strong discretion precisely because it is application of mere judgement, and as a result the judgement required for this will fall within the ambit of the law.

For Dworkin, the main difficulty with this defence of the positivists' position lies in the fact that if they are correct as to the existence of an ultimate test of legal validity, such as Hart's rule of recognition, then it follows that principles are not binding law.[25] But at the same time, they require that at least some principles count as law, and as a result are binding on judges, for otherwise very few rules could be said to be binding on them either. This is because the higher courts will not often reject established rules, and if the courts have discretion to do this then no rule can be said to be safe. The positivists must therefore argue that there are binding standards that determine when an established rule may be overturned. In order to establish this it would first be necessary, though not sufficient, that there exists some principle that justifies the change. For example, in *Riggs v. Palmer* this was the principle that no man shall profit from his own wrong. This alone will not suffice, for if just any principle could do this, once again no rule could be said to be sage. Therefore it is necessary that the judge in such a case takes account of "some important standards that argue against departures from established docrtine".[26] These will again largely consist of principles, as well as doctrines such as that of precedent.[27] Therefore, when we say that a particular rule is binding, we imply that is so because it is positively supported by principles that the court must take into account and that these 'outweigh' the principles arguing the other way. Otherwise the judge will imply that any change would be condemned by the conservative principles and doctrines that argue against changes from the established rules. Often it will be the case that both are implied for these conservative principles "are usually not powerful enough to save a common law rule or an aging statute that is entirely unsupported by substantive principles the court is bound to respect".[28] Of course this does not solve the dilemma for positivists relying on the first defence as this treats a body of rules and policies as being law in the same sense as rules.

The first defence has not proved to be one relied on most heavily by positivists. In fact, Dworkin claims only Professor Jospeh Raz appears to be a full adherent to it.[29] Raz's basic contention is that no standard may be called a law unless it meets what he terms the 'sources test', which is his version of the ultimate criterion of legal validity. Whilst he accepts that judges often appeal to principles not established by prior legislation, and that judges characteristically treat these principles as being grounded in political morality and not social fact, for that very reason we would deny them the status of law, and instead view them as extra-legal standards. In order to set out Raz's arguments on the first defence we shall concentrate on his views as they are expressed in his article 'Legal Principles and the Limits of Law',[30] and his subsequent postscript to this article.

In the first section of his article Professor Raz constructs his argument around the claim that every theory about the logical types of law presupposes a doctrine of the individuation of laws.[31] An examination of this underlying doctrine is then a necessary component of any critique of a theory of law, and Raz applies his insight in an attempt to reveal the flaws in Dworkin's distinction between rules and principles. Raz thus focuses his argument on the question of which principle of the individuation of laws we would choose to adopt. He claims that, although we could construct a principle of individuation such that each rule would contain all its qualifications, and as a result no rules would conflict, nevertheless this would not be desirable. To do so would entail the construction of a few rules of enormous complexity, each containing a great deal of repetition. It would also distort the function of adopting a principle of individuation which should be used in order for us to refer separately to the different sections of our legal system.

Raz instead proposes that we should adopt a principle of individuation whereby individual rules are kept to a more manageable size[32] as this better reflects the way in which lawyers think of the law, and additionally illuminates the connections between various laws. By adopting this principle we would have a larger body of laws that "interact with one another, modifying and qualifying each other".[33] The conclusion for Raz that with such a principle of individuation rules and principles may conflict with one another. This conclusion should however be rejected. The difficulty with this argument is that he appears to be undecided whether to use his principle of individuation as a strategy of exposition, or as a method for answering the problem of what law is. As a result, in Dworkin's view, he claims too much when he views this question of being of vital importance to any theory of law. Where it is instead treated as a strategy of exposition, then Raz fails to adequately justify his own preferred principle of individuation over the numerous other potential strategies.[34] This seems to be the result of Raz's somewhat unusual notion of conflict. He argues that where there are only a few large rules no conflicts will arise between them, but that where we instead have more rules of a manageable size conflicts will occur. As Dworkin points out, this argument seems to rest on a "bizarre notion of what a conflict is".[35] Raz clearly views rules that provide exceptions as being in conflict with the rules that they refer to. However in that situation there is clearly no question of a judge having to choose between the two rules, as both will be applied where they are relevant, and thus no conflict will arise. Indeed, it is hard to see how an exception to a rule can ever be converted into a conflicting rule simply through the process of individuation, for that merely deals with the form in which a rule is expressed, and not with the content of the rule itself.[36]

Raz's argument proceeds from this to a comparison of rules and principles in conflict. We have seen that Dworkin argues that where two rules are in conflict one will always prevail over the other. By contrast he argues that should two principles come into conflict consequentialist arguments would come into consideration, and thus in different situations the outcome may vary. However, Raz refuses to accept that this distinction is a logical one. Instead he points to the situation in which a rule and a principle conflict, as here the two standards will be treated alike. Raz concludes that the distinction cannot be grounded in logic but must instead be the result of legal policy. This however seems to rest on a misreading of Dworkin's distinction. For Dworkin, rules "often represent a kind of compromise amongst competing principles",[37] according to the weight prescribed to them by the court. Thus it would be incorrect to regard a rule as in conflict with a given principle, for in fact the relationship is more subtle, and is dependent on the weight given to the principle in comparison to its competitor. Rules can thus be said to reflect principles, rather than to conflict with them.[38]

The final element of this section of Raz's argument looks at the nature of legal principles in order to cast doubt on Dworkin's definition of them. Raz refers to the rule that a will is invalid unless signed by two witnesses. He argues that this is not a norm as it will affect the reasons for action only indirectly, by qualifying the meaning or application of laws that are norms. Raz argues that such a rule is often known as a principle, especially where it governs a wide field of law. However, in that it is not a norm, it falls outside Dworkin's definition of principles.[39] Dworkin is solely concerned with principles of obligation, and as a consequence not all legal principles fall within his definition. It is doubtful that the term 'principles' is in fact used in a sense that Raz describes. It certainly seems ill-suited to the example given here. In any event, the issue is not an important one for Dworkin, who himself describes the difference between rules and principles as sometimes "almost a matter of form along".[40] Raz's argument seems to be an attempt to widen the category or principles, but unconvincingly.

In the second section of his article, Professor Raz defends positivist theories against Dworkin's claim that the existence of legal principles undermines their view that there is an ultimate criterion of legal validity.[41] As we have seen, Raz adopts the first line of defence suggested by Dworkin that argues that principles are extra-legal standards. However, he adds a gloss to this by taking the position that judges do have a duty to consider certain principles that are determined by 'judicial custom' and consequently consistent with a criterion of validity. This builds on a possibility that Dworkin discussed in relation to the other defence of positivism.

Raz introduces this argument with a discussion of Dworkin's theory of judicial discretion. Raz argues that if courts cannot exercise strong discretion then "all reasons, rules, and principles which they are entitled to rely on are part of the law".[42] If this is so, and we also accept that the courts are entitled to rely "on every reason which is endorsed by part of the community for some purpose or other"[43] then it follows that the notion of a criterion of validity will be defeated to the extent that it claims to distinguish between legal and non-legal social standards. If however courts do possess strong discretion, in those cases in which they are entitled to exercise it they will be acting on extra-legal standards. In this situation the criterion of validity will be of use in order to distinguish these standards from legal ones. Thus Raz tends to consider the question of whether judges do ever have strong discretion. For Raz, Dworkin's argument against the existence of strong discretion rests on his claims for the existence of legally binding principles. However, Raz argues that their existence "has never been denied by anyone, least of all by the positivists".[44] Dworkin's mistake is in assuming that the positivists use the term 'rules' in the same sense that he does. For example, Hart used the word to refer to "rules, principles, or any other type of law (whether legal or social)".[45] Raz concludes that if Dworkin is to make his case against strong discretion, then he must show that a set of principles will always dictate the result in a case, and this "he does not even try to establish".[46]

Raz then seeks to explain the various sources of strong discretion in a legal system. He argues that it can arise through vagueness in the principles themselves, through the imprecision that arises in ascribing weight to principles, and finally in principles which actually guide the exercise of discretion by stipulating what type of goals and values the judge may consider. This particular type of principle, which Raz terms 'principles of discretion',[47] rather than negating strong discretion actually presupposes its existence and guides it.[48] He therefore concludes that the existence of some principles depends on the existence of strong discretion and that consequently we must reject Dworkin's argument for the absence of this degree of discretion. Unfortunately this argument seems to rest on a comprehensive misunderstanding in Dworkin's doctrine of discretion. Throughout his argument Raz seemingly confuses Dworkin's first weak sense of discretion with the stronger sense.[49] For example, Raz's claim that judges possess strong discretion, on the basis that Dworkin fails to show that a sense of principles always dictates the result in a given case, misses the point that even when judges disagree as to the relevant principle in a particular case, they will treat the issue as one of judicial responsibility.[50] Thus they will exercise discretion in the first weak sense in that they have to apply judgement in reaching their decisions according to certain standards, and they will not have to resort to the application of extra-legal standards. Raz makes a similar error in discussing the various ways in which discretion may arise. Here, all of his examples are examples of the exercise of weak, not strong, discretion. For example, 'principles of discretion' are those that require the exercise of judgement, for as Raz himself points out, they seek to direct and guide judges to their decision. Raz's argument here does not then pose a serious threat to Dworkin's attack on positivism.

The final argument of Raz's discussed here focuses on the possibility of there being a criterion of identity. We have already seen that Dworkin's main argument against this possibility was based on the idea that Hart's sharp distinction between the acceptance and validity of rules would not hold for principles with their dimension of weight. This was so because if we were asked to argue for the existence of a given legal principle we would cite any institutional support it may have received, but in so doing we would speak as much to its acceptance as to its validity. Raz rejects this proposition because he claims that the notions of weight and institutional support are not logically related concepts. After all, it is possible that a principle might have been referred to frequently by the courts as binding, but have little weight.[51] Raz does however accept that some legal principles are indeed law because of judicial acceptance and that in consequence some modification is necessary to Hart's criterion of identity. However, he argues, in asserting that once we admit this to be the case we fail to distinguish law from other social norms, Dworkin claims too much,[52] for although social customs may be binding, they must first pass certain tests. If these tests are not set out in a statute or other law they will be identified by the rule of recognition. Thus general community customs can be captured by a criterion of validity. Principles evolved by the courts will become binding through what Raz terms 'judicial custom'. They are part of the law because they are accepted by the courts and not because they are validated by the rule of recognition. Raz modifies Hart's criterion of identity so that a legal system will consist of "all the customary rules and principles of the law enforcing agencies and all the laws recognised by them".[53] Thus in this way Raz seeks to avoid the difficulties that we have seen Dworkin identify in relation to Hart's concept of customary law. Raz's argument therefore is that, in order to understand the role of principles in legal reasoning, we need an adequate explanation of the concept of the customary norm, and that nevertheless Hart has provided such an explanation notwithstanding the need to make some adjustments to it.[54]

The problem with linking principles to the notion of judicial custom is that the particular characteristics of principles are often unamenable to the idea of custom. Dworkin points out that, at least as to their weight, the great bulk of the principles and policies judges cite are controversial and thus unsuited to a notion that looks to judicial consensus. Furthermore, many appeals to principles are to those that have yet to be the subject of any established judicial practice, and hence would not be covered by judicial custom.[56] Raz's notion would therefore uncover few of the principles that judges take into account in practice. This leads to the conclusion that for Raz to be correct that only those principles identified by judicial custom are legally binding, his argument that judges have no duty to consider other principles must be particularly ineffective. This is a challenge that he cannot meet.

Raz added a new postscript to his original article.[57] The object of this was to argue that, whilst the defence of positivism set out above remained sound, it was no longer relevant to an assessment of Dworkin's then current views on law and positivism, and Raz found it difficult "to fit the old arguments into the framework of the new theory" as expounded in a later article called 'Hard Cases' published in 1975.[58] The new approach, as Raz saw it, stemmed from the fact that in 'Hard Cases' Dworkin used the term 'principle' to refer to any standard establishing a right, which could clearly embrace rules too. The main part of this article introduces Hercules, the ideal judge, and describes how he decides cases according to the institutional morality of the law. However, Dworkin denies that he altered the 'weaponry' of his earlier argument, but maintains that Raz's argument is in fact unsound.[59]

In discussing Raz's arguments here we shall concentrate on his comments about discretion as these are the most important part of his attack. Raz focuses on the idea that "the discretion allowed in most legal systems is much in excess of that required to deal with the inevitable indeterminacy of any legal system".[60] Raz points to the existence of rules which are deliberately inconclusive and also to the discretion given to the courts to change a determined and clear law.[61] This he seems to regard as decisive evidence of the existence of discretion, and evidence that arguments about discretion do not entirely depend on the fate of the indeterminacy thesis, which is to say, the idea that there are legal statements which are neither true nor false because law is 'gappy'. This is significant for Raz since he claims that the arguments in 'The Model of Rules I' are "essentially arguments against indeterminacy only".[62] However, once again Raz confuses Dworkin's three senses of discretion. Laws that deliberately create discretion lead only to the first weak sense of discretion in that judgements according to given standards need to be exercised. More importantly, the power of the courts to change established law is expressly dealt with by Dworkin's second weak sense of discretion. Additionally, we have seen that Dworkin offers a detailed argument in 'The Model of Rules I' as to the conditions necessary for such a change in which he points out that without the existence of binding principles no rule can be said to be safe from such change.[63]

In detailing the supposed shift in Dworkin's attack on positivism, Raz argues that Dworkin's later arguments "are addressed against discretion regardless of whether its source is indeterminacy or a power to change the law".[64] We have already cast doubt on whether this actually represents any change in emphasis in Dworkin's arguments. However, Raz seems to hold a mistaken view of the purpose of some of these later arguments. Dworkin's arguments in 'The Model of Rules I' are largely directed at the proposition that strong discretion is not exercised by the courts, but that the positivists cannot capture the existence of principles if judges have only a weak discretion. Some of the subsequent arguments Raz cites[65] do indeed go beyond this,[66] but to show why strong discretion is undesirable. These are them complementary to the arguments in 'The Model of Rules I'. The other arguments are concerned with the descriptive deficiencies of positivism, and as such they develop points made in 'The Model of Rules I'. Again this is consistent with the earlier arguments.

Dworkin on the Second Defence We must now consider what the consequences for positivism would be if we were to adopt the second description of principles, and consequently argue that they are binding in the same way as legal rules.[67] This has proved to be the more popular of the two defences.[68] This necessitates a consideration as to whether the positivists' tenet that law can be identified by a criterion of legal validity such as Hart's rule of recognition would need to be abandoned. This question arises in Dworkin's view because, whereas rules are identified by a test of pedigree, this is not the case with principles as by definition their authority and weight are inherently controversial. Whilst it is indeed true that if challenged we would argue for the existence of a particular principle by citing any cases in which it had featured, or any statute that seemed to exemplify it, nevertheless we would be unable to construct any formula to determine when a principle becomes a legal one. For in arguing for the existence of a particular principle we are "grappling with a whole set of shifting, developing and interacting standards".[69] Much of the problem originates from the fact that Hart's sharp distinction between acceptance and validity does not hold in the case of principles. When we cite institutional support in arguing for the existence of a principle we refer as much to acceptance of the principle as to its validity. Indeed the concept of validity seems itself to be inappropriate in a discussion of principles as "validity is an all or nothing concept, appropriate for rules, but inconsistent with a principle's dimension of weight".[70]

If we were asked to defend a particular doctrine of precedent that we have used, as well as citing the practice of others using that doctrine, we would cite other general principles that we believe supported it. This, Dworkin says, introduces a "note of validity into the chord of acceptance".[71] However, this passage of support would not finally lead us to an ultimate principle resting solely on acceptance but instead to the conclusion that at this level- of abstraction our principles "rather hang together than link together".[72] It would appear then that principles lack a direct enough contact with the official acts of legal institutions to enable them to be captured by an ultimate criterion of legal validity.

Another possibility is that we might be able to account for principles on the basis that they are analogous to customary rules. Hart allowed that the ultimate criterion of legal validity must stipulate that some custom was to count as law prior to its recognition by the courts.[73] However, this raises difficulties for Hart which he did not face in that he failed to set out the criteria necessary to recognise a custom as a legal one. If Hart's intention, which is unlikely, was simply that those rules regarded as morally binding were sufficient, then no distinction is made between moral customary rules and legal ones, and of course not all of a community's customary moral obligations are enforced at law. If instead only those rules regarded as legally binding will suffice, then, Dworkin says, "the whole point of the master rule is undercut", at least for this class of rules, for the master rule is meant to provide a test for determining social rules of law "other than by measuring their acceptance".[74] To allow that some rules, other than the rule of recognition, can be binding through their acceptance, is to chip away at Hart's neat distinction between acceptance and validity. All of this suggests of course that Hart would be unlikely to widen the spread of this damage by seeking to bring principles within the ambit of customary law. Therefore Dworkin's conclusion is that we cannot modify the rule of recognition so as to capture principles as well as rules. We cannot formulate a test of pedigree in order to relate principles to legislative acts, nor can we adopt Hart's concept of customary law so as to embrace principles. One final possibility is that the principles themselves could in some way constitute the rule of recognition. However Dworkin is quick to dismiss this as tautologous, for it would simply lead us to the claim that law is the law.[75]

Broadly speaking, there have been two responses to the second defence by positivists. We shall examine them by concentrating on responses put forward by two theorists who best reflect positivist approaches here. Firstly we will look at Neil MacCormick's arguments in his book *Legal Reasoning and Legal Theory*[76] and in particular in its title chapter[77] in which Professor MacCormick seeks to incorporate Dworkin's insight into the role of principles in legal reasoning within a positivist framework. He accepts the importance of principles within legal reasoning and the need for a clear conceptual distinction between rules and principles, but argues that Dworkin's account does not succeed in providing this. Instead, MacCormick argues that this is best achieved by recognising the possibility of reconciling the existence of legal principles with that of an ultimate criterion of identity. MacCormick also considers Dworkin's theory of discretion and is led to argue that it should be rejected as neither strong nor weak discretion accurately describes the restraints placed on judicial activity. MacCormick is not concerned simply to dismiss criticisms of positivism. He instead constructs his own theory that builds on Dworkin's insight but retains the positivist framework. We shall also consider the arguments put forward by Jules Coleman in his article 'Negative and Positive Positivism'.[78]. With MacCormick, Professor Coleman also argues that Dworkin is correct to identify the controversial nature of some legal reasoning, but he argues that there is a form of positivism based around conventions that incorporates this view, and at the same time avoids Dworkin's objections to positivism. This position has come to be known by Dworkin as soft conventionalism.

MacCormick first considers Dworkin's "destructive arguments".[79] His argument here is that whilst Dworkin is correct in identifying the important role of principles in legal argument, his theory is inadequate as a means of explaining that role. We have seen that one distinction Dworkin draws between rules and principles is that whereas rules have an all or nothing quality, principles possess a dimension of weight, and hence two principles may compete with each other without either being invalidated.

MacCormick argues that this is an exaggeration on the basis that the reason behind argument by analogy is that rules can contribute to cases to which they are not of direct relevance. It is also possible for such analogies to compete with one another without the losing analogy being invalidated. MacCormick also points out that the notion of 'weight' is a misleading one when applied to principles, for it appeals to a quality of material objects that is objectively measurable, whereas this is not the case with principles. He also makes the converse point that in problems of interpretation rules effectively compete with principles and are not invalidated should they lose out. For example, in the *Anisminic* case[80] the House of Lords construed the relevant statute narrowly, for reasons of principle. This did not imply the invalidity of the relevant section but merely determined the ambit of the rule within a given context. MacCormick therefore argues that we must seek an alternative to Dworkin's account if we are to achieve the clear conceptual distinction between rules and principles that is required.

We can however criticise this argument on the same grounds that we rejected Raz's arguments with regard to the rule - principle distinction. For instance, MacCormick's chosen example of the *Anisminic* case is clearly one in which principles of interpretation are competing in order to determine the ambit of the rule in that context. By deciding to construe the statute narrowly the House of Lords clearly attributed greater 'weight' to the principle of interpretation which advocated such an approach. The section was not disregarded or even amended in their view. The judges addressed themselves to the question of what the section meant in a particular context. This appears to be a more satisfactory explanation of the court's process of reasoning than that given by MacCormick.

The claim that Dworkin's account cannot explain the role in legal reasoning of arguments by analogy requires closer examination. Throughout, *Legal Reasoning and Legal Theory* one of MacCormick's concerns is to show the extent to which the judiciary applies arguments by analogy. Such arguments are also dealt with by Dworkin in 'Hard Cases' in which he argues that a past decision exerts "a gravitational force on later decisions even when these later decisions lie outside its particular orbit".[81] In some cases, all the judges may agree as to the relevant precedents but disagree as to what rule or principle these precedents should be taken as establishing. Thus in adjudication "the arguments *for* a particular rule may be more important than the argument *from* that rule to the particular case".[82] Judges then are agreed that past decisions have gravitational force even though they will disagree as to what that force is. Dworkin concludes that the doctrine of fairness offers the only adequate account for practice of precedent and that gravitational force will be limited to the extension of the argument, a principle necessary to justify those decisions. In this way we capture the full practice of precedent which goes beyond simply looking at the enactment force of legislation, to look at the fairness of treating like cases alike. This account appears to be consistent with MacCormick's view of argument by analogy, but Dworkin's emphasis here is firmly on the moral reasons that lie behind the use of these arguments, examining the interaction of fairness and legal principles.[83]

MacCormick's view of the role of legal principles differs from Dworkin's. He argues that the better view is that principles are "relatively general norms which are conceived of as 'rationalising' rules or sets of rules".[84] We know which rules are to be rationalised because of our criterion of legal identity. There is then an indirect relationship between the principles of law and the criterion of legal validity. Rules are rules of law by virtue of their pedigree and principles are principles of law because of their function in relation to those rules. In this way MacCormick argues that the existence of legal principles can be reconciled with that of an ultimate criterion of legal identity, and hence Dworkin's argument to the contrary must be rejected.

This might appear to suggest that the law is not after all value-free. However that in itself is not inconsistent with positivism for in recognising that this is the case, one "does not have in any sense to share in or endorse these values ... in order to know that law exists, or what law exists".[85] MacCormick accepts that the law must have practical, and therefore moral, virtue, and this is one of the fundamental arguments in *Legal Reasoning and Legal Theory*. He argues that the application of principles in the law is one method of making these underlying values explicit. However, this process "is a matter of making sense of law, as much as of finding the sense which is. already there".[86] In this way MacCormick seeks to maintain the positivist separation of law and morality.

It would therefore be wrong to assert that principles that are legal are so because they are determined by the ultimate criterion of legal identity. Indeed there may be more than one set of normative generalisations that can be advanced to rationalise the rules governing a specific area of law. However, over time the governing principles will become settled as they represent more or less widely-received viewpoints. We might argue at this point that MacCormick is trapped in a logical circle, for whilst those principles that are legal are determined by the rules of law, at the same time these rules are qualified in the light of, and fully understandable only by reference to, the principles that are legal. MacCormick's answer to this apparently serious problem is to view the circularity as a reflection of the dynamic process of the law as it seeks to furnish answers to new problems as they arise, whilst continuously seeking to update previous decisions to bring them into line with current thinking. Thus, far from being vicious, the circle is required if our account is to be accurate.

MacCormick's description of the role of legal principles initially appears to be powerful and persuasive. It reconciles the existence of principles with an ultimate criterion of legal identity, which we have seen Dworkin deny is possible. Further it would seem that Dworkin has never repudiated this argument.[87]

What, then, might Dworkin's reply be? It seems that the main difficulty with MacCormick's argument is its failure to give any precise test for identifying principles as legal. Instead they are recognised because of their function in relation to the rules of law identified by the criterion of validity. But, as MacCormick freely admits, more than one set of principles may be advanced in this way, and thus they only become settled over time. This disjunction between the legal roles of principles arises because of the positivists' insistence on the separation of law and morality. By arguing that the legal principles are those that make sense of the law, MacCormick manages to maintain this distinction.[88] However, difficulty persists when we turn to the consideration of how this would actually operate in a hard case. The judge will be able to identify the relevant rule, and any principles that he must take into account, but his criterion of legal identity will give him no guidance as to what the application of the rule should be, for in such cases there will be no official practice to guide him. MacCormick is faced with two options in this situation.[89] He could argue that the judge may simply exercise discretion to select the 'best' justification of the law. This however leads MacCormick towards a pragmatic position whereby the judge can act as he desires unconstrained by precedent. Clearly, this would not fit with MacCormick's theory, with its emphasis on judicial constraints. Alternatively, therefore, he could argue that we should look for a more abstract example of official practice by which to determine the result. This however appears to lead to the position known as soft conventionalism, which we consider in the section on Professor Coleman,[90] and which also seems to lack the clarity which is one of the main virtues of a system based around a criterion of identity. Therefore MacCormick's description of the role of principles is problematic.

MacCormick also puts forward a critique of Dworkin's theory of discretion and the claim that underlines that theory, the one-right-answer thesis. MacCormick argues that this thesis cannot hold for the disagreements we find in hard cases. Furthermore, he argues that whilst judges do not have strong discretion in hard cases, they cannot be said as a result to be exercising weak discretion with all that is implied in the notion of weakness.

MacCormick's concern in the first part of his argument is therefore with Dworkin's contention that the very fact that reasonable people may genuinely disagree as to the right answer in a given case reveals that there must in principle be a right answer even though we may not be able to discover it in practice. MacCormick contends that, whilst the argument from genuineness of disagreement is a forceful one, it is also false because it fails to account for an ambiguity within the idea of disagreement. This is that disagreements may be over both conflicts of opinion as to speculative questions on the one hand, and conflicts relating to projects for practical action on the other. MacCormick's thesis is that whilst Dworkin's one-right-answer thesis holds for conflicts of opinion as to speculative questions, it will not suffice where the conflict relates to a project for practical action. In hard cases it will often be the latter form of conflict that arises. This argument is perhaps best understood through the use of examples. For instance, if we were to genuinely disagree as to the distance between Exeter and London, this would be an example of a speculative disagreement for although our conflict is genuine we can in principle achieve an objectively correct result, or right answer. If however our disagreement were instead to be about which painting we should buy to hang in our house the conflict would be of a different nature. One of us may prefer impressionist works whilst the other favours pre-Raphaelite styles. Here, even after we have resolved the speculative disagreements as to the order of our preferences, we will still be faced with the practical problem of which painting to buy, given our differing aesthetic judgements. This disagreement is a genuine one, but it is also one that appears to lack a right answer.[91]

Many of the disagreements we are faced with in the law are analogous to this in that they deal with the questions of what it is best, all things considered, to do. These are not speculative disagreements in which we must recognise the existence of a unique correct answer. The fact that this is the case does not mean that the outcome is of no consequence, and a decision must be reached. Therefore the force in MacCormick's argument is not based on an analogy between aesthetic and legal standards, but on the reality of "the difference between disagreeing over what to do and disagreeing over what is the case".[92]

Professor MacCormick has subsequently been persuaded to relax this argument in response to a lecture given by Dr Knud Haakonssen in

Australia.[93] In this, Haakonssen argues that the distinction drawn between speculative and practical disagreements is insufficient to found MacCormick's argument. This is because, whilst the distinction is perfectly appropriate to the situation in which we must buy a painting, that is taken from the point of view of our motivation for acting, and is thus subjective in viewpoint. Once we turn to view the case objectively, in the sense of seeking to rationally justify our selection, we cannot ever know whether the disagreement is speculative or practical. This can be seen if we further examine our original example. In disagreeing about which painting to buy, we may have to accept that we cannot progress beyond our point of disagreement. However this does not mean that it is in principle impossible to get any further. For example, in the instant case it may be possible to construct an aesthetic theory within which our aesthetic standards can be compared and thus a rational selection arrived at. In other words our practical disagreement would become merely speculative, and thus objectively verifiable. However difficult it may be to imagine the construction of such a theory, we can neither know nor prove that it cannot be achieved, for a proof of non-existence is a logical impossibility.

Whilst this argument appears somewhat illogical when applied to aesthetic questions, once transferred to the social sphere, as with MacCormick's original distinction, it takes on more meaning. The main point is that we cannot know or prove that there exists no way to resolve disagreements arising in hard cases. Haakonssen does however point out that "there is a good deal of difference between asserting that there is a right answer in disputes, as Dworkin does, and asserting that there is no proof that there is no right answer".[94]

In his reply to Haakonssen, MacCormick is prepared to accept the force of this argument and to examine its effect on his theory. We have seen that MacCormick's difficulties arise from a confusion between the subjective and objective aspects of practical reasoning in that he seeks to use the solution to the problem of what motivates us to solve the problem of what will suffice to rationally justify a normative conclusion. However this argument appears to similarly damage Dworkin's claims as Haakonssen argues that Dworkin uses the untenable idea of genuine disagreement on a subjective level to reach his objective conclusion that there is one right answer. MacCormick takes up this point, and argues that the 'un-provenness' of both claims necessitates a procedure for conflict resolution. In law this is provided by the courts. It is the acceptance of value-pluralism that reinforces this conclusion for MacCormick, based on the arguments in Finnis's book *Natural Law and Natural Rights*.[95] Whilst

MacCormick accepts that differing subjective choices may be objectively reasonable he argues that it is absurd to conclude that only one set of political principles and goals, in one particular arrangement, is objectively reasonable. We must conclude, he argues, that whilst it does not follow that there "is no right way of getting an answer", on many points of decision "more than one outcome remains discursively possible".[96] It is for this reason that we have the law, and the courts of law.

Dworkin's response to this revised argument might be a simple one. Both MacCormick and Haakonssen base their attacks on the premise that Dworkin is advancing the proposition that there are right answers in hard cases. In fact, Dworkin's purpose in 'No Right Answer?' was purely a defensive one, in that his argument was that it is insufficient to claim that there are no right answers simply because they cannot be proved or demonstrated.[97] Dworkin does not however provide any arguments in favour of right answers.[98] This would appear to accord with the argument advanced by Haakonssen in that both seem to be effectively asserting that there is no proof that there is no right answer.

Once we recognise that Haakonssen was mistaken in arguing that the one-right-answer thesis was intended to provide an objective resolution to a subjective disagreement we can see that Dworkin and Haakonssen are actually largely in agreement. The reason for their apparent argument lies in the inadequacies of the demonstrability thesis itself. The main problem with this is that the thesis operates to refute itself. The thesis can be stated as asserting that "only those propositions that can be demonstrated, or proved, to be true, are capable of being true or false".[99] Here we clearly cannot fulfil the test as far as the thesis itself is concerned, for we can neither demonstrate nor prove it to be true. Simply because we cannot demonstrate or prove the one-right-answer thesis does not necessitate its rejection.

MacCormick also raises an argument against Dworkin's definitions of discretion. He argues that judges characteristically exercise neither strong nor weak discretion in hard cases. The basis of this argument lies in MacCormick's contention that in hard cases, where we must look beyond the rules for a solution, judges will not possess strong discretion, but instead must account for authorising principles (coherence), consistency, and consequentialist arguments, with the latter being the critical factor. MacCormick argues that this means that judges are "cribbed, cabined, and confined in the exercise of the great powers which they wield".[100] Judicial discretion is therefore limited, but it should not be considered weak because, whilst we are told what modes of argument will operate to justify a decision, we are not told what decision is in the end completely justified.

This argument is a disappointing one, as it seems to rest on a purely semantic argument about the word 'weak'. The form of discretion MacCormick is proposing is of course clearly within Dworkin's definition of weak discretion, and indeed both seem to have a similar view of the nature of judicial discretion. However, MacCormick seems to feel that the idea of weakness implies inferiority and thus is keen to stress the benefits of his theory of discretion. This is mistaken, for Dworkin also wishes to espouse the benefits of this more limited form of discretion. It therefore seems that MacCormick's argument is a misguided one, in particular because on Dworkin's model the only alternatives are weak and strong discretion. MacCormick is clearly not advocating strong discretion, and thus must be proposing a weaker form. MacCormick's error is to read too much into the term 'weak' and to look for "all that is implied in that",[101] whereas Dworkin merely uses the term to distinguish it from the strong or wider version of discretion. MacCormick's further point, implicit in his theory of discretion, that we are not told which decision is in the end completely justified and that consequentialist arguments will be critical here, cannot do the work set for it. MacCormick argues from this proposition that these arguments will provide reasons for according supremacy to a given principle but that this is 'ascribing to it', rather than finding in it, the greater 'weight'.[102] Thus there is no prospect of an objective resolution. Again, this assumes that Dworkin is seeking an objective resolution which as we have seen is mistaken.

We now turn to examine briefly the arguments presented by Jules Coleman in his article 'Negative and Positive Positivism'.[103] In this Professor Coleman distinguishes three different versions of positivism and concludes that his own version based around judicial conventions can meet Dworkin's criticisms.

Coleman first examines what he terms 'negative positivism' which claims that the positivist insistence on the separation of law and morality simply entails that there is at least one legal system imaginable in which the criterion of legal identity does not entail that a law must be a principle of morality in order for it to be valid. Coleman terms this 'negative positivism' in order to acknowledge the "character and weakness of the claim it makes",[104] and he accepts that this version of positivism is not Dworkin's target in 'The Model of Rules I'.

Coleman next examines a version of positivism that he terms 'law as hard facts'. Coleman notes that the positivist tenets that Dworkin appears to be attacking in "The Model of Rules I' are the model of rules itself, the concept of judicial discretion, and the use of a 'pedigree' test to identify law.

However it is far from clear that there is a version of positivism that is actually committed to these tenets. Coleman argues that we could view Dworkin as attacking Hart's version of positivism, but that it is not clear from this which elements of Hart's version are essential to positivism in general.[105] Coleman therefore constructs the 'law as hard facts' version of positivism to illustrate the force of Dworkin's arguments. On this model, the positivist distinction between law and morality is motivated by the need for law that is "apparently concrete and uncontroversial",[106] in contrast to the uncertainty that surrounds morality. This entails that the law consists in "knowable, largely uncontroversial fact".[107] Thus to be meaningful on this view, law cannot be essentially controversial. Once positivism is characterised in this manner Coleman argues that Dworkin's basic tenets become plausible and as a result his criticism is compelling. Additionally, Coleman notes that the arguments for hard facts becomes even more plausible and interesting if it relies on semantics, as is the case with Hart's theory. Thus, Dworkin's criticisms of Hart and the 'law as hard facts' version of positivism is persuasive. However Coleman maintains that there is a version of positivism that falls outside this picture and thus escapes the criticism.

Professor Coleman terms this version of positivism 'law as social convention'. The basic idea behind this version is that there must be a test for "distinguishing moral principles that are legally binding from those that are not",[108] and therefore that principles can be incorporated within a criterion of legal identity. Dworkin has argued against this possibility in *Taking Rights Seriously*[109] on the basis that such a criterion would be inherently controversial, and as a result it cannot be a social rule, for it would not be conventionally accepted. Coleman however argues that there are two ways to avoid this difficulty. One alternative would be to reject the social rule theory in favour of "some other theory concerning the way in which conventional or social rules give rise to duties".[110] This would be based on the expectations arising from efforts to co-ordinate behaviour. Coleman however follows the second strategy,[111] which restricts the duty imposed by a social rule "to the area of convergent practice".[112] Here then where controversy arises we must look for a concordant practice amongst judges for its resolution. There will thus be a legal duty even in controversial cases. Thus Coleman's claims to "do justice to Dworkin's insights while rendering his objections harmless".[113]

Dworkin's response to this is brief.[114] He argues that wherever judges disagree we will always be able to discover some more abstract convention that is accepted by the officials, leading us towards the most abstract convention of all, that judges should make their decisions "in the way such decisions ought to be made".[115] This obviously trivialises the theory.

Notes

1 Dworkin 1977 pp. 14-45.
2 See Hart 1961.
3 These basic tenets are set out in Dworkin 1977 at p.17.
4 This is based on Hume's well-known distinction between factual and normative propositions. See Hume 1739.
5 In other words, the non-vegetarian can coherently use normative language reflecting views with which he does not agree, taking the sense of another's set of values. In so doing, what he is saying is that, given adherence to a set of values, this is the conclusion the vegetarian ought to arrive at.
6 As such, secondary rules can be both duty-imposing and power-conferring.
7 A hard case, in broad terms, is one where there are no plain facts of the law which determine the issue in question in any particular way.
8 Dworkin 1977 p.22.
9 115 NY 506, 22 NE 188 (1889).
10 Id. at p. 509 and p. 189 respectively.
11 Id. at p.511 and p.509 respectively.
12 32 NJ 358, 161 A2d 69 (1960).
13 These are set out by Dworkin 1977 at p.24.
14 Id.
15 These options are described in Dworkin 1977 at p.24.
16 The two options are set out here in reverse order to that given in Dworkin's discussion to prevent some confusion that may arise in his article.
17 These definitions are set out in Dworkin 1977 at pp.31-32.
18 Id. at p.32.
19 For example, we can distinguish between the elderly and the young, and the existence of the category of middle-aged does not break down the distinction. Indeed, it would be impossible without it. See further, Guest 1992 at p.217. It is interesting that this criticism is made against Dworkin by Raz in Raz 1984 at p.81. See too Raz 1972.
20 See further Guest 1992 at pp.217-218.
21 Dworkin 1977 at p.34.
22 This argument is set out by Dworkin id. at pp.35-39.
23 Id. at p.35.
24 This is, of course, in contrast to the all-or-nothing character of rules.
25 Dworkin 1977 at p.36.

26 Id. at p.37.
27 Dworkin sets these out at pp.37-38.
28 Id. at p.38.
29 See Dworkin 1984 at p.261.
30 Raz 1972, the second part of which is reprinted in Cohen 1984 at pp.73-81. In addition, this reprint is accompanied by a Postscript to the original article at pp.81-86. It is important to note that in this Postscript Raz asserts that he still believes his original article is sound (at p.82). However, he does point out that Dworkin's thesis has subsequently changed.
31 Raz 1972 at p.831.
32 Id. at p.832.
33 Id.
34 See Dworkin 1977 pp.75-76. Dworkin points out the ambiguity in Raz's discussion of the principle of individuation, and discusses the consequences of this in greater detail.
35 Id. at p.74.
36 Dworkin's argument on Raz's notion of conflict is located at pp.74-75.
37 Id. at p.77.
38 See further id. at pp.77-78.
39 See Dworkin 1977 at p.27 where he states that anyone who knows something of American law must take the law on the witnessing of wills as stating a rule.
40 Id. at p.27.
41 This is the section of Raz's article reproduced in Cohen 1984. All page references from this section of the article are to this book.
42 Id. at p.74.
43 Id. Raz asserts here that he believes this to be "true ... on various occasions".
44 Id. at pp.74-75.
45 Id. at p.75.
46 Id.
47 This is in contrast to substantive principles. See further id. at p.76.
48 Id.
49 This conclusion intitially appears unlikely, given that Raz himself actually quotes Dworkin's distinctions in his article (at p.73) but, as we will see, this is the only plausible meaning of Raz's arguments.
50 Dworkin 1977 at p.70.
51 In Raz 1984 at p.79.
52 Id. at p.80.
53 Id.
54 Id. at p.81.
55 Dworkin 1977 at p.65.
56 Dworkin argues that many of the principles cited in the *Henningsen* case are of this description.
57 Raz 1984 pp.81-86.
58 In this article Dworkin sets out the "soundest theory of law". It can be found

in Dworkin 1977 at pp.81-130.

59 In Dworkin 1984 at pp.260-263.

60 Id. at p.83.

61 Id.

62 Id.

63 Dworkin 1977 at pp.37-38.

64 In Raz 1984 at p.83.

65 In particular Raz refers to two arguments that view discretion as "offensive to our democratic beliefs and to our condemnation of retroactive legislation". See id.

66 Dworkin agreed that his critique of positivism was now broader in scope than it was earlier. See Dworkin 1984 at p.262.

67 The defence is discussed by Dworkin in Dworkin 1977 at pp.39-45.

68 See for example Lyons 1977 and Soper 1984.

69 Dworkin 1977 at p.40.

70 Id. at p.41.

71 Id.

72 Id.

73 This is a problem for positivist theories in general for many rules of older origin have never actually been enacted by a legislature or created by a court.

74 Dworkin 1977 at p.42.

75 Id. at p.44.

76 Published in 1978.

77 Chapter Nine.

78 Coleman 1984 at pp.28-48.

79 MacCormick 1978 at p.230.

80 *Anisminic Ltd v. Foreign Compensation Commission* [1969] 2AC 147.

81 Dworkin 1977 at p.111.

82 Id. at p.112.

83 This argument is further developed by Dworkin in *Law's Empire*. See further here, Stephen Guest 1992 at pp.57-60.

84 MacCormick 1978 at p.232.

85 Id. at p.233.

86 Id. at p.234.

87 Of course, as we shall see, the arguments developed in the initial chapters of *Law's Empire* are aimed at positivist theories in general, and in seeking to expose the fundamental flaw in their theories, this acts as a reply to all those theorists who have criticised Dworkin on the basis of positivist arguments.

88 This is similar to Dworkin's solution to this problem in *Law's Empire*. See in particular pp.96-98.

89 This situation is the same as that discussed by Dworkin in relation to the interpretive theory of conventionalism in *Law's Empire*.

90 This thesis is made explicit by Dworkin in Dworkin 1977(a) at pp,58-84.

91 See further MacCormick 1978 at pp.247-248. This example is taken from

MacCormick's account.
92 Id. at p.248.
93 Haakonssen 1981. MacCormick's reply follows this at pp.504-509.
94 Id. at p.501.
95 Finnis 1980.
96 MacCormick 1981 at p.509.
97 This is known as the demonstrability thesis. See Dworkin 1977(a).
98 In a later article (See Dworkin 1991) Dworkin re-affirms the weakness of his claim here, asserting that it is simply a claim made within legal practice and that it can be "sound or correct or accurate to say, about some hard cases, that the law, properly interpreted, is for the plaintiff (as for the defendant)." (At pp.365). If we can ever ourselves make such a claim about a hard case, then we have also rejected the no-right-answer thesis. The claim is not then metaphysical, but legal.
99 This definition is set out in Guest 1992 at p.143.
100 MacCormick 1978 at p.251.
101 Id. at p.251.
102 Id. at p.254.
103 Coleman 1984.
104 Id. at p.31.
105 This is not something Dworkin denies. In *Taking Rights Seriously* he states that he wishes to examine the soundness of legal positivism, particularly "in the powerful form that Professor H L A Hart has given to it" (Dworkin 1977 at p.16). Further, in setting out the positivist tenets that he wishes to attack, Dworkin asserts that "though not every philosopher who is called a positivist would subscribe to these in the way I present them, they do define the general position I want to examine (id. at p.17). In other words, it is indeed possible to be a positivist, and to have a theory that does not subscribe to the basic tenets as set out by Dworkin, but such theorists do not concern him.
106 Coleman 1984 at p.32.
107 Id. at p.33.
108 Id. at p.35.
109 Dworkin 1977 Chapter 2, and especially Chapter 3.
110 Coleman 1984 at p.43.
111 As does Charles Silver in Silver 1987. He agrees with Coleman that there will be a legal duty to solve theoretical disagreements where conventional legal practice dictates it. He also acknowledged Coleman's influence and argues that "as Jules Coleman has shown, legal positivism can deny that the truth of propositions of law necessarily turns on historical events; that is, they can deny that law is always a matter of plain fact (as pp.388-389). Silver's argument here is, as he freely admits, almost entirely derived from Coleman's (see p.389 n.15).
112 Coleman 1984 at p.43.
113 Id. at p.47.

114 Dworkin 1984 at pp.252-254.
115 Id. at p.253.

2 The Interpretive Theory

In *Law's Empire* Dworkin's legal theory takes new directions with the introduction of his interpretive theory of law. However, although he takes new routes, the old destinations remain. Many of the aims of his earlier work stay intact in *Law's Empire* but the methodology he utilises is substantially different. In the Preface he specifically mentions that his attacks on legal positivism and the no-right-answer thesis remain intact from *Taking Rights Seriously.* However, the attack concentrates on the interpretive aspects rather than the phenomenological defects previously targeted, although the failings are essentially the same. Most briefly, Dworkin's new theory can be said to be that law is best understood as a social practice seen in its best light as to interpret is to make the best of something that it can be.

The new emphasis on interpretation is an important one that reflects new directions and interests in other branches of philosophy and the study of language. However, the concept of interpretation itself is complex and its meaning is far from settled in this context. A basis feature would seem to be that the process of interpretation is the pursuit of the meaning of something, but this does not take us very far. This picture of interpretation immediately raises a number of further complex questions.[1] Not everything has meaning and we therefore need to identify what sorts of things have meaning. To seek the meaning of something may be to suggest that we are attempting to discover an objective truth about what it is we are interpreting, and this gives rise to various complicated and controversial issues regarding the nature of objectivity and subjectivity. We also need to understand why it is that we think the search for meanings is important. So it can be seen that even by stating what would appear to be a self-evident truth about what interpretation is we have already stepped into difficult terrain.

An initially attractive starting point in considering what it means to interpret something would seem to be that it somehow involves the discovery of a truth in the sense that it seeks to reveal the intention of the creator (the author) of what it is to be interpreted (the text). We can interpret works of art because there is human action involved in their creation and therefore volition and intention investing those works with a reflection of their creator. We can interpret a novel because we seek to get into the mind of the author to discover what it was that he meant by what he wrote, how he intended us to understand his creation. But this clearly does not exhaust common and readily recognisable concepts of interpretation, although it reflects a view that objects in nature (be they cloud shapes, rock patterns, molecular structures or whatever) cannot have meaning as such. We also recognise as interpretation a reconstruction, or a novel construction, of texts (in the very widest sense of that word), which are not intended by authors. For example, even a view of Othello that seeks to explain his behaviour and his psyche by references to illnesses unknown to Shakespeare, and which he therefore clearly could not have intended in any sense to be a part of the person of Othello in the play, we nevertheless acknowledge as legitimate interpretation. Indeed, it is often the form of interpretation that comes most naturally to an actor. Hence Laurence Olivier, in his autobiography, states that he has "reason to feel that Othello's fit is not the result of accelerated self-hypnosis, but a plain cause of physical dysarthria, which is also brought about by over-heightened emotional distress".[2] What this type of attempt at the discovery of meaning may seek to be is an understanding of a character or events as if they were true. In real life events happen, and people are as they are, for an infinite number of facts and reasons about which those involved are entirely ignorant. This form of interpretation can therefore be seen as attractive and legitimate when applied to fictional texts because it treats them as if they were not fictional. This is what authors ask us to do, even if they do not envisage that we will *believe* their texts to be true. It is not even necessary to say that this form of interpretation is only legitimate when there are lacunae in an author's intention. We may interpret a text, give it a meaning, which is at odds with the intentions of the author. Even though the author has particular relevant intentions with regard to his text and might object to contrary interpretations, we nevertheless can (although not necessarily) recognise interpretation as legitimate which ascribes to that text contrary meaning. We may say, for instance, that an author of a novel completely misunderstood the motives and reasons for actions of a character in his book. We may do so by seeking to provide an explanation that better fits the facts of the character, the novel, and also the world at large as we know them where the author's understanding is in some way defective. Whilst some people may stand back a little from viewing this approach to a novel as justifying interpretation, as legitimately-labelled interpretation, considering it better viewed as meddling with the text, it is in fact a concept very familiar to lawyers. Although one view of the correct interpretation of a statute is that which reflects parliamentary intention at the time of the Act's passage this is by no means regarded as the only proper way to interpret an Act. Old statutes are routinely applied to new situations of which Parliament could not possibly have envisaged at the time the Act was passed. No lawyer finds this at all odd.

A theory of interpretation that makes of an object to be interpreted the best that that thing can be is a form of interpretation on the model just described. The best that something can be does not require a reference to intentions, although of course it might. The best way to understand what a person meant in conversation would normally involve seeking to determine what that person intended by what he said. For this reason, Dworkin refers to such intention-based theories of interpretation as conversational interpretation.[3] But the best light that an object of interpretation may be put in may be shed over a wide area going beyond the object itself. For example, the best interpretation of a character in a novel might involve looking at other novels in the canon in which it is placed. Likewise the best light in which a statute may be placed might be that which can only be determined after reference is made to the law in general and this may be something about which the authors of that law, or the legislators, were themselves not addressing in the process of passing that statute. An important factor here is clearly the desirability of consistency, coherence and the avoidance of contradiction. That interpretation is best that prevents inconsistency, incoherence or contradiction.

On this altar may be sacrificed (if it is ever thought desirable in a given context) the intention of the author of the object in question. In fact, this sacrifice may be an important one. Whilst consistency and similar virtues are clearly highly desirable so that the law speaks with one voice, the abandonment of authors' intention to these desiderata may involve the loss of much that is morally and democratically desirable. We might for example think that a major feature of any democratic process should be that the intentions of those who are elected to democratic institutions should be reflected in the interpretation of what they enact, even at the price of some inconsistency or contradiction. The price is not so high to pay in other areas of interpretation.

Even given the desirability of adopting an intention-based interpretation there are often very difficult barriers to overcome in so doing. For example, in dealing with an institution rather than an individual, the discovery of intention is problematic precisely because possibly a large number of people are involved, each with their own intentions and understandings. One therefore needs to ask such questions as whose view is to count, as the opinions of all involved will not necessarily, in fact will rarely, be convergent. Will those of government ministers carry more weight than those of backbenchers? Will the views of government-side backbenchers voting for a measure that is passed carry more weight than those of opposition members on the losing side of a vote? To what extent are the views of the drafters of the legislation, not members of a democratic assembly passing a particular statute, relevant? And then there are the views of ordinary citizens writing to legislators who may affect the way those legislators vote. There are also difficulties in determining how, once we have determined whose views are to count and by how much, those views are to be discovered, and when they are discovered how they can combine to form a single institutional intention. Does the majority view represent best that institutional intention or is it perhaps just the largest single voice in that body, even if it represents a minority overall? Or is the best approach to take a representative view, in effect by constructing an intention closest if not identical to that of most of the legislators overall? Dworkin considers each of these problems at some length in *Law's Empire*[4] in a critique of intentionalism described by Jeremy Waldron as so powerful "that it is surprising to find it appearing in anything other than a trivial form in respectable academic jurisprudence".[5] Nevertheless he feels that it is possible to construct an argument for the intentionalist thesis which is "almost persuasive" if democratic considerations are eschewed, and that Andrei Marmor has done so.[6] We shall not consider those arguments here, but suffice it to be said that intentionalism when abandoned in favour of some other form of interpretation, such as a best light approach, may be abandoned not because it is less viable than those other approaches, but because it may not be viable at all.

Nevertheless, the best light approach is also in a similar position. It is not that we do not necessarily characterise our interpretive practices most accurately by concentrating on adopting meanings which place an object to be interpreted in its best light. It is not at all clear that we adopt this approach when we interpret certain objects at all. For example, Balkin has made the telling point that when we seek to interpret in some contexts the best light approach is inappropriate. In seeking to adversely criticise a work of art, for example, we are engaged in interpretation but we do not seek to put it in its best light, but take the contrary stance. This also seems to be true of social practices of which we disapprove, such as injustices.[7]

The Nature of Legal Disagreement

From this brief introductory examination of interpretation we must now move on to consider Dworkin's views in more detail to see how his approach to interpretation has affected his thinking on legal practice.

In *Taking Rights Seriously* disagreements in hard cases were viewed on the positivist model as arising in the penumbral areas of the law in which there is no fixed core of meaning. Dworkin's challenge to positivism was based on the argument that in such cases judges do not run out of law but characteristically have recourse to legal principles which it is their duty to consider. This position was illustrated by cases such as that of *Riggs v. Palmer*.[8] In this case a man murdered his grandfather knowing that the grandfather's existing will bequeathed to him the bulk of his estate. However he worried that his grandfather would alter the will in the light of his recent remarriage. The court called on a principle that no man shall profit from his own wrong, in order to prevent the grandson from inheriting under the will. Dworkin argued that this showed that judges in hard cases have only a weak form of discretion consisting in the exercise of judgement. In *Law's Empire* Dworkin raises the subject again in order to introduce and explain his development of an interpretive theory of law. The arguments he gives here may thus be seen as a reply to positivist critics such as MacCormick who challenged this area of his account, and to semantic theorists in general.

Dworkin points out that lawyers and judges frequently disagree about the law governing a particular case, and indeed even as to the right tests to use in order to identify it. However at the same time it is generally assumed that whilst some propositions of law can be said to be true others are false. Propositions of law he describes as statements and claims people make about what the law allows or prohibits or entitles them to have. Dworkin's point is that these propositions are not similar to statements such as those of taste or opinion which are in a sense arbitrary or at least subjective. We are able to make these claims because the law is parasitic upon more familiar propositions, which furnish what Dworkin terms the grounds of law. Grounds of law for Dworkin are the reasons why something. is the law, for example that it has been passed by the legislature. As a result we can idenfify two types of disagreement here. Firstly, we may agree about the grounds of law, about when the veracity of other propositions determine the truth of a particular proposition of law, but disagree about whether these grounds are satisfied in a particular case. Dworkin refers to this as an empirical disagreement. This contrasts with another form of disagreement which he terms theoretical. This arises when we disagree as to the grounds of law, even though we may agree as to the empirical facts. Thus an empirical disagreement will arise, for example, when we disagree as to the words in a statute, whereas a theoretical disagreement will occur when we are in agreement about what the statutes and past decisions have to say on a particular matter but disagree as to what the law is because we disagree about whether statute books and judicial decisions exhaust the pertinent ground of law.[9] This form of disagreement is clearly more problematic. Dworkin's contention is that many of the disagreements that we encounter within the law are theoretical in nature,[10] but that this has not been recognised either by laymen or jurisprudential theorists. The influence of the plain fact view of law has largely been the reason for this, as it holds that such disagreements refer to what the law ought to be, and not to what it actually is. The popularity of this view amongst both theorists and the public explains why we are commonly more concerned that the courts exercise fidelity towards the law, than with what the law actually is.

Our concern with fidelity may be for one of two reasons. More usually, it will be because we believe that judges should follow the existing law and not to seek to improve upon it, or, indeed, be allowed to make it worse. Alternatively, it may be because we feel that judges should seek to improve the law whenever appropriate. However, whichever of these provides our reason for concern, both may be based on the thesis that law is a matter of plain fact. Where the law is either silent or vague the plain fact view of law stipulates that the judge must exercise discretion to fill the gap in the law. The question of fidelity is thus replaced by that of what judges should do in this situation. There are some critics[11] who draw the radical conclusion here that past decisions almost always fall into this category and thus that there is never any law on a particular topic. Thus an acceptance of the plain fact viewpoint seems to lead us from the belief that the law covers everything to the conclusion that it in fact covers nothing. This is a direct consequence of its claim that theoretical disagreements are, in fact, disguised political discussions for the more we examine the law the more contentious it appears. This argument is an interesting one as Dworkin appears to apply a distinction similar to that used by MacCormick[12] in order to criticise those who espouse a plain fact view of law, such as MacCormick himself. The complex nature of legal disagreement, which MacCormick sought to utilise in his critique of Dworkin's theory of discretion, instead serves to undermine the plain fact view of law with its emphasis on clarity and simplicity. However, whereas MacCormick's distinction was seen to break down under Haakonssen's analysis this does not occur here because Dworkin remains at the level of subjectivity and thus does not seek to draw objective conclusions from his distinction between subjective disagreements. In order to substantiate this argument Dworkin must provide a framework that will explain the role of theoretical disagreements within the law, whilst enabling him to maintain his theory of discretion.

Drawing the Semantic Sting

Dworkin's interpretive approach to the law views moral argument as necessary in order to identify what the law is. Dworkin identifies three stages in the interpretation of a practice which will involve both a prescriptive and a descriptive element. Firstly, there must be a pre-interpretive stage in which the rules and standards taken to provide the tentative content of the practice are identified.[13] This will itself, of course, involve an element of interpretation. Then there must be an interpretive stage at which the interpreter settles on some general justification for the main elements of the practice identified.[14] This requires an element of 'fit' with the details of the practice. Finally there will be a post-interpretive stage in which the interpreter adjusts his sense of what the practice 'really' requires[15] so as to better serve the justification given at the interpretive stage. With regard to the law 'better' in this context means better in a moral sense. The effect of this for semantic theories of law can be seen in Dworkin's discussion of the consequences of the existence of theoretical disagreements within the law. As we have seen, semantic theories of law argue that what appear to be theoretical disagreements are in fact illusions for here the argument is not about what the law is but about what it ought to be. The reason for this is that the word 'law' makes law depend on certain criteria that cannot be challenged. In other words semantic theorists suppose that lawyers and judges apply essentially the same criteria in deciding whether propositions of law are true or not. Lawyers therefore agree on the grounds of law. Semantic theories that have been the most influential[16] state that the shared criteria make the truth of propositions turn on specified historical facts (such as legislative acts) although they differ as to what these are.

Dworkin elects to concentrate on positivism as an example of a semantic theory, rather than natural law theories or legal realism, as positivism supports the plain fact view of law and thus rejects the existence of theoretical disagreements within the law.[17] Positivism however produces a much more sophisticated defence of this view. This is because it stresses that there are both core and penumbral uses of the word 'law'. We will all apply a slightly different set of criteria to identify the law and this will manifest itself in the penumbral cases. Thus in cases such as *Riggs v. Palmer* the disagreement is merely a verbal one, equivalent to an argument about whether Buckingham Palace is a house. The theory may therefore be regarded as being about repair, about what the law should be, for we will understand our legal practice better if we use 'law' simply to describe the core aspects of that concept. This view, however, does raise a practical problem. If this is an accurate description, and arguments in hard cases do fall within the penumbral areas of law, then how could lawyers think that they had arguments for one view of what would essentially be arbitrary disputes?[18] The positivist argument here does not seem practicable, and indeed Dworkin describes it as "worse than insulting".[19] The reason for this is that it fails to recognise the importance of a different type of distinction. Sometimes we may disagree about the appropriateness of the use of the word because we disagree as to the criteria for using it on any occasion, not just in penumbral situations. In hard cases arguments will often be of this fundamental nature and thus fall into the category of what Dworkin terms 'pivotal' cases. Here the disagreement goes to the core and not to the penumbra.

If Dworkin is correct, and legal argument sometimes revolves around pivotal cases, then it means that lawyers cannot be using the same criteria in determining what is to count as law. Their arguments are about which criteria should be applied. On a semantic viewpoint this means that, were we to argue about the truth of a particular legal proposition, we would not really be disagreeing about anything but instead would simply be talking past each other, because of the different criteria we would be applying.[20] This is the 'semantic sting' and it arises because disagreement in the law is typically of a theoretical, not empirical, nature. Semantic theories offer us too crude a picture of legal disagreement, and we must instead turn to the alternative - an interpretive theory of law.

Philip Soper has said that Dworkin's sting is harmless.[21] Professor Soper argues that Dworkin takes up the internal participants' point of view, where as semantic theorists take the viewpoint of disinterested outsiders. Thus to some extent Dworkin's method is incompatible with that of the semantic theorists. This difference arises according to Soper because, whereas semantic theorists are concerned with either defining or describing the legal system, Dworkin is by contrast engaged with the coherence problem. He wishes to show how our concept of law can be used both to justify the use of force, and refer to social facts, from the standpoint of an insider. That is to say different purposes require, or justify, differing methodologies. The conclusion Soper draws from this is that the two enterprises are different, and hence the sting is harmless. However Soper does allow that in some sense there is room for meaningful comparison. In discussing this, it is clear that Soper views the main disparity between semantic and interpretive theories as arising because of the difference over the basic concept of law we apply. But he does see a connection between these theories, as even those theorists whose work is definitional "have never been entirely able to resist the temptation to apply their models of law to insider concerns".[22] Soper argues that this indicates an uncertainty as to which viewpoint is the appropriate one for the pre-analysis of the definitional enterprise. This therefore indicates a "logical connection between the two enterprises".[23]

Much of this argument seems to arise from a failure to distinguish between Dworkin's pre-interpretive and interpretive stages of interpretation. The descriptive versions of positivist theory provided detailed accounts of the relatively uncontroversial pre-interpretive stage of interpretation. Where positivists apply their theory to hard cases they are in the interpretive stage. This explains why Dworkin's concern lies in the nature of disagreement in hard cases, and why Soper admits that semantic theorists do discuss such matters. This is particularly apparent in the case of the positivists when they argue about the existence of core and penumbral cases. Indeed the argument in the previous chapter as to the existence and role of legal principles only makes sense if such arguments fall within the positivist enterprise. This is perhaps why Soper feels that there is confusion as to the appropriate pre-analytical viewpoint.

Another source of confusion here seems to arise from Dworkin's criticism of the semantic approach to hard cases. Soper seems to think that the two enterprises are to some extent incompatible because Dworkin is engaged in what Soper terms the coherence approach, whilst semantic theorists are engaged in definition or description. But the whole point of this part of Dworkin's argument is to reveal that the semantic approach is misguided, and therefore it should not surprise us that Dworkin suggests a different approach to the discussion of controversial areas of law.

A Threshold Objection

Law's Empire does not cover more than a few issues of concern to legal theory. Dworkin notes[24] that this lays him open to the charge of being too narrow in that he does not consider, for example, questions of fact or what he calls the practical politics of adjudication, namely the compromises judges accept in order to make their own views attractive to other judges. He also concentrates on formal adjudication and in particular the judiciary rather than other actors in the legal drama. He recognises that the charge may not be restricted to selectivity but that he is also wrong because to be so selective is to misunderstand the legal process. Theories need to pay particular attention to the social and historical contexts of law. Dworkin believes that such a charge (which he calls a threshold objection) fails because it overlooks the fact that legal practice, unlike other social phenomena, is argumentative and this aspect is crucial. It can be studied from two points of view, the internal and the external. The latter is taken by the sociologist or historian who asks why certain patterns of legal argument develop in some periods or circumstances and not in others. However, their interest is not finally historical, he says, by which he seems to mean descriptive, but practical. As such, he argues, it needs to take into account the internal point of view too, which is to say the examination of legal practices through the eyes of those participating in it. In other words, "[w]e need a social theory of law, but it must be jurisprudential just for that reason".[25]

This argument has been attacked by Nigel Simmonds. In his article 'Imperial Visions and Mundane Practices',[26] he argues that Dworkin treats history and sociology as being concerned "to offer causal explanations"[27] only and thus considerably underestimates their role. For Simmonds this can be seen if we look closely at Dworkin's interpretive theory, for Dworkin seems to ignore the possibility of "historical and sociological enquiries taking an interpretive form".[28] Here, we are not seeking to reproduce the views of the participants of the practice we are interpreting, but instead seeking the best interpretation from a moral perspective.[29] Therefore if a particular practice is in our view despicable, our interpretation must be "a fully skeptical one",[30] entailing the rejection of our project to constructively interpret it. Thus the idea of constructive interpretation can be seen to be dependent on its social context. If we instead look at the arguments presented in a typical case before the courts, many conflicting standards will be used and abstract concepts applied. If a historian or sociologist were to enquire into the meaning of these practices, or what was happening, he would no doubt locate the practices within their wider social context. If we must instead answer by looking at the practices in isolation we have more difficulty. We are left with two options. One is to attempt to reproduce the beliefs and opinions of the participants, and the second is to argue that the participants have shared criteria of what constitutes good and bad argument. This poses a problem for Dworkin, for both options are ruled out by this theory. Simmonds concludes that the internal/external distinction can only be said to be a contrast between "interpretation, on the one hand, and causal explanation on the other",[31] for if we claim anything further Dworkin is forced to adopt a position excluded by his own theory. If Dworkin is instead merely claiming that a social theory of law cannot take law for granted, this amounts to little of content for it does nothing to justify the converse proposition that a theory of law may ignore its social context. This would result in the conclusion that Dworkin has provided us with simply the first step towards a full theory of law. It is therefore argued that in its detachment from these factors Dworkin offers a theory "not of Socratic self-awareness, but of narrowness and blindness".[32]

If we were forced to accept it this conclusion would be a damaging one for Dworkin. However, although Simmonds' argument is forceful it appears to subtly misrepresent Dworkin's view of the interaction between the internal and external perspectives. Dworkin states that "both perspectives ... are essential, and each must embrace or take account of the other".[33] It is clear that he sees the two perspectives as being parasitic upon one another, and the main thrust of Dworkin's argument seems to be directed at the proposition that the two are inter-dependent. Simmonds criticises this for saying little indeed, as this will not justify a theory of law that ignores law's social context. However that does not appear to be an accurate description of the enterprise Dworkin is undertaking. For whilst it is true that he intends to concentrate his attention on legal argument from the judicial viewpoint, equally he understands the importance of social context within the law. We noted in a previous section that Soper asserts that there is a logical connection between the two enterprises and that recognition seems to form the intent behind Dworkin's reply to this threshold objection. Additionally, whereas Hart argued that "to be occupied with a penumbra is one thing, to be preoccupied with it is another",[34] and provided only a general scheme for the answering of insider questions, Dworkin instead provides a distinction between the grounds and force of law in order to distinguish the question of what the law is from that of whether it should be enforced or obeyed.[35] Further, Dworkin's theory of community, which we will examine later,[36] seems to place law within a central framework. Therefore, whilst Simmonds' argument is of use in indicating the wide role played by sociological concerns within the law, his substantive thesis that this undermines Dworkin's project appears to be exaggerated.

One Right Answer?

We have already noted that Dworkin maintains in the Preface to *Law's Empire* that his new interpretive approach to law does not entail the abandonment of the one-right-answer thesis to the effect that in all types of cases, including hard cases, it is possible for a judge of sufficient quality to discover the one right answer. He argues that, contrary to the positivists' claim, the argument that there can be uniquely correct answers is one based on morality not metaphysics, and that the no-right-answer thesis is 'deeply unpersuasive' in morality as well as in law.[37] In other words, where Dworkin had based his earlier arguments in *Taking Rights Seriously* in the positivists' own territory on the open texture of language and judicial discretion, he argues in *Law's Empire* that, even given these difficulties, it is always open to a judge at the end of the day to determine a hard case on a basis of political morality. Despite this, Brian Bix has suggested [38] that it may be significant that at the end of *Law's Empire* Dworkin abandons the language of one right answer, referring instead to a "right way ... to decide a hard case".[39] However, in the light of Dworkin's claims elsewhere, this may be being a little too pedantic. It is not in any event clear how a uniquely right way to decide a hard case would give rise to a range of possible answers without adhering to a theory of strong discretion.

Nevertheless it would be true to say that, despite Dworkin's firmly-stated continued allegiance to the one-right-answer thesis, in *Law's Empire* this is manifested only implicitly through a number of other arguments. For example, Dworkin insists in *Law's Empire* that there is a pre-existing right in one party in a law suit to win. It is inconsistent with principle, he argues, to hold parties liable in ways in which they had at the time of so acting no duty not to act.[40] This does not reject the idea of novel decisions, of course, but roots them in law as integrity which can furnish the best solution to a hard case to a Herculean judge, ascertainable in advance. The existence of a right answer and its annunciation are distinguishable.

Despite this, George Christie has argued that Dworkin has abandoned his claim that legal questions, if properly analysed, have only one right answer.[41] Professor Christie points out that Dworkin concedes that judges acting in good faith, and even applying Dworkin's own methods, may still arrive at different solutions to particular legal problems. Although they may strive to reach the best solution that they can, that is the case with anyone who does not simply decide on an arbitrary basis. However, Christie points out that Dworkin does attempt to "maintain a semblance of consistency"[42] with his former position by insisting that it is meaningful to talk of right answers even where it is arguable what the right answers are. To this Christie's response is a blunt "so what?", for this is "an admission that we shall never be able to agree on what the right answer is".[43] Christie therefore feels that Dworkin has trivialised his former and more interesting argument.

Christie's position appears to rest on a misunderstanding of Dworkin's original argument. He seems to believe that Dworkin's former position was that there is one right answer that can be shown to be objectively right, when all along Dworkin has stressed the difference between the question whether we can have reason to think that an answer is right, and the question whether it can be demonstrated to be right.[44] That two judges may disagree as to the right answer is an indication of this, and also a vindication of it, for it suggests that we believe that there are right answers to be discovered, and act on this belief.

However, it is possible even in Dworkin's analysis for judges to reach differing conclusions and, as Bix has commented, Dworkin does not seem to find this troubling.[45] Bix cites various reasons for this, such as the divergence in moral and political opinion from one person to another, and the absence in Dworkin's theory of any indication of the degree of fit required to be satisfied in judicial decision making. But all this does is to highlight the difference between an ordinary judge and the Herculean judiciary in Dworkin's writing. Hercules will not differ in his moral and political views from his Herculean brethren precisely because he is who he is. Likewise, the absence of any indication of degree of fit will not trouble Hercules because he will not need to be constrained by any shortfall of ability to establish a best possible fit. It is no answer to say, as Bix does, that there will be a different best answer for each judge in a case because this can only be so if there exists relevant differences between judges, and the perfection of the Herculean judiciary will not allow this. Therefore the point Bix makes can amount to no more than that the real judiciary is not Herculean. This is not an insight. For the same reason, where the law allows a range of possible answers, any one of which will not be overturned on appeal, this is not to say that there are a number of right answers in any other sense than that there are a number of answers that will not be considered to be wrong. But there is a difference between an answer which is close enough to a uniquely correct answer to be acceptable and an answer which is as right as any answer could be. In other words, that an answer is acceptable does not make it right, but not sufficiently wrong, except in the sense that any answer allowable by a legal system is in some sense right, a Realist response with which few today would agree.

As we noted earlier[46] Dworkin has recently reaffirmed the weak nature of the thesis, and pointed out that it is a "claim made within legal practice rather than at some supposedly removed, external, philosophical level".[47] He maintains that this has always been the case,[48] but that commentators seem to have an "apparently irresistible impulse" to insist that he must mean something more than this.[49] Dworkin then does not seek objectivity, and indeed admits that his claim is "a very weak and commonsensical legal claim".[50]

Given that Christie has misinterpreted Dworkin's former argument, it seems that he would wish to argue that Dworkin's thesis has, all along, been a trivial one. The claim of "so what?", or "that's interesting", seems to ignore the moral status of Dworkin's argument, despite his recent assertions. This is developed by Dworkin in *Law's Empire*[51] in his distinction between external and internal skepticism, no doubt as a riposte to critics such as Christie. Dworkin's claim seems to be that legal argument is, like moral argument, about making decisions, and that both always demand the best decision possible. Skeptics would argue that there could be no right answers, only different ones. The skeptic who stands outside the enterprise and declares that truth is not possible because it is not demonstrable, and there is no 'real' counterpart, is what Dworkin terms as an 'external' skeptic. He is disengaged from the interpretive exercise, and thus cannot threaten their project. The internal skeptic does not rely on metaphysics, but instead argues that one view is indeed right, that being the view that to be successful an interpretation must provide a level of unity that it is impossible to achieve in the particular case. This claim must compete with our other conceptions as an interpretation of our practice.

The main point to note here is that from the internal viewpoint we must regard one interpretation of our practices as being the best, even if this is the argument of the internal skeptic. Thus in a case the judge does not operate as if there were no right answer, but instead must imply what he thinks is the best interpretation of the case before him. This point equally applies to the critics of judicial decisions, who are arguing that there is, in fact, a better answer.[52] For this reason the no-right-answer thesis is unpersuasive as an interpretation from the internal viewpoint. Similarly, Dworkin argues that where we make a moral judgement, for example that slavery is wrong, we also presume that there is a right answer to the question. of slavery. Dworkin argues from this, that there is no difference between making the claim that slavery is wrong, and in claiming that it is objectively wrong, for "we use the language of objectivity, not to give out ordinary moral or interpretive claims of a bizarre metaphysical base, but to repeat them ... to emphasise or qualify their *content*".[53] Thus for Dworkin, there is no important difference in philosophical category or standing between "the statement that slavery is wrong and the statement that there is a right answer to the question of slavery, namely that it is wrong".[54] Thus in this way Dworkin links our moral and legal claims, and concludes that the no right answer claim is unpersuasive in morality as well as in law.[55]

Different Methodology, Same Argument?

Dworkin's move from an analytic to an interpretive theory of law represents a change in his methodology, but many of his former arguments have survived this and remain intact, if in a different form. In *Taking Rights Seriously* Dworkin argued that the positivists offered too simplistic an account of the law in failing to account for legal principles. In *Law's Empire* the problem instead is their failing to recognise the existence of theoretical disagreements within the law. We must recognise that law is an interpretive concept in order that we may account for our disagreements in hard cases. Therefore both methods offer arguments against semantic theories based on the idea that such theories are too simplistic to account for the realities of argument in hard cases. However, whereas in 'The Model of Rules I' Dworkin showed that positivists could not explain the nature of legal argument in hard cases, he now focuses on why they cannot. This change is illustrated by the respective uses Dworkin makes of the case of *Riggs v. Palmer*. In 'The Model of Rules I', it was viewed as a case in which the court applied a legal principle as opposed to the existing statutory law. In *Law's Empire* however it is instead used to illustrate the interpretive method, with the court seeking to ascertain the meaning of the statute ascertained in its morally best interpretations This would seem to be a more accurate representation of what actually occurred.[57] Dworkin's arguments in *Law's Empire* therefore seem to complete the project started in *Taking Rights Seriously* by indicating that it is a failure to notice the existence of theoretical disagreements that explains the defects in positivism noted previously.

Similarly, the one-right-answer thesis remains a feature of Dworkin's theory. Here the form of the argument is unaltered, Dworkin explaining that the thesis takes hold within legal practice, and thus is not subject to those who criticise it from a position of external skepticism. Dworkin also develops an argument in *Law's Empire* as to the objective status of interpreting the moral claims that we must examine in discussing his theory of law as interpretation. The argument here then serves to clarify, rather than alter, Dworkin's thesis. It is however important to note that whilst Dworkin appears to have successfully completed his attack on positivism, this rests on the semantic version of that theory which is based on the plain fact view of law. We have seen that Dworkin's own interpretive approach to the law views moral argument as being integral in identifying what the law is, and that the presence of theoretical arguments in law is indicative of this. However, this does not seem to provide an argument against those versions of positivism that recognise controversy in the law and seek to explain it within a positivist context. The argument advanced by Jules Coleman, for example, clearly recognises this controversy and seeks to explain it through the use of judicial conventions.[58] For this reason, Dworkin must provide an additional argument here, in order to explain why these alternatives are also unsuccessful. This is the focus of the next chapter with Dworkin recasting such arguments in the interpretive conception of conventionalism, and lies behind the need for Dworkin's own theory of law as integrity to be convincing.

Notes

1 Moore 1995 pp.2f.
2 Olivier 1982 pp.268-269.
3 Dworkin 1986 pp.51-52.
4 Id. pp.313-327.
5 Waldron 1995 p.329.
6 Mannor 1992.
7 Balkin 1993.
8 (1889) 115NY506, 22NE 1 88.
9 Dworkin 1986 p.5.
10 Dworkin outlines four cases as examples of this. See id.pp.15-30.
11 In particular the Critical Legal Studies movement, and American Realists adhere to this view.
12 See Chapter One on the second defence.
13 Dworkin 1986 pp.65-66.
14 Id. at p.66.
15 Id.
16 This refers to positivism, and particularly the versions espoused by John Austin and HLA Hart.
17 Dworkin also points out that the other two types of theory are deeply unpersuasive if viewed as semantic theories - Dworkin 1986 p.35.
18 This, of course, includes those studying the law. Why would one spend so much time studying hard cases, and formulating arguments as to why certain of these should, in the future, be overruled, if such disputes were concerned with the essentially arbitrary decisions to use a word one way rather than another? See id. p.41.
19 Id.
20 Dworkin gives the example of a disagreement about 'banks' where one person refers to savings banks and the other to river banks. See id. at p.44.

21 Soper 1987 at p.1174.
22 Id. at p.1175.
23 Id. at p.1176.
24 Dworkin 1986 11f.
25 Id. p.14.
26 Simmonds 1987 at pp.480-483.
27 Id. at p.481.
28 Id.
29 Id. But it seems that this negates the point that Simmonds previously made. We form our own interpretive judgements, rather than simply examining those of other participants, which already points to the fact that Dworkin has recognised the interpretive nature of legal history.
30 Dworkin 1986 p.105.
31 Simmonds 1987 p.482.
32 Id. at p.486.
33 Dworkin 1986 pp.13-14.
34 Hart 1983 p.72.
35 Dworkin 1986 pp.108-113.
36 See Chapter Five.
37 Dworkin 1986 p.ix.
38 Bix 1993 p.107.
39 Dworkin 1986 p.412.
40 Id. p.244.
41 Christie 1986 p.184.
42 Id.
43 Id. at p.185.
44 See Chapter One in the section discussing the second defence of positivism for a critique of the demonstrability thesis.
45 Bix 1993 p.109.
46 See Chapter One.
47 Dworkin 1991 p.365.
48 See id. at p.382 n.l where Dworkin states that "for better or for worse" he has not changed his mind about the character and importance of the one-right-answer claim.
49 Id. at p.365.
50 Id.
51 Dworkin 1986 pp.76-86.
52 See Guest 1992 at pp.146-147, for the entertaining example of a judge in a competition for a jingle advertising a breakfast cereal! Guest points out that even here the judge must form an understanding of what is required by the competition, and would not be expected to choose randomly.
53 Dworkin 1986 p.81.
54 Id. at p.82. This reveals the error in the external skeptics' position.

55 This argument is developed in Dworkin 1986 from an argument in Dworkin 1986(a) at pp.171-174.

56 Dworkin 1986 at pp.15-20 and 122-123.

57 See Christie 1986 at p.182 n.186. It should be noted that the *Henningsen* case is not referred to in *Law's Empire*.

58 Denise Reaume points out that Joseph Raz explains the role of morality through the notion of a 'directed power', which is a law-making power coupled with a duty to use it, but ordy in order to achieve specific objectives. Thus Raz argues that moral argument only becomes law once the decision is actually rendered, as is the case with a directed power. Reaume concludes that although this does now show that the moral considerations judges take into account are not law, because of the defensive nature of Dworkin's argument, it does mean that Dworkin has not provided an account which shows that they are. See Reaume 1989 at pp.381-388.

3 Conventionalism, Pragmatism and Interpretation

As we have seen the main innovation in *Law's Empire* is Dworkin's shift from an analytic to an interpretive theory of law. This views the judge as being involved in an act of creative interpretation of the practices of law in deciding the case. For Dworkin the correct interpretation of a practice will be that which makes it the best practice it can be, and this involves both a descriptive and prescriptive element. This is represented in the stages of interpretation (pre-interpretive, interpretive and post-interpretive) Dworkin sets out. This provides the basic framework for the interpretive theory around which Dworkin discusses the question as to which conception of law we should adopt, and it is to this that we now turn. In this chapter we focus on the conceptions of conventionalism and pragmatism before turning in the next chapter to introduce law as integrity.

Concepts and Conceptions

Dworkin employs the distinction between concepts and conceptions that was developed by Gallie[1] and has been influential with a number of leading philosophers, notably John Rawls. The idea is that we can have different conceptions of an object of interpretation, and argue amongst ourselves which is the best conception. The object which is the subject of our conceptions is the concept. The contrast between concept and conception here is "a contrast between levels of abstraction at which the interpretation of the practice can be studied".[2] Therefore with the concept agreement collects around discrete ideas that are uncontroversially employed in all the interpretations, whereas with our conceptions the controversy latent in this abstraction is identified and taken up.[3] In Dworkin's terms this sees the concept operating to furnish a plateau on which we can argue the merits of our various conceptions. Therefore, rival interpretations of our legal practices will amount to rival conceptions of law. In Dworkin's words, "interpretations struggle side by side with litigants before the bar".[4]

The next step is therefore to apply this analysis to the law itself. Dworkin's argument is that "we might understand law better if we could find a similar abstract description of the point of a law", although he is careful to add that "neither jurisprudence nor my own arguments .... depend on finding an abstract description of that sort".[5] Dworkin argues that our discussions about law generally assume that "the most abstract and fundamental point of legal practice is to guide and constrain the power of government".[6] This is achieved by licensing coercion only where rights and responsibilities "flow from past decisions of the right sort".[7] This provides us with a shared understanding, or plateau, from which to argue about our conceptions of law, and Dworkin asserts that it seems "sufficiently abstract and uncontroversial" to give us "the structure we seek".[8] We will thus be able to question the controversy latent in our basic concept, namely whether the supposed link between law and coercion is justified, if so how it is justified, and finally, which rights and responsibilities should flow from past decisions.[9]

It will be helpful here to briefly survey the three conceptions of law proposed by Dworkin as possible interpretations of our practices. However, it is important to note that these are not meant to precisely reflect 'schools' of jurisprudence, but instead to capture prominent themes and ideas and organise them into interpretive claims. As a result, Dworkin admits that "perhaps no legal philosopher would defend either of the first two as I describe it".[10] The first conception discussed is that of conventionalism. This accepts the idea of law and legal rights, and argues that law's constraint arises because of the need for predictability and procedural fairness. Legal rights and responsibilities will flow from the explicit extension of past decisions, or from that which can be made explicit by conventionally accepted techniques. The second conception is that of pragmatism. This denies the benefit of legal rights flowing from past decisions. Instead it proposes that judges should do what is best for the community's future. Law as integrity is the final conception. This accepts our idea of law and legal rights, and sees law's constraints as a benefit, not just for predictability, but also because by securing equality it makes a community more genuine and as a result increases the moral justification for exercising power.

This use of the concept-conception distinction by Dworkin has drawn criticism from other theorists. In his article 'Why Conventionalism Does Not Collapse Into Pragmatism'[11] Nigel Simmonds argues that Dworkin's choice of basic concepts distorts our view of the three conceptions. He argues that this supposedly abstract description is in fact "an essential underpinning" for Dworkin's later arguments against conventionalism.[12] The whole point of the abstract description should be to give a shared structure to the conceptions we are considering, resulting in conceptions that correspond to the abstract concept. However it is clear that pragmatism actually denies the essential assumption on which our plateau is constructed, for it does not accept that the imposition of coercion must flow from past political decisions. Simmonds also argues that, although conventionalism does fit the abstract description, "a more natural and obvious version"[13] of that theory does not. Instead of adopting Dworkin's 'fair warning' view of conventionalism, he proposes an account which focuses on the need of society to require the regulation of conduct by rules. Simply put, this sees the purpose of law as being to create rules giving rise to stable expectations rather than seeking to secure expectations through the device of legal rules. (We shall examine this in more detail below.) As a result the only conception that finds the concept a comfortable fit is Dworkin's own theory of law as integrity.

Philip Soper has also been critical of Dworkin's choice of basic concept.[14] Soper argues that, having condemned semantic theories, Dworkin has effectively introduced his own semantic rule for the term 'law' by constructing an abstract account of law that in effect amounts to a semantic rule. This is because he says we use the term 'law' to indicate when the collective use of force is justified. Soper is sceptical about Dworkin's claims that our choice of abstract concept is unimportant, arguing that these are "semantic quibbles (at least as annoying as semantic stings)".[15] Because all the conceptions are tested for fit and justificatory force against the abstract concept, it is in fact "a device by which the argument of the rest of the book proceeds".[16] Even more worrying for Soper is the knowledge that Dworkin does not defend his choice of abstract concept, but simply asserts it. This leaves Dworkin open to the charge of having assumed the point in issue, for positivist theories "typically go to some lengths to defend the opposite view - that the abstract concept of law refers to collective force simpliciter, not to justified collective force".[17]

Allan Hutchinson has also taken up this point,[18] but from the standpoint of the skeptic. The skeptics are not even allowed on Dworkin's plateau,[19] for it is located "in a theoretical environment and at a level of philosophical abstraction that preempt their participation".[20] Dworkin does argue, however, that pragmatists will accept the plateau as the right one for argument about the nature of law, but of course only to adopt a skeptical stance. This hardly amounts to an uncontroversial, shared, concept of law. In this way, Hutchinson says, Dworkin has stage-managed his "enactment of the jurisprudential Armageddon" but "it is this very kind of apolitical theorising, with its loaded epistemological standards and reduced hermeneutic horizons, that the Critical project is most at pains to deconstruct and reject".[21] Hutchinson also points out that Dworkin appears here to have forgotten his own injunction that "there is no position of interpretive neutrality" and concludes that once the fragile plateau of rough consensus begins to break down, Dworkin's Empire will begin to crumble. This presents a serious problem for Dworkin, appearing as it does to undermine his discussion of the three conceptions of law. Stephen Guest has attempted to defend Dworkin on this point by arguing that the choice of basic concept is "difficult to deny and accepting it does not mean that we are bound to accept Dworkin's conception of law".[22] If Guest were to argue that it would be difficult to deny that law can justify, and does justify, the use of collective or state force, then we can readily agree. What is much more difficult to accept is that this is the best abstract concept of law that we can achieve, at least without a great deal more by way of argument from Dworkin. Simmonds puts forward a possible alternative, as we have seen, but there are many others. A great deal of the law is private law which attempts to regulate the relations between private individuals. A concept of law which saw law as regulating these relations for the advancement of community welfare, even though the state also has a collective interest in the maintenance of good order, would be prima facie defensible. However, it would be difficult to view this as *primarily*, and uncontroversially, about the justification of collective force.

One possibility not explored by Guest is to view the basic concept as a necessary pre-analytic tool. Whether we see ourselves as being engaged in revealing semantic criteria, or as interpreting practices, it is necessary that we start with a pre-interpretive view. The basic concept would thus on this account furnish Dworkin's pre-interpretive view of the law, with the three conceptions being the possible interpretations of this at the interpretive level. In this way Dworkin could avoid the difficulties his basic concept seems to give rise to. This argument however appears to be ruled out by Dworkin. himself. The pre-interpretive stage seems to require more content. Dworkin stated that the pre-interpretive stage is that in which "the rules and standards taken to provide the tentative content of the practice are identified".[23] Additionally, at this stage, whilst some kind of interpretation is required, the classifications it yields "are treated as given in day-to-day reflection and argument".[24] Yet discussing the basic concept, Dworkin treats it as being "useful in several ways",[25] but not essential. It thus differs from the pre-interpretive view which is a necessity.

One further possibility, mentioned by Guest, is to argue that positivism is best viewed as reflecting the basic concept.[26] Indeed it now seems that Dworkin regrets not making it clear that he regards Hart's theory as best understood as a conventionalist theory.[27] Because this claim also includes the additional one that conventionalism should be seen as reflecting Dworkin's basic concept, this is more controversial than it initially appears to be. In Dworkin's terms, Hart's concept of law amounts to an exhaustive account of the pre-interpretive model of law, followed by an argument as to whether that model should be restricted simply to those rules deemed morally acceptable. Hart's conclusion was that it should not, hence preserving the individual's moral judgement from the incursion of the law's demands on him. It can be argued that Hart's purpose here is not normative, but instead interpretive. Hart is advocating a particular version of law, which has as its point the promotion of clarity and objectivity. Hart's theory may then serve as a basis for Dworkin's claims at the pre-interpretive stage, and there is likely to be disagreement between them at the interpretive level. Thus, whilst Hart's theory initially appears antagonistic to the basic concept, this is because its initial attraction lies in its simplicity and clarity. Once it is viewed as being interpretive it takes on a new aspect, and can be viewed as a conception of the concept of coercive state power, with Guest suggesting that for Hart "the importance of distinguishing law from morality lay in the preservation of individual conscience against the state's demands".[28] For Hart the virtue of his account of law was his commitment to clarity and certainty, and similarly conventionalism argues that the best interpretation of legal practice is to view it as a matter of enforcing and respecting legal conventions. Hart's version of positivism does indeed appear to be best viewed on the conventionalist model, provided that he would accept Dworkin's basic concept. This is questionable, for that concept is not the "abstract description of the point of law most legal theorists accept"[29] that Dworkin claims it to be. Indeed, we have noted that many positivists do deny this, and we cannot be certain that Hart would not also do so. Nevertheless, even if Hart were to accept it, theorists such as Soper and Coleman would probably not do so, and we must bear this in mind in examining Dworkin's discussion of conventionalism.

Strict and Soft Conventionalism

In *Taking Rights Seriously* Dworkin argued that, unless some principles were accepted as binding on judges, no rules could be said to be binding on them either.[30] This was because it is common, particularly in the higher courts, for judges to directly overturn or radically alter the existing rules. If courts had discretion to do this, then these rules could not be said to be binding on them and would thus not be law on the positivist model. Dworkin therefore argued that we must accept the existence of legal principles, which guide the circumstances in which an existing rule may be overturned. In seeking to accommodate these insights, we have already seen that positivist theorists such as Raz, MacCormick, and Coleman were led either towards legal realism, or soft conventionalism.[31] In *Law's Empire*[32] this argument has been fleshed out and clarified, with the basic argument being cast as the collapse of conventionalism into pragmatism.[33] Since the conventionalist wishes to treat judges as being bound by rules, whereas the pragmatist treats rules only as a factor to be considered, this collapse, if inevitable, would refute the conventionalist position. Dworkin completes his project here by considering the status of soft conventionalism. Conventionalism differs from the plain fact account of the law in that its nature is neither semantic nor descriptive, but instead makes the interpretive claim that the best interpretation of our legal practices is to view them as a matter of enforcing and respecting legal conventions.[34] Legal conventions are identified by reference to the plain facts of legal practice. Conventionalism makes the two post-interpretive claims that judges must respect established legal conventions except in rare cases, and that there is no law other than that drawn from past political decisions by conventional techniques. The appeal of conventionalism lies, according to Dworkin, in its application of the ideal of 'protected expectations', which it serves by giving a 'fair warning' of when coercion will be invoked.[35] This ideal is served in two ways. Where a convention covers the point in issue it will be clear to us what the law requires. Where, however, there is a gap in the law, law cannot be appealed to and the ideal is served because judges are not permitted to act as if they were applying a past decision. Everything is thus out in the open.

When we turn to look at how well this is reflected in our practices we encounter a problem. Conventionalism requires us to show that the behaviour of judges generally converges sufficiently to allow us to term it a convention. However, judges often disagree about how statutes and past decisions should be interpreted. Whilst we may agree on an abstract formulation of these conventions, we take an interpretive attitude towards this abstract composition. We must therefore distinguish between the 'explicit' and 'implicit' extensions of the convention. Dworkin defines the explicit extension as being that set of propositions that almost everyone said to be a party to the convention actually accepts as part of its extension.[36] This contrasts with the implicit extension which covers the set of propositions that "follow from the best or soundest interpretation of the convention",[37] regardless of whether these form part of the explicit extension.

This distinction entails another. We can now distinguish two forms of conventionalism. The first is what Dworkin terms 'strict' conventionalism, and restricts the law of the community to the explicit extension of its legal conventions. This is distinct from 'soft' conventionalism, which insists that the law includes everything covered by the implicit extension of these conventions. If conventionalism is best viewed as strict conventionalism, then no guidance is offered to judges in hard cases, thus giving a very narrow conception of law. For this reason recent philosophers have been attracted to the soft version of the theory.[38] In this way they can argue that the theory is relevant to hard cases, for the instruction is for judges to decide according to their own interpretations of what is required, even though this may be controversial. Whilst strict conventionalists may claim a gap in the law, soft conventionalists need not, for they can always draft a more abstract proposition that everyone is agreed upon where there is argument as to the content of the abstract convention in question. In the end the soft conventionalists can always fall back "on the most abstract convention of all: judges must follow the best understanding of what the law requires".[39] For this reason Dworkin argues that we can see that soft conventionalism is "not really a form of conventionalism at all", but is rather "a very abstract, under-developed form of law as integrity".[40] Clarity which is at the heart of conventionalist theories is not present here, and there is nothing to guarantee, or even promote, the ideal of protected expectations. Dworkin therefore contends that if conventionalism "is to provide a distinct and muscular conception of law ... with even remote connections to the family of popular attitudes we took it to express, then it must be strict, not soft, conventionalism".[41] For Dworkin it is therefore strict conventionalism that we must test against the dual interpretive constraints of fit and justification.

Before we turn to look at this, however, we must first turn to the response of the soft conventionalists to Dworkin's argument. Not surprisingly they have tended to regard their dismissal as unfair and demand reinstatement. Philip Soper argues that there is a crucial difference between soft conventionalism and law as integrity. Even if it is in practice equivalent to law as integrity, "it is so only contingently".[42] This is because it will only remain thus as long as society is "content with the particular decisions judges reach in their search for the 'best' interpretation that political theory can offer".[43] If society is no longer content it can alter the convention and reverse the decisions. Soper argues that this appears to fit our practice, given the frequency with which controversial judgements are met with calls for constitutional amendments. However, this argument seems to assume that law as integrity for Dworkin is a practice outside conventions, and Dworkin never argues that. Integrity for Dworkin presupposes conventions, and if those conventions are altered this does not involve an abandonment of integrity. Integrity remains within the context of different conventions. As Dworkin says: "like conventionalism, law as integrity accepts law ... wholeheartedly".[44]

Nigel Simmonds has also responded to Dworkin's argument here.[45] He identifies the difference between the two theories as lying in the area central to Dworkin's interpretive theory, namely the account of the purpose of law. Whilst Dworkin argues that legal practices of argument, involving concern with rules and principles "have as their fundamental point or object a deep concern with equality", Simmonds argues that conventionalist theorists are concerned with order and predictability.[46] This may be so, but this is not a criticism which is damning to integrity as such, for it is possible to construct a theory in law as integrity which is concerned with law as preserving order and predictability. In other words, equality as law's purpose stems from Dworkin's concept of law rather than deriving necessarily from his preferred conception.

These arguments focus on Dworkin's assertion that soft conventionalism is really an underdeveloped version of Dworkin's own conception, law as integrity. They do not deal with the main reason behind Dworkin's dismissal of soft conventionalism on the ground that it does not conform to the main ideal behind that theory. The argument put forward by theorists such as Soper and Simmonds is therefore not based on the premise that Dworkin is wrong to choose to test strict conventionalism as a conventionalist theory, but instead that he should also test the soft version, not as a conventionalist theory, but on its own terms. His failure to do so, and to recognise the difference between this position and his own, effectively means that he ignores a potential competitor to law as integrity. The problem would appear to arise in Dworkin's wish to examine particular ideas and themes, and not schools of jurisprudence. This should have led him to create a broad canvas on which to conduct this. However, in selecting his abstract concept he seems to have artificially limited himself, and one of his victims is soft conventionalism for which a place in Dworkin's picture is not forthcoming.

We must now look at Dworkin's analysis of the fit and justificatory force of strict conventionalism, whilst considering whether the arguments he offers against that conception could equally be applied to its soft counterpart.

Fit and Justification

For Dworkin an interpretation must have both a descriptive and a prescriptive aspect. It must both accord with the requirements of 'fit', and make the practice into the best that it can be. We will first consider Dworkin's arguments against conventionalism on the first dimension.[47]

Fit

The first argument we consider is that, paradoxically, our judges actually pay more attention to conventional sources of law than strict conventionalism allows them. According to the conventionalists, a judge will first inspect judicial practice to see if there is agreement to a convention, and then if he finds that there is none, he will proceed to turn to the legislative stage of exercising his discretion. This however does not seem to reflect the actual practice in hard cases,[48] which appears to assume that judges have an obligation to enforce the law, even where it is controversial as to what it is - that is to say, that it is controversial *whether* it is law, not that its content is controversial. This does not mean that a conventionalist judge would simply ignore statutes and precedents once it becomes apparent that their force is controversial, but instead that he would no longer treat them as sources of law. They will now be relevant to him in deciding what will be the best new law for the future, for every lawmaker must be careful to make the new law consistent with the old, and this is particularly true of the conventionalist judge, for "his power to change existing law is very limited".[49] Here then our concern is with consistency in *strategy*, and this does not require us to seek the 'best' interpretation of a statute, or the 'correct' reading of a precedent, where these are controversial issues.

Consistency in strategy must be distinguished from consistency in principle, which requires that the state's use of coercion should be consistent in expressing "a single and comprehensive vision of justice".[50] Acceptance of this means that we would show concern for the principles that should be understood to justify statutes and past decisions, and it is in such acceptance that law as integrity differs from conventionalism. Therefore the conclusion follows that "anyone who thinks that consistency in principle ... must be at the heart of adjudication, has rejected conventionalism, whether he realises he has or not".[51]

Simmonds argues that this objection is not relevant to his account of conventionalism, but only to the bilateral version proposed by Dworkin whereby a party who has a clear rule in his favour is entitled to win his case, with the judge in other cases having a choice which he can exercise on grounds such as justice or policy. The flaw in that account lies in making a clear distinction between cases in which the rules apply, in cases in which discretion must be exercised. Simmonds' account differs in this respect, because he views the law as seeking "to reflect a structure of informal rules and expectations",[52] and thus we must interpret the legal rules in the light of surrounding expectations, which may be both tacit and diffuse. As he puts it: "the scope of a rule is then not a matter of some verbal formulation taken in abstraction" but "understood against the wider structure of informal rules and understandings".[53] Thus the case law in such a system will develop by means of the "gradual crystallisation of informal rules and expectations".[54] In this situation, Dworkin's distinction between strategy and principle cannot be maintained because there is no distinction between interpreting and applying a rule and applying a principle implicit in it. Additionally, Simmonds points out that, even where the law does not reflect pre-existing informal rules, it may still embody a moral principle for judges will still be concerned with consistency and coherence "as a part of the wider project of creating stable and interlocking structure of rules and expectations".[55]

This defence is of course open to the attack that Simmonds is putting forward a version of soft conventionalism, and thus ignoring the central tenets of conventionalist theories. This seems particularly to be the case where Simmonds talks of "the wider structure of informal rules and understandings".[56] However this argument runs both ways. For although Dworkin is correct to be dismissive of this theory as a version of conventionalism, he is wrong to simply dismiss it as an under-developed version of law as integrity. Simmonds himself acknowledges this when he states that "instead of being in defence of conventionalism ... my argument will amount to the claim that Dworkin neglects an important alternative theory".[57] Thus Simmonds' theory appears to be safe from the attack of Dworkin's first argument against the dimension of fit in conventionalism.

The second point that Dworkin raises as to the fit of conventionalism employs a distinction between convictions and conventions. Dworkin's argument is based on the idea that consensus may be achieved both by means of conviction or convention, but the difference has important consequences. The difference is this. If we think that a particular proposition is true by reason of convention, then we will not require any substantive reason for accepting it.[58] Where, however, our consensus is a result of conviction then dissent will not be considered out of order in the same way. This is because our convictions depend on the substance of the argument, not on whether others agree with us. Here the consensus will last only as long as the convictions supporting it are widely held. Dworkin's arguments here are based on the idea that the notion of 'bare' agreement as being at the centre of legal argument will be insufficient to explain the complexity of such argument. It is more descriptively accurate to talk of the agreement that arises between judges as being a consensus of conviction. In this way we are able to explain how differences of opinion can arise between judges, even where the end result will be the same.[59] When judges report their decisions they do so in a manner much more complicated than a simple amalgam of conventions, and their arguments usually arise within the rules, not around them. The conclusion Dworkin draws from this is that our legal practice is largely shaped by conviction, for it is usually in response to arguments made in the context of adjudication that the law is altered, and not in "special miniconstitutional conventions".[60]

Simmonds argues against this portrayal on the basis that, although conventionalism does require some degree of convergence in official conduct, it does not need to claim that this is a matter of convention rather than conviction.[61] Indeed, all that conventionalism does need to claim is that conventionalist reasons are the *best* reasons for conformity.[62] For conventionalists, the sources of law need only be accepted by the judiciary through consensus. The convictions behind that consensus may be based on reasons many and varied without destroying that consensus. In any event, as Simmonds points out, there would be evidentiary difficulties present in ascertaining the motives for compliance within a pattern of behaviour. Simmonds claims that his account enables us to see more clearly how a practice may undergo change when "the substantive convictions ... become transiently dominant over the conventionalist attitudes".[63]

Simmonds appears to ground his argument in his contention that a judge who believes that conventionalism presents legal practice in its morally best light offers a legitimate interpretation of his legal system, despite the fact that the other judges' convergent practice is not the result of a shared convention requiring its participants to regard the conformity of other participants as providing part of their own reasons for conformity. This would involve "treating the attitudes of participants in the practice as a part of the 'text' which is to be interpreted".[64] However, such criteria of fit must be weighed against criteria of appeal, and were Dworkin to give 'infinite weight' to participants' attitudes, his theory would be transformed into one in which there is "no potential for the radical re-interpretation of established practices".[65] Dworkin's theory of interpretation does however seem to treat participant attitudes in just this way. For Dworkin an interpretation "must nevertheless flow throughout the text",[66] and his discussion of *McLoughlin v. O'Brian*[67] stresses the importance of fit in interpretation.[68] Participant attitudes must be included within this 'text' for otherwise we would have no means of determining whether a particular conception of law was of satisfactory fit in explaining the features of our legal system.

Professor Stanley Fish has offered an intriguing argument.[69] He states that the possibility of being a conventionalist 'depends on the assumption that explicit or literal meanings do in fact exist', and it is his contention that they do not.[70] There is in fact "no possibility of a direct or uncontroversial application"[71] either of the institution of legislation or of anything else. This is because even meanings which appear to leap off the page are in fact meanings flowing from interpretive assumptions "so deeply embedded that they have become invisible".[72] Thus someone who stands on a literal or explicit meaning is actually standing on an interpretation, even though that interpretation is at present unassailable. For example, the seemingly clear provision in the US Constitution that no-one shall be eligible to be president who has not attained the age of 35 years looks absolutely clear. But when one has in mind the assumptions and the concerns of the framers behind it, and the changing factors of life expectancy, course of education and similar cultural conditions, it is clear that the literal or explicit meaning of the words nevertheless stands on an interpretation.[73]

This then represents not merely an attack on conventionalism itself, but also on Dworkin for presenting conventionalism as a viable conception of law. However, the charges made by Fish do not seem to adhere to Dworkin's description of conventionalism. If a proposition is accepted as being true by convention, it is true "just because everyone else accepts it".[74] In addition to this, convictions may be altered over time, although this occurs outside rather than within the practice. Thus no difficulty would appear to arise from Fish's idea that conventions are deeply embedded interpretations, for what is crucial with conventions is that they are accepted as a matter of course. Indeed, Fish seems simply to have provided us with a description of conventions, not an attack on them.

Justification

We now turn to Dworkin's arguments against conventionalism on the justificatory power of strict conventionalism.

Conventionalism aims to remove many of the elements of surprise that are perceived as existing in the law. It does so by giving fair warning of the application of coercion and protecting the expectations created by this.

This then assumes that the reduction of surprise is a valuable and important goal of political morality. Dworkin however argues that surprise in general is not unfair. It is not unfair, for example, to someone who has gambled on a horse in a race if it loses, even if beforehand it looked likely that it would win. However, surprise is unfair where "a prediction has been specifically encouraged by those who deliberately defeat it".[75] But this, for Dworkin, is just one special circumstance. Therefore, surprise itself must be undesirable for some other reason, such as its inefficiency. If this were not the case, and we were solely concerned to eliminate surprise *per se*, then Dworkin argues that we should adopt 'unilateral conventionalism'. This insists that the status quo be preserved, unless some rule within the explicit extension of a legal convention requires otherwise.[76] In other words, if a rule is clearly in favour of a party to a case he is entitled to win, otherwise he loses. This is compared with 'bilateral conventionalism' whereby either party with a clear rule in his favour wins. If neither has such, the judge has a choice which he can exercise on some other grounds, such as fairness. In limiting the plaintiff to the explicit extensions in unilateral conventionalism surprise is minimised by eliminating those hard cases in which the court grants a new remedy. However, Dworkin argues that "our legal practice is not unilateralist in this way over the broad reaches of the private law",[77] and thus this interpretation does not fit our practice. We should therefore turn to a bilateral approach which will of course necessitate further justification. This may be provided by the fact that bilateral conventionalism preserves a balance between reliability and flexibility.

We therefore have a two stage defence of conventionalism. First of all, wise adjudication consists in seeking the right balance between predictability and flexibility, and secondly, this is achieved by respecting only past explicit decisions of political institutions. Dworkin argues that this is similar to the situation facing a pragmatist judge, but with the difference that although a pragmatist judge will usually enforce past political decisions he is under no duty to do so. The conventionalist judge is by contrast arbitrarily restrained in this situation. Dworkin therefore argues that if we are seeking to obtain the best balance between predictability and flexibility, it would be more rational to adopt a pragmatic attitude, as it is much more adaptive and is best carried out on a case by case basis in that the consequences of a trade off between the two values will vary from situation to situation.. Thus conventionalism can be seen to collapse into pragmatism.

Simmonds argues that, whilst this argument is valid, it is valid only against the 'fair warning' version of conventionalism.[78] If the enforcement of rules does turn on the existence of fair warnings and protection of the expectations generated by this, then it would indeed be irrational to rigidly enforce the existing rules for the strength of the argument for enforcing the rules will be determined by how far the expectations are dependent upon the warning which is given. But, this argument turns on the adoption by us of such an account, which itself turns on our acceptance of Dworkin's abstract concept. This is because the idea of fair warning is a constraint on the pursuit of governmental objectives which is central to the abstract concept. This is, as we have seen, a controversial issue.

Simmonds contends that if we approach this question with a fresh outlook we will not be drawn to the fair warning version as a "natural and obvious account of conventionalism".[79] Instead we are led to adopt this account simply because it fits the abstract concept. Simmonds argues that we must break away from this in order to produce a better account of conventionalism. Instead he offers a rival and, he alleges, more natural account of conventionalism. This is based on the central proposition that "social order requires the regulation of conduct by rules".[80] Whilst it is possible to achieve order in other forms of society, such as those with interlocking kinship structures, it is probably not useful to regard such societies as being of a legal nature. In those societies dispute resolution will be by means of compromise, and this means that the existence of distinct individual rights cannot be achieved, and consequently that liberty cannot be adequately protected. Simmonds concludes that the "maintenance of order consistently with liberty therefore requires the enforcement of rules".[81] In the complex society these rules will need to be of relatively precise and clear scope, and thus informal social rules will not suffice. Additionally, an authoritative organ will be required to pass judgement on any disputes that may arise out of these rules. If these decisions are treated as being generally authoritative in scope, then obviously this will operate to reduce the number of future disputes.[82] We can also entertain a different consideration here. Our ability to devise and execute plans for the future are largely dependent on the degree of predictability illustrated by society. In order for there to be sufficient continuity here, Simmonds contends that the society must be governed by rules.[83]

Simmonds therefore argues that we require the existence of a system of rules for two distinct but related reasons. Firstly, in order to define entitlements and thus enable the authoritative resolution of disputes consistent with overall liberty, and secondly, to give a stable set of expectations and thus enable us to pursue projects giving future benefits. This "echoes themes" to be found in writers such as Hart, Fuller and Hayek and, Simmonds argues, offers a more natural account of conventionalism than the fair warning version proposed by Dworkin.

We are now in a position to see why Simmonds argues that conventionalism will no longer collapse into pragmatism. This is because, as we have seen, the point (rather than the consequence) of rules is, at least to some extent, the creation of a stable set of expectations. However, when a pragmatist weighs up the arguments in favour of enforcing a rule, they will be "a function of the expectations actually created by the rule".[84] This makes it extremely hard for rules ever to create stable expectations for we will not know whether to expect their enforcement until we have examined the expectations of our fellows, but they also find themselves in this position.[85] The conclusion then is that the best strategy for the creation of stable expectations will be a prior commitment to rule-enforcement, and thus that conventionalism is superior to pragmatism on this model.

Stephen Guest has commented that Simmonds' argument is an "interesting interpretation of the ideal of conventionalism",[86] but that the arguments that Simmonds presents do not depend on an interpretation of conventionalism which is the same as Dworkin's. Guest asks us to note that Dworkin's description of conventionalism is a *possible* model of law based on his making the best sense of 'the ideal of protected expectations'.[87] This does not seem to address the main points raised in Simmonds' article. His argument is intended not to defend conventionalism but instead to show that Dworkin neglects an important alternative theory.[88] In this is the further claim that Dworkin's choice of abstract concept blinds him to such possible alternative interpretations. Clearly Simmonds grasps the point that his theory does not exactly correspond to Dworkin's account of conventionalism,[89] but then that is an essential feature of his alternative. To point out, as Guest does, that Dworkin's model is only a possible one based on the ideal of protected expectations is to miss the point that Dworkin presents his interpretation as being the 'best' account of that conception, and as one constructed around a basic concept that is supposedly both abstract and uncontroversial.[90] Thus in presenting an alternative account of conventionalism Simmonds draws attention both to the extent of Dworkin's reliance on his abstract concept and the existence of an alternative conception of law not considered by Dworkin.

Pragmatism

Dworkin paid little attention to theories of legal realism in his previous work or, as he terms it, pragmatism. Indeed Andrew Altman has complained that he devotes approximately one page to the movement in *Taking Rights Seriously.*[91] This, however, has not been the case since the publication of *Law's Empire* in which Dworkin discusses both pragmatism and skepticism. Whereas in *Taking Rights Seriously* Dworkin was content to simply point out how positivism could lead to realism unless the existence of principles were accepted[92] in *Law's Empire* he examines the consequences of the collapse of conventionalism into pragmatism. Additionally Dworkin uses this discussion of pragmatism to lead into his own theory of law as integrity.

We have already observed that pragmatism starts out at a disadvantage to the other two conceptions discussed by Dworkin in that he denies the assumption at the centre of the abstract concept in placing little store by past political acts, particularly precedents.[93] Pragmatism[94] denies that past decisions create rights that bind judges in future cases, and instead argues that judges should be free to decide what is the best decision unencumbered by precedent, although they may act 'as if' people had legal rights in order to serve society better in the long run. In allowing such flexibility we have seen that Dworkin argues that pragmatism is superior to conventionalism. However, pragmatism does have considerable problems of fit.

Dworkin first considers what strategy a "self-conscious and sophisticated"[95] judge employing a pragmatist outlook would adopt in acting as if people had legal rights.[96] He would seek to strike the right balance between predictability and flexibility and this would probably lead him to hold that those rights that clear legislation purports to create should be amongst his 'as-if' rights. Similarly, as-if rights declared by past decisions will generally be recognised. However, not all statutes or past decisions need be honoured in this way. For example, he may decide that older statutes no longer serve a useful role in co-ordinating social behaviour. Therefore, a sound as-if strategy will lead us to produce an attenuated doctrine of respectable statutes and precedents. A sophisticated pragmatist might well decide to disguise this and pretend to follow a statute or precedent when really he is ignoring it. He might present this as a surprising 'interpretation' of the statute or precedent[97] in question. Dworkin describes this strategy as the 'noble lie', and it is used by pragmatists where they believe it will serve their community better in the long run if their actual decision is disguised. The decision to employ such a strategy is therefore itself a strategic one.[98]

One obvious benefit of this approach is that if people knew that a new rule would be applied retrospectively then they would behave in the manner that they believe the courts would find to be in the public interest were the matter to be litigated. This will give much of the benefit of such rules, without the need to actually litigate or enact them. Thus as against conventionalism pragmatism "tells a more promising story".[99] However, like conventionalism, pragmatism encounters difficulties when it seeks to explain why judges show concern for explicating the 'true' force of a statute or precedent, even where this is controversial. Although as we have seen, a pragmatist judge will have some sort of attenuated doctrine of precedent, the justification for respecting precedent will not hold where the scope of that past decision is unclear and controversial. Here we can only defend the fit of pragmatism on the basis of a noble-lie reason. This however is somewhat implausible, for the public will not be outraged if it is told that precedents will be confined to their facts, and the power of precedents to guide behaviour will not be much affected "if judges refuse to follow them when the advice they give is garbled or murky".[100] Thus Dworkin concludes that pragmatism can only be rescued here by means of "procrustean machinery that seems wildly inappropriate",[101] and can only be tolerated if pragmatism "is so powerful along the second dimension of legal interpretation ... that it merits heroic life support".[102] On this dimension, namely justification, we have seen that pragmatism rejects the central contention of Dworkin's basic concept: it does not take legal rights seriously.[103] Instead it views legal rights as "servants of the best future".[104] It is sometimes argued that the reason for this is that pragmatism is the subject of an over-arching convention that judges should decide cases in this way. However this marriage of conventionalism and pragmatism appears to be inadequate. We have already seen that conventionalism is a weaker conception of law than pragmatism, and thus is unlikely to improve the case for pragmatism. Further, the necessary convention simply does not seem to exist, for the pragmatist explanation of judicial activity is not sufficiently widely accepted. A much more promising line here is to exploit the pragmatists' skepticism about legal rights and argue that we should not slavishly follow rights for their own sakes. Here we are led to question how consistency in principle can be important in its own right and not simply a "fetishism of doctrinal elegance",[105] particularly in those cases where there is controversy as to what consistency really requires. It is this that integrity must answer in order to establish its own credentials, and see off the pragmatist challenge.

We have seen that Dworkin describes the sophisticated pragmatist as employing a 'noble lie' strategy in order to best be able to serve his community's best interests in the long term. In this way his pragmatic conception of law will effectively be disguised, although he may be as "openly pragmatic as he dares, disguising only those elements ... that the community is not quite ready to accept".[106] It is at this point that the suspicion arises that Dworkin himself may be something of a 'sophisticated' pragmatist,[107] disguising his pragmatism under the guise of giving surprising and insightful interpretations of the law. If we examine Dworkin's analysis of those cases referred to in his work, then it is noticeable that he often reaches a conclusion that differs from that of most comentators, and indeed may well not have occurred to the judges in the case. For example, Larry Alexander cites Dworkin's discussion in 'The Bork Nomination'[108] as an example of a situation in which Dworkin forsakes conversational standards of interpretation in favour of seeking "the most abstract conception of the author's normative intentions".[109] Similarly in his discussion in *A Matter of Principle* of the case of *Steelworkers v. Weber*[110] when he examines the majority opinion written by Justice Brennan, Dworkin argues that two arguments are put forward, one explicit and one that "must be reconstructed from independent remarks".[111] It is the second argument that Dworkin finds more successful, and which he makes more explicit for the purposes of his discussion of the case. This gives the impression that Dworkin, whilst putting forward his argument as a surprising interpretation of the case in question, is in fact employing a noble lie strategy. Indeed, it comes as little surprise that Dworkin's reconstructed interpretation sees Justice Brennan employing Dworkin's own principle/policy distinction in order to argue that the law should be concerned with consistency in principle.[112] Further, whilst Dworkin criticises the pragmatists for lacking fit in acting only as if they were enforcing pre-existing legal rights, he is himself prone to use this metaphorical device.

Stanley Fish has written a highly dismissive account of Dworkin's version of pragmatism which nevertheless seems to miss the point.[113] Fish's argument is that the picture Dworkin paints of the pragmatist is not believeable as no-one could operate in the way Dworkin describes. It is not possible, Fish says, for a judge to reach the 'best' decision in the case without reference to the history of decisions, statutes and precedents that preceeded it. He writes: "the very ability to formulate a decision in terms that would be recognisably legal depends on one's having internalised the norms, categorical distinctions, and evidentiary criteria that make up one's understanding of what the law is".[114] This criticism misses the mark for this reason. Dworkin does not argue that a pragmatist can be free of the past in making his decisions in cases, but rather he merely argues that the past and its materials do not form the reasons why the pragmatist judge comes to the decisions he does. He does not decide a case in a particular way because of the past, but he nevertheless does not ignore it in that he will frame his decisions in terms that those familiar with the past and its materials will be able to accept. He would not, after all, be a pragmatist unless he had his eye on that. Dworkin puts it this way: "[The pragmatist] denies that past political decisions in themselves provide any justification for either using or witholding the state's coercive power".[115] It is important to recognise that this is what Dworkin is arguing. We may feel that his pragmatist judge is something of a straw man but it would be wrong to see him constructed entirely of straw. Pragmatists by definition could not be that.

Notes

1 Gallie 1965.
2 Dworkin 1986 p.71.
3 Id.
4 Id. p.87.
5 Id. p. 93.
6 Id.
7 Id.
8 Id.
9 Id. p.94.
10 Id.
11 Simmonds 1990.
12 Id, p.66.
13 Id. p.67.
14 Soper 1987 at p. 1 170.
15 Id.
16 Id.
17 Id.
18 Hutchinson 1987.
19 See Dworkin 1987 pp.266-275 and p.430 n.4.
20 Hutchinson 1987 p.658.
21 Id.
22 Guest 1992 p.37.
23 Dworkin 1986 pp.65-66.
24 Id. p.66.
25 Id. p,92.
26 Guest 1992 pp.28-31.
27 Id. p.44 n.26.
28 Id. p.37.
29 Dworkin 1986 p.93.
30 Dworkin 1977 p.37.

31 See Chapter One.
32 This argument will generally follow that set out in Dworkin 1986 pp.114-150.
33 Id. pp.139-150.
34 Examples of conventionalists given by Dworkin are Postema, Hayek and David Lewis. (See Dworkin id. at p.433 n.13 and n.14). Lewis seems to have largely influenced this development of positivism - see Coleman 1984 at p.43 where Coleman refers to Lewis as providing the theoretical foundations for such an alternative. We have also seen above that Hart may arguably be best viewed as a conventionalist.
35 This then adheres to Dworkin's basic concept.
36 Dworkin 1986 p.123.
37 Id.
38 See id. at p.431 n.4 where Jules Coleman, Philip Soper and David Lyons are given as examples of this modern trend. Coleman has argued that Hart seemed to reject the interpretation of his views given by Soper and Lyons.
39 Guest 1992 p.202.
40 Dworkin 1986 pp.127-128.
41 Id. p.128.
42 Soper 1987 at p.1178.
43 Id.
44 Dworkin 1986 p.95.
45 Simmonds 1990 p.77.
46 Id.
47 These arguments appear in Dworkin 1986 at pp.130-139.
48 See id. p.131 for examples here.
49 Id. p.133.
50 Id. p.134.
51 Id. p.135.
52 Simmonds 1990 p.76.
53 Id.
54 Id.
55 Id.
56 Id.
57 Id. p.65.
58 Dworkin 1986 p.136.
59 For example, in a decision of the House of Lords, where each judge finds in favour of the same party, but each differs in his reason for so holding.
60 Dworkin 1986 p.137.
61 Simmonds 1990 p.78.
62 Id.
63 Id. at 79.
64 Id. at 78.
65 Id.
66 Dworkin 1986 p.230.

67 [1983] 1 AC 410.
68 Dworkin 1986 pp.238-250.
69 Fish 1989 at pp.356-371.
70 Id. at 358.
71 Id.
72 Id.
73 Id. at pp.358-359.
74 Dworkin 1986 p.136.
75 Id. p.141.
76 Id. p.142.
77 Id. p.143. Dworkin does allow that criminal law practice is close to unilateralism. However, his concern is with private law.
78 Simmonds 1990 p.70.
79 Id. p.71.
80 Id.
81 Id.
82 The themes in this passage are drawn from Hart 1961. See Simmonds 1990 at p.72 n.19.
83 Here Simmonds develops themes in Fuller 1969. See Simmonds 1990 at p.72 n.20.
84 Simmonds 1990 p.72.
85 Simmonds assumes here that we have seen through the deceits of pragmatism - id. n.21.
86 Guest 1992 p.223 n.6.
87 Id.
88 Simmonds 1990 p.65.
89 Id. p.63.
90 Dworkin 1986 p.93.
91 Altman 1986 p.205.
92 Dworkin 1977 p.37.
93 Although, as we have already seen, Dworkin claims that pragmatists "accept that concept as the right plateau for arguments about the nature of law" but then "frame their theories as skeptical on that plateau" (Dworkin 1986 p.430 n.4). Given their skepticism, it is however surprising that they would accept this plateau. Dworkin summarises their conception as being that "there is no law" (id. p.430 n.4) and thus they are viewed as accepting the plateau furnished by the basic concept, in order that they may criticise it. However, this appears to be contradictory.
94 Dworkin gives no examples of pragmatist theorists, although it is clear that he regards the legal realists as early members of this movement (See Dworkin 1986 at p.153). Stephen Guest refers to John Griffith as an example of a pragmatist theorist (See Guest 1992 pp.208-209). Since the publication of *Law's Empire* there seems to have been something of a renaissance in pragmatist thinking with numerous legal scholars now claiming the title of

pragmatist - see Smith 1990 at p.409, especially n.7.

95 Dworkin 1986 p.154.

96 Dworkin's argument here is set out at id. pp.154-160.

97 Id. p.155.

98 Another reason for the noble lie strategy is that were decisions instead to be 'prospective-only', then people would not be prepared to litigate novel cases and hence the law would become static.

99 Dworkin 1986 p.157.

100 Id. p.159.

101 Id.

102 Id. p.160.

103 This discussion is set out at pp.160-164.

104 Id.

105 Id. p.163.

106 Id. p.155.

107 This argument is one adapted from one put forward by Steven Smith in Smith 1990, especially pp.414-420.

108 Dworkin 1987.

109 Alexander 1987 p.425 n.14.

110 (1979) 443 US 193. See Dworkin 1986 (a) pp.316-331.

111 Id. p.326.

112 Id. p.327.

113 Fish 1989 pp.360-361.

114 Id. p.360.

115 Dworkin 1986 p.151, italics added.

4 Integrity and Interpretation

Having rejected both conventionalism and pragmatism as candidates for the best interpretation of our legal practices Dworkin turns to his preferred account of law as integrity. Central to this notion is Dworkin's theory of community which has at its base the idea of fraternity. We shall examine this in some detail in the next chapter. In this we will explore his views on integrity from three angles. Firstly, we shall consider Dworkin's argument that integrity is a distinct political virtue alongside justice and fairness. Then we shall discuss his view that legal practice is best explained as a chain of reasoning explicable by analogy with the writing of chain novels. Finally we shall examine his views on the role of authorial intention in the law.

Integrity as a Virtue

Dworkin identifies three ideals that ordinary politics shares with utopian political theory. These are those of a fair political structure, which he labels 'fairness', a just distribution of opportunities and resources, which he terms 'justice', and the equitable process of enforcing the rules and regulations needed to establish these, which is procedural due process. However, it is Dworkin's contention that ordinary politics adds a fourth to these, not present in utopian axiomatic theory. Whilst this may be captured in the expression that 'we must treat like cases alike', Dworkin prefers to refer to it as the virtue of 'political integrity'.[1] This requires government to speak with one voice and act in a principled and coherent manner towards all its citizens.[2] Dworkin states that he has chosen the title of 'political integrity' in order that we can more clearly see its relation to the parallel ideal of personal morality. For, as with personal behaviour, we insist that the state acts on a single coherent set of principles even when its citizens are divided about what the right principles of justice and fairness really are.[3] Integrity therefore assumes a deep personification of the state or community. If we accept integrity as a distinct political virtue we have a general non-strategic argument for recognising legal rights, and thus a means of defeating pragmatism. Dworkin's argument is then "that integrity rather than some superstition of elegance is the life of the law as we know it".[4]

This argument is challenged by Denise Reaume on the basis that integrity is not an independent virtue but instead parasitic upon the other ideals.[5] This is because each of the ideals will itself be made up of a set of principles, or a single principle, and thus will require internal consistency. Reaume argues that this is true of whatever principles one may accept for each requires consistency on its own terms.[6] For example, if we regard slavery as unjust we will regard all instances of slavery as unjust. To allow slavery would be to violate our principle of justice - we do not require the existence of a separate ideal to explain why this is the case. Dworkin himself appears to recognise this in drawing his distinction between 'pure' and 'inclusive' integrity.[7] He defines pure integrity as arising in a situation where judges are free simply to pursue coherence in the principles of justice which flow through the law.[8] This is what, for Dworkin, the law gropes towards. However, he recognises that for the present the judge must instead aim for an inclusive integrity whereby he constructs his theory of the law "so that it reflects, so far as possible, coherent principles of political fairness, substantive justice, and procedural due process, and reflects these combined in the right relation".[9] This clearly seems to point to the parasitic nature of integrity, particularly in the case of its pure form. In a case of inclusive integrity, as Reaume points out, Dworkin's argument appears to suggest the need for "a principle of some sort that determines the outcome of conflicts between substance and procedure or determines the right mix of other ideals" rather than for the independent ideal of integrity.[10] Thus in order to counter this Dworkin needs to provide a more convincing argument for the independence of integrity. This he attempts to do with his 'checkerboard' statute argument.[11] Dworkin asks us to imagine the existence of a law in which similar events are treated differently not because of any rational or reasoned grounds, but on the basis of arbitrary decisions for the purpose of reaching compromise. Dworkin claims that we reject such compromises because we accept integrity.

Dworkin envisages the situation where a legislator passes a law on abortion having decided that a compromise is necessary between justice and fairness due to a division of opinion in society. As a result the right to have an abortion is granted in proportion to the numbers of citizens who are pro-abortion and anti-abortion. Why should we condemn such a solution as a means of resolving divisions over the matter of principle? After all, we can find no defect here on the basis of fairness, for such a compromise is by hypothesis fairer than the possible alternatives. This way both points of view are represented which is not so with the winner-take-all strategy some may regard as preferable. Can we then argue that we have reasons of justice for rejecting such a compromise? Here we must be careful, for many single checkerboard solutions will provide more examples of injustice than at least one of the alternatives, and fewer than another. However, there will be controversy over which alternative would be more and which less just. Our question is instead that of whether we have a reason for rejecting such compromises on the grounds of justice in advance. We could argue that simply by reason of treating people differently, without any justifying principle, justice is offended. But the fact remains that some instances of injustice which would otherwise occur will be prevented by this solution, and we cannot say that justice requires not eliminating any injustice unless we can eliminate all.[12] To reject a checkerboard solution will appear perverse when the alternative is the implementation of the alternative we oppose. Thus, if in our example we were in the minority in arguing a pro-abortion stance, it would appear perverse of us to desire a solution whereby abortion was proscribed as one in which a minority of applicants were entitled to an abortion.

Perhaps, Dworkin says, we are looking for a reason of justice in the wrong direction. Instead we might argue that no-one should actively seek to reduce what he believes to be injustice. A checkerboard statute can be enacted only by a majority vote, and by definition will contain some injustices, and therefore will be passed only if a majority of legislators votes in favour of a provision they believe to be unjust. However, this seems to beg the question at issue, for even if we were to accept that no-one should vote for such a compromise, we still have no reason for rejecting it as an outcome in advance. It is very easy to imagine a system where such outcomes would be achieved as a matter of course without any legislator, being asked to vote for the compromise as a package.[13] We therefore seem to have strong reasons of fairness for endorsing such a compromise. Yet, as Dworkin surely correctly states, our instincts condemn it.[14] For this reason, he argues that our instincts about internal compromise suggest another political ideal standing between justice and fairness.[15]

This explanation of the existence of the virtue of integrity, and consequently of the role of consistency in principle, has been criticised. Philip Soper argues that integrity "does not ... seem adequate to the task Dworkin has set for it: that of showing why pragmatism is an inferior normative theory".[16] Soper discusses Dworkin's own example of *McLoughlin v. O'Brian*,[17] the facts and issues of which we have detailed before, in relation to a pragmatic judge. Dworkin uses this case in order to show the benefits of the pragmatist position. Soper characterises Dworkin's argument here as being that the pragmatist who believes that there should never be recovery for emotional distress "can deny this plaintiff recovery without wondering whether he can distinguish in a principled way McLoughlin's case from other precedents".[18] However, Soper argues that this "assumes that the pragmatist judge cannot overrule the prior precedents which is exactly what integrity would lead him to do".[19] Soper instead argues that a pragmatic judge considering this case would either be correct that damages for emotional distress could not be recovered or he would have a means of distinguishing the precedents on 'strategic' grounds. Either way he would not be worried about past political decisions except for reasons of strategy. Thus Soper concludes that Dworkin begs the question, for the pragmatist thinks everything can and should be decided on the basis of policy and therefore will never have to act in an 'unprincipled' manner. He therefore needs some independent prior argument for preferring principle over policy.[20]

Soper's account of this is misleading. Much of the confusion that arises here seems to stem from the fact that he discusses the issue of checkerboard statutes, and the consequent argument for the existence of integrity as a virtue, from within the pragmatist viewpoint. Problems arise because the case of *McLoughlin v. O'Brian* is not an example of a compromise, and because Soper seems to misunderstand Dworkin's discussion of the case. Soper states that Dworkin's argument assumes that the pragmatist judge cannot overrule the prior precedents.[21] This is clearly mistaken. One of the main themes of Dworkin's discussion of pragmatism is that in not being bound to follow precedent pragmatism does not seem to fit our practices. Indeed, the discussion of *McLoughlin v. O'Brian* that Soper is referring to is intended to show that the pragmatists, skeptical approach to legal rights may appear more sensible and less like doctrinal elegance.[22] Soper's error seems to arise from reading Dworkin's pragmatist appraisal of the McLoughlin case as if he were setting out the sole option for pragmatists when in fact he simply states what a pragmatist judge would be likely to do if faced with such a case. From this, Soper compounds his error by arguing that the application of integrity to *McLoughlin v. O'Brian* would lead the judge to overrule the prior precedents, whereas this will not be the case with a pragmatist approach. This is mistaken, as in fact the distinction is that the judge applying integrity will distinguish the case on the grounds of principle, whereas the pragmatist judge will distinguish on grounds of strategy. Both Dworkin and Soper recognise this,[23] but for some reason Soper seems to believe that Dworkin has failed to do so. Having reached this point Soper then concludes that Dworkin has begged the question in failing to answer why the pragmatists should abandon policy. This conclusion seems to result from the confusions we have noticed. Soper views it as following from the distinction he has drawn between pragmatists and those applying integrity, and he goes on to argue that we need some independent, prior, argument for preferring principle over policy. Soper has got things back to front. In choosing to discuss checkerboard statutes within the context of pragmatism, Soper seems to miss the point that Dworkin's checkerboard statute argument is intended to produce the reason for preferring principle to policy, namely that integrity reflects the need for principled decisions.

Thus Soper first puts forward the argument that pragmatists need only worry about past decisions for strategic reasons, which is already accepted by Dworkin. Then secondly, because of the order of his argument he believes that this provides a distinction that Dworkin must tackle. However, Dworkin has done just that in his discussion of checkerboard statutes. Hence we must conclude that Soper's argument is both confused and confusing. Perhaps a better argument along these lines would have been to point out that pragmatists are not bound by checkerboard statutes, and can ignore them on strategic grounds because they offend our intuitions. However, whilst this achieves the desired result it fails to indicate why these compromises offend us, and it also ignores the fact that we object to them *ab initio*, in that we do not consider them and then reject them on policy grounds, but instead reject them from their inception. We regard them as lacking fit and therefore do not need to consider their substance.

A more promising defence is undertaken by Robert Westmoreland.[24] Westmoreland's argument is that Dworkin adopts an unusual maximising view of justice in discussing checkerboard statutes and that a more appropriate version would lead us to reject such compromises on the grounds of justice and not integrity. Westmoreland argues that the idea that justice does not condemn checkerboard statutes depends on a view of justice that appears nowhere else in Dworkin's work, and is inimical to his Rawlsian conception of justice as bound up with a foundational right to 'equal concern and respect'.[25] The maximising conception to have been adopted by Dworkin appears to be an example of what Robert Nozick has termed a 'utilitarianism of justice'[26] whereby the state seeks to minimise the amount of violations of rights according to the level of seriousness. This then presents a problem for Dworkin for, as Westmoreland indicates, if the state employs a non-maximising conception of justice, "as Hercules' neo-Kantian state surely does",[27] then it will be this that condemns the checkerboard statute on the grounds that it offends the inviolability of persons. Thus Dworkin is in a bind, for it would now appear that "whether or not the state accepts a maximising conception of justice, it is justice, not 'integrity', that determines whether or not such unequal treatment is condoned".[28] This means that, although law as integrity may in the end endorse the kind of equality that condemns checkerboard compromises, we no longer have a reason for defeating the pragmatism of justice, for it is respect for reason and for persons that leads to the rejection of checkerboard statutes and not respect for institutional history.[29]

Westmoreland's conclusion is essentially a sound one. However, some aspects of his argument require clarification. Dworkin affirms his basic commitment to a Rawlsian conception of justice in *Law's Empire*,[30] and he has in the past interpreted Rawls' original position as providing the right to equal concern and respect,[31] and indeed he goes so far as to state that "justice as fairness rests on the assumption of a natural right of all men and women to equality of concern and respect".[32] Thus it seems fair to say with Westmoreland that it will be justice and not integrity that inspires Hercules' rejection of checkerboard compromises. However, we could argue that Dworkin's argument here is intended to clarify his earlier views and, as we have seen, Dworkin expressly deals with the possibility "that a checkerboard solution is unjust by definition because it treats different people differently for no good reason".[33] But, Dworkin points out that it can hardly be a good reason to fail to eliminate injustice because we cannot eliminate all.[34] Here, however, we may feel that Dworkin's argument begins to falter. The example that Dworkin uses to justify his proposition is the situation where we can rescue only some prisoners from tyranny,[35] but this is not an example of a compromise because the only options available are rescuing some prisoners or rescuing none. If there were an option to rescue all such prisoners then clearly justice would direct us to seek that. This is the difficulty with Dworkin's argument. Where there are two plausible alternatives representing different principles, we have no need of the checkerboard compromise. However, where one of the two alternatives is no longer plausible then the compromise looks more attractive. Thus in Dworkin's own example, if the option to rescue all the prisoners of tyranny were no longer plausible, we would compromise and seek to rescue as many as possible. If integrity would argue against this compromise, then it would be the consistency of integrity that offends our intuitions. Much of the apparent difficulty with these compromises arises here because of the criteria Dworkin applies to them.[36] If we argue for a compromise on the grounds of justice, then the criteria we apply to determine this compromise must also be consistent with our principles of justice. In his example of a statute on abortion, Dworkin suggests a compromise whereby only women born in even years are permitted abortions. This clearly employs an unjust selection criterion, and ignores the obvious alternative that the stage of pregnancy be used.[37] In this way, principles of justice such as the need for equal concern and respect will play a part in our decision whether to accept or reject checkerboard compromises. This reflects the need to apply justice consistently but does not show integrity to be an independent virtue.

There is one area of Westmoreland's argument that is difficult to accept. This is his claim that Dworkin adopts "a curious maximising view of justice"[38] in his discussion of checkerboard statutes. Instead, although this is not made clear, it seems that Dworkin's argument is actually based on the maximin view of justice that also appears in Rawls's work. This is the notion that in any pay-off any inequalities should be arranged so that they are to the greatest benefit to the least advantaged. The checkerboard solution is an attractive alternative as it allows that, whichever side is 'correct' as to a particular decision, by adopting a compromise *some* justice will be done whatever. We are therefore in a position to maximise the amount of justice that can be done within a context of minimising as much injustice as possible. Westmoreland is therefore mistaken to argue that Dworkin applies an unusual view of justice here, but his substantive argument, that injustice and not integrity explains our reaction to checkerboard statutes, is not affected by this.

Integrity and the Chain of Law

Dworkin describes his theory of law as being interpretive in nature. Understood in this way law is a deeply political activity, and lawyers and judges are unable to avoid engaging political theory in making legal judgements. However, it is Dworkin's argument that we can comprehend the nature of legal interpretation only be comparing it with interpretation in other disciplines, and in particular literature. Dworkin argues that the interpretation of social practices and works of art are linked under the heading of 'creative interpretation' as both are *essentially* concerned with purposes rather than mere causes.[39] Creative interpretation is itself a form of what Dworkin terms 'constructive' interpretation, for the purposes in play "are not (fundamentally) those of some author but of the interpreter"[40] who should aim to impose purpose on the object or practice he is interpreting such as to make it the best possible example of the genre to which it is taken to belong. Thus creative interpretation involves an interaction between purpose and object, and it is this that leads Dworkin to make an analogy between the practice of legal interpretation and the writing of a chain novel. This analogy lies at the heart of Dworkin's theory of legal interpretation, and has initiated a lengthy debate between him and Stanley Fish.

In his original essay entitled 'How Law is Like Literature,[41] Dworkin argues that the interpretation of a work of literature strives to show which way of reading that work reveals it in its best possible light. This is the 'aesthetic hypothesis', and different schools of interpretation will hold different views as to what will be required for its satisfaction. However, it is Dworkin's claim that, despite appearances, the hypothesis is "neither so wild or so weak nor so inevitably relativistic as might first appear".[42] This then provides the starting point for Dworkin's theory of interpretation. However, the theory of interpretation in *Law's Empire* appears to differ from that in Dworkin's earlier articles on this subject and this would seem to be largely as a result of the criticisms put forward by Stanley Fish. We will therefore examine Dworkin's theory as it appears in his first essay on the subject, and then turn to consider the subsequent development in his thesis in the light of Fish's critique.

In 'How Law is Like Literature' Dworkin commences his examination of interpretation by considering the constraints placed upon literary critics in reading a text. Here, Dworkin argues that the text provides one severe constraint[43] in that all the words must be accounted for, and none may be altered in the quest to interpret the work in its best light. However, Dworkin does allow that this requirement will be sensitive to the particular critic's own theoretical beliefs as to the nature of the canonical text.[44] Another constraint will be that of the interpreter's own artistic opinions as to the need for coherence or integrity. The aesthetic hypothesis will not be satisfied by an interpretation that renders much of the text irrelevant, or the style unintegrated. Thus Dworkin argues that an interpretation would fail which interpreted an Agatha Christie novel as a treatise on the meaning of death, not simply because it would be "a poor tract less valuable than a good mystery",[45] but because such an interpretation would make the novel a shambles with all but one or two sentences irrelevant to its supposed theme. Dworkin does accept that some works of detective fiction, such as those of Raymond Chandler, have been 'reinterpreted' as being of wider critical merit, but that the fact that this succeeds with the works of Chandler and not with those of Christie simply shows the constraints imposed by integrity. Here we can see Dworkin already moving towards establishing a link between the interpretation of law and of literature through the need for both to be coherent and thus to apply integrity. However, as with judicial practice, Dworkin allows that there is much room for disagreement in the interpretation of works of literature, not only as to what is required to satisfy coherence, but also more widely about the function or point of art conceived more broadly. Although we may not realise that we possess such beliefs, anyone interpreting a work of art will rely on beliefs of the theoretical character about identity and other formal properties of art as well as more explicit normative views as to what constitutes good art. There will thus be a form of reciprocity between our general theory of art and our specific approach to the interpretation of a particular work. This leads Dworkin into his discussion of the chain of law, with its twin criteria of fit and substantive values. In this way the constraints of the text, and the role of our convictions as to what constitutes the 'best' that an object can be, are joined together in a single enterprise that Dworkin argues is equivalent to the role played by judges in the legal system. This is because it unites the role of the author and the critic in an enterprise which should produce a single, unified work. Similarly the role of the judge, particularly in common law cases, is both to interpret the law that has gone before, and to show the value of that law in political terms by demonstrating the best principle or policy it can be taken to serve.[46] As with the chain novel, the judge has a duty to advance the continuing enterprise of the law rather than strike out in some new direction of his own.[47] Thus the enterprise of the chain novelist and that of the judge are linked, and Dworkin has a means of explaining how constraints of fit and opinions of substantive value combine together in a single enterprise in which the roles of critic and creator must be played by a single figure.

The literary critic creates his own theory of coherence or integrity in order to "tutor and constrain"[48] his working theory of fit, and in the same way the judge will also develop his convictions. However, in those frequent 'hard' cases in which more than one possible interpretation meets this theory of fit the judge, as with the critic, must apply his substantive political theory in order to adjudicate between these possible decisions. Here the decisive factor as to the best interpretation will be the consequence of beliefs that judges need not share.[49] This poses a problem for Dworkin as to the inherent subjectivity of these judgements. However, it is one that he recognises and deals with. As Dworkin himself points out, since it is the case that we all hold our own opinions on what constitutes good art, the aesthetic hypothesis "abandons hope of rescuing objectivity in interpretation except, perhaps, among those who hold very much the same theory of art".[50] Interpretation therefore becomes on this view a concept around which there are various theories competing as conceptions. However, Dworkin argues that it is an open question whether these judgements can be said to be true or false, despite the impossibility of demonstrating any particular claim. This then returns us to the idea put forward by Dworkin in rejecting the demonstrability thesis in relation to his one-right answer thesis, which we examined in earlier chapters. Here he concludes, as he did previously, that from the subjectivity of these judgements it "does not flow that no normative theory about art is better than any other".[51]

Having thus set out Dworkin's views as they appear in 'How Law is Like Literature' we now consider the response to them of Stanley Fish, for Fish's critique appears to have influenced the subsequent development of Dworkin's views. In order to do this we shall consider Fish's critique and the resultant developments to Dworkin's interpretive theory under two broad headings, reflecting the different issues that we have highlighted in Dworkin's argument. These are the nature of interpretive constraints in the chain of law, and the subjectivity of interpretive claims. Whilst these overlap to some extent, they do represent different aspects of Dworkin's thesis here.

The Nature of Interpretive Constraints

We concentrate firstly on Fish's criticism of Dworkin's depiction of the constraints placed upon those operating on the chain of law. In that Fish's critique derives much of its force from his view of the substantive nature of our interpretive judgements, this overlaps with his comments on the objectivity of Dworkin's theory. However, the possibility of objectivity in interpretation remains a distinct issue, and hence will be dealt with separately. We begin by examining Fish's criticism of Dworkin in his article 'Working on the Chain Gang'.[52]

Fish's basic argument is that, in elaborating his chain of law, Dworkin makes two related and mutually reinforcing assumptions: "he assumes that history in a form of a chain of decisions has, at some level, the status of a brute fact; and he assumes that wayward or arbitrary behaviour in relation to that fact is an institutional impossibility".[53] These two assumptions enable Dworkin to explain how an independent agent is bound by the self-executing constraints of the text he is interpreting. It is Fish's argument that these constraints exist anyway, through the tacit awareness of the interpreter as to what constitutes an acceptable interpretation. With regard to these assumptions, we have seen that Dworkin argues that the judge is bound by the history as he finds it, and he cannot invoke a 'better' history to suit his preferred interpretation. The difficulty with this idea, as Fish indicates, is that the idea of legal history is itself an interpretive one. We can only decide what constitutes the relevant legal history to a particular case by making an interpretive judgement, and this may often be controversial. Dworkin states that the judge must seek cases "arguably similar"[54] to the one before him, and Fish points out that it must be argued *for*, as "similarity is not something one finds, but something one must establish".[55] Dworkin seems to recognise this when he states that the judge must interpret this history because he has "a responsibility to advance the enterprise in hand rather than strike out in some new direction of his own".[56] However, this assumes that it would be possible for a judge not to make an interpretive judgement of that history, and this is not the case. How could he strike out from something he had not constituted in his mind? Further, for a decision to be recognisably judicial it would have to be made in judicial terms, and thus would not be seen as striking out in a new direction. If we put forward a decision not made in such terms, we would "simply not be acting as a judge".[57] Thus, the difficulty for Dworkin here lies in the idea that to view a case as being part of a chain of previous decisions is "to reconceive that chain by finding in it an applicability that has not always been apparent".[58] For Dworkin's fear that judges might strike out in a new direction to be plausible there would have to be some hard core of historical facts to be avoided, yet we have seen that this is not the case. This point can be illustrated by Dworkin's use of the example of the novels of Agatha Christie to reinforce his claims on interpretive constraints. Dworkin argued that an interpretation of a Christie novel as a tract on death would be a failure, not only because it would be a poor tract, but also because it would make the novel a shambles. If this were presented as Dworkin's own interpretive judgement it would be acceptable. However, it is instead given the status of fact. That this is problematic becomes apparent when Fish points out that there have in fact been a number of academic studies of Christie's work that put forward the interpretation that Dworkin claims cannot be successful.[59] Dworkin seems to miss the point that the text itself must be interpreted, and thus no core to it can exist, although obviously most sections of a text will be interpreted identically by most readers with variations only where the text is complex.[60] This point is perhaps best brought out in Dworkin's discussion of Shakespeare's *Hamlet*.[61] Dworkin comments that we might argue that the play would have been improved had Hamlet been portrayed as a more forceful man of action,[62] but that this does not mean that the play as it actually is really is like that. In other words, Shakespeare's text exercises a constraint on such an interpretation. This is a better example simply because of its acceptability to the modern reader of Hamlet, as the interpretation of Hamlet as a procrastinator is now the standard reading of the text. However, it appears that the reading of Hamlet as a man of forceful action was for many years the standard reading of the character, only to be superseded by our current interpretation.[63] This indicates that our view of the character of Hamlet is a deeply embedded interpretive belief which does not carry the status of being at the core of the text. This brings out the error that Dworkin appears to make, for he seeks constraints in the text itself whereas in fact those constraints appear internally in the interpreter's analysis of that text. Readings that appear to be at the heart of the text are in fact deeply embedded interpretations which will therefore be highly popular accounts.

Dworkin's initial response to this criticism appears in his brief article 'On Interpretation and Objectivity'.[64] Dworkin protests that Fish has misunderstood his original argument. Dworkin argues that in his original article his point was that we should understand our interpretive judgements as "special and complex aesthetic claims about what makes a particular work of art a better work of art".[65] Thus Dworkin states that he recognises that "interpretive claims are interpretive ... and so dependent on aesthetic or political theory all the way down",[66] and that on his account the text itself is the product of interpretive judgements.[67] We have however already seen that this does not seem to be the case with certain of Dworkin's arguments in 'How Law is Like Literature', whatever he may protest to the contrary. Indeed, this protest seems more to indicate confusion on Dworkin's part between what he wishes to say and the implications of what he does say. This is a notable feature of Dworkin's articles on interpretation, with Dworkin providing much of his own critique without realising he is doing so. For example, in 'How Law is Like Literature' he argues that integrity or coherence acts as a constraint on our interpretation of a text. But in the next sentence he acknowledges that there is "room for much disagreement among critics about what counts as integration",[68] thus indicating that this constraint is interpretive. Yet he has just used that constraint to strike down a potential interpretation of Agatha Christie's novels. He does not present that as simply being his interpretation of the constraint of integrity, but instead as being ruled out by the text. Dworkin seemingly fails to see the incompatibility of these arguments, and thus his protestations in 'On Interpretation and Objectivity' fall somewhat flat.[69]

However, Dworkin does provide arguments beyond his simple claims of being misrepresented. He also deals with the objection that the text can exercise only illusory constraint over the result of an interpretive judgement.[70] The argument here is that Dworkin anticipated this objection by arguing that "interpretive convictions can act as checks *on one another*" in that our interpretive convictions as to fit are "sufficiently disjoint" from our convictions about substance to constrain them.[71] Whether or not this is the case it does not answer the point at issue which relates to the possibility of there being a fixed core within a text which provides an external measure of fit, as Dworkin's arguments seem to require. Dworkin simply denies that this is the case, without then explaining how his arguments can be understood if this is not so.[72] Instead he selects to concentrate on the possibility of there being some sort of distinction between our internal convictions. Thus Dworkin's reply here does not seem to answer the difficulties raised by his original article.

Fish's response to this appears in 'Wrong Again'[73] which essentially is a reiteration and expansion of the points made previously. He does however provide the additional example of our understanding of Milton's *Paradise Lost* which was once thought to lack the coherence and psychological plausibility we would expect in a novel, but was subsequently reinterpreted such that it "turned the verse into just the flexible instrument everyone had always known it wasn't",[74] and in a manner found convincing by many conversant with Milton. The point of this, of course, is to indicate the extent to which apparently deeply embedded interpretations are capable of change, and also to indicate that what may appear to be at the core of the text is actually only a widely held interpretation of that text.[75] However, Fish does recognise that this point is one that is increasingly present in Dworkin's analysis[76] and in a discussion of Dickens's *A Christmas Carol* he deals with Dworkin's more recent arguments. In his article 'My Reply to Stanley Fish (and Walter Benn Michaels)' Dworkin uses the example of a chain novelist called upon to provide an ending to Dickens's book.[77] Here Dworkin is clearly moving towards Fish's position in his argument that "most chain novelists would think that certain interpretations of Scrooge's character would be incompatible with the final sections of *A Christmas Carol*, but not with the opening pages alone", and that as a result a novelist at the end of the chain "will have more difficulty seeing Scrooge as inherently evil than a novelist second in line would have".[78] Fish simply makes the point to this that, whilst it is true that our context constrains our interpretation, that context is itself the product of interpretation, and this is variable as a constraint. Dworkin does appear to implicitly recognise this, and is simply arguing how he feels most people would interpret that context. This becomes more explicit in *Law's Empire* which continues Dworkin's process of clarification based on Fish's arguments.

In *Law's Empire* Dworkin retains many of his former arguments on interpretation, but seems much clearer as to their implications. He retains the idea of the chain of law, and also maintains the distinction between judgements of fit and judgements of substantive value. However, whereas Dworkin previously stressed this distinction in order to "bring something of the great complexity of these judgements to the surface",[79] he now views it as a "useful analytical device that helps us give structure to any interpreter's working theory", and recognises that the distinction is "less crucial or profound than it might seem".[80] This would appear to be something of a reply to Fish's point about the interpretive interdependence of these constraints,[81] although Dworkin does hold that these constraints remain distinct enough to give the "possibility of contest" as it is this that distinguishes the chain novelist from the creative writer.[82] This distinction remains unsatisfactory however in that the creative writer necessarily still interprets the text that he is writing, and whilst we might maintain that he has the opportunity to alter his previous chapters in order to better accommodate his interpretation of his work, in the same way legal history is constantly being rewritten.[83]

Dworkin also returns to his discussion of Dickens's *A Christmas Carol* and the constraints on novelists at various points of its completion. Here Dworkin reprises much of what he previously stated. However, his discussion is more detailed, and it is much clearer that he sees the individual interpreter's convictions as the root of the enterprise. Dworkin asserts that he does not mean that no interpreter could possibly think Scrooge inherently evil after his supposed redemption,[84] but then goes on to assert that it would be a poor interpretation based on all the criteria so far described.[85] Dworkin seems to be sliding back towards the difficulties we noted in his discussion of Agatha Christie's novels. It would be better for Dworkin here to state that on his criteria, and probably on that of most people, this would be a poor interpretation. This seems to fit better with the substantive point he is seeking to make. This is illustrated by Dworkin's discussion of the role of the chain novelist within *A Christmas Carol* whom he concludes is neither free nor constrained for "each must in some way be qualified by the other".[86] This seems to strongly echo Fish's comment that the interpreter is free *and* constrained.[87] The final indication of this shift comes with Dworkin's discussion of 'the misleading objection',[88] which refers to the possibility that the chain novelist may depart from the novel in progress with which he has been furnished. He now regards this as no longer being an option as "he has nothing he *can* depart from or cleave to until he has constructed a novel-in-process from the text".[89] Any proper disagreement here will arise over the interpretive and aesthetic convictions employed by the interpreter. This will be a disagreement as to what respecting the text requires. This represents a considerable move forward in Dworkin's theory and significantly alters his previous position as to the possibility of judges striking out on their own.[90]

It is interesting that much of what appears in *Law's Empire* on this issue is also present in the first article 'How Law is Like Literature', but that Dworkin seems to have managed now to avoid most of the conflicts that appeared to arise in that earlier work. This is largely a result of the clarification Dworkin has been forced to make in the face of Fish's attack, although some of his arguments have also been revised. We must now undertake a similar examination into Dworkin's discussion of the subjectivity of interpretive judgements.

Interpretive Judgements and Subjectivity

We now consider the debate as to whether our interpretive claims possess the status of pure subjective opinion or attain objectivity. Many of the arguments on this issue parallel those encountered in our discussion of interpretive constraints, and thus similar points are raised. This argument derives from Fish's article 'Working on the Chain Gang', and in particular his argument that in 'How Law is Like Literature' at certain points Dworkin makes the assumption that there can be a core to a text which cannot be challenged in interpreting that text. Fish concluded that it is not the case that interpretation is constrained by "what is obvious and unproblematically 'there'".[91] Although Dworkin claims, as we have seen, that this was not what he was saying, Fish's argument nevertheless led Dworkin to discuss the status of interpretive claims.

Dworkin's argument here is best understood by reference to his article 'On Interpretation and Objectivity'.[92] In this Dworkin commences by stating that he sees no point in making a general argument in order to show that our moral or interpretive judgements are objective since he has no arguments for the objectivity of interpretive judgements except interpretive arguments.[93] However, if we consider a specific example, such as the assertion that slavery is unjust, then Dworkin claims that although we have arguments for this view, if pressed on the point we would be forced to admit that these relied on convictions for which no further arguments could be produced. If we were then asked if we had any further arguments to the view that slavery is objectively or really unjust, then Dworkin argues that we would not, because "it is not a further claim at all but just the same claim put in a slightly more emphatic form".[94] This forms the basis of Dworkin's argument, and is the reason why he does not seek a general defence of the objectivity of his claims. Dworkin however still feels the need to deal with

Fish's comments that his views assume that judgements can be objectively right and wrong, that there are answers 'out there'. Dworkin experiences difficulty with this point for, as he freely admits, he cannot see the difference between the proposition that slavery is unjust and the proposition that the injustice of slavery is part of the furniture of the universe.[95] However he does consider a contemporary explanation of how this might be the case which takes the form that, were we to stand outside the enterprise in which we are engaged, we would know that no such proposition can be really or objectively true.[96] The difficulty of this for Dworkin is that it assumes that it is possible to distinguish our enterprise from the real world "and that is exactly what we cannot do",[97] for words such as 'objectively' cannot change the sense of interpretive judgement. The reason for this is that he regards the problem of objectivity as a 'fake' as the distinction that could give it meaning, between substantive arguments within and skeptical arguments about social practices, is itself a fake.[98]

This leads Dworkin into a discussion of internal and external skepticism which we have already seen is a feature of *Law's Empire*. The conclusion in both works is that external skepticism cannot trouble our, enterprise for we cannot step outside it in order to check our interpretive judgements against an external reality, and that we are thus left only with he possibility of internal skepticism. If external skepticism is to be persuasive then Fish needs to produce a normative argument to that effect, and "must abandon, as inconsistent, his own favourite interpretations of texts".[99] Dworkin therefore attacks Fish on the basis of the impossibility of external skepticism, which means that the only way Fish can justify his "extravagant claim" that "any text allows any interpretation whatsoever"[100] is to turn instead to internal skepticism.

Fish gives only a limited response to this argument in 'Wrong Again', choosing instead to concentrate on the defects in Dworkin's own interpretive theory. He does however reject Dworkin's attribution to him of the extravagant claim that any text allows any interpretation on the basis that such a claim makes no sense given that the text itself is an object of interpretation, and thus "it does not survive the sea of changes that a succession of interpretation brings".[101] Such changes will be the result of persuasion within the relevant profession. Fish also makes the point that Dworkin seems to seek independent confirmation of his interpretive judgements, but if an interpretation is grounded in the interpreter's beliefs then it goes without saying that the interpreter believes in his interpretation.[102] If that is the case then it necessarily follows that he believes that interpretation to be better than another, for otherwise he would not have made it. From this we need no further explanation of why he believes it to be better, for clearly it is "flatly impossible for him to think anything else".[103]

Applying Fish's argument here it seems that we can furnish a rejoinder to Dworkin's thesis as to the status of interpretive claims based on the incommensurability of these claims. In order to illustrate this point consider the following example. As a frequent viewer of films over a lengthy period a person will have gradually evolved his own aesthetic standards as to what he seeks from any particular viewing experience. From this he obviously regards certain films as particular favourites, others in a lesser light, and from this he could if he so desired set out his own personal selection of pictures that he regarded as being the 'best'. Having compiled this according to his own aesthetic standards he could then compare this list with that of fellow viewers and no doubt here he would find a considerable, if not total, difference of opinion. The reason for this difference is that everybody possesses their own distinct aesthetic standards. For instance, he may be particularly interested in film noir, whilst someone else may prefer westerns. His position as to this difference of opinion would be to accept that on his criteria certain films would be regarded in a favourable light whilst accepting that on other criteria they would not. Nevertheless he would still be able to argue that his aesthetic theory was superior to others. If he did not believe this, he would simply alter his theory to bring it into line with others. Thus it is impossible to make any interpretive claim that does not seek the status of objectivity without having to adopt the position of the internal skeptic. Dworkin does not seem to recognise that putting forward an interpretive argument is the same as arguing that the interpretation is part of the furniture of the universe.[104] The possible reason for this becomes clearer once we consider the claims of the incommensurability thesis.[105] This arises where we regard two values as being incommensurable, as there is no common currency by which to evaluate them. If we regard certain reflections as being incommensurable then it could be argued that we are simply putting forward a version of the skeptical thesis in that we cannot measure these beliefs against one another. Therefore all such beliefs possess equal status.[106] This is the basis of Dworkin's argument that Fish is bound to take up the position of the internal skeptic. However, this apparent conclusion does not follow, for in assigning equal status to these beliefs they have in fact been ranked. As Joseph Raz points out, in saying that two options are of equal value one is passing a judgement about their relative value whereas saying that they are incommensurate does not.[107] Therefore one can hold the view that certain beliefs are incommensurable and at the same time regard one's own beliefs as superior without any logical conflict arising. Thus to return to our examples of judgements as to the status of various films, in assessing the merits of our respective aesthetic judgements we have no common value by which to evaluate the relative merits of westerns as against film noir thrillers. Thus these values seem to be incommensurate, and in the same way this seems more accurately to reflect the status of our interpretive claims on law and literature.

What are the implications of this conclusion for Dworkin's theory? We saw in the previous section of the argument, in discussing the nature of interpretive constraints, that Dworkin still maintains his distinction between fit and substantive interpretive judgement in *Law's Empire*. Dworkin maintained that these could still 'check one another', based on the complexity of such judgements.[108] Indeed, Dworkin goes so far as to claim that such checks are a necessity if we are to view someone as genuinely interpretive at all.[109] Whilst Dworkin accepts that these constraints are 'internal' to the particular interpreter, and thus that the precise nature of the constraint will differ from person to person, he nevertheless argues that it "is a familiar part of our cognitive experience that some of our beliefs and convictions operate as checks in deciding how far we can or should accept or give effect to others".[110] However, Dworkin seems to go back on the insight that our interpretive convictions are all inter-connecting when he maintains the "possibility of contest" between these convictions.[111] Thus, as Simmonds points out, although our convictions about fit are interpretive in nature, for Dworkin we can only be interpreting "if the criteria of fit are independent of the substantive interpretation offered".[112] This perhaps states the point too strongly - Dworkin does after all allow that there will be some overlap - but Simmonds's substantive point remains. Dworkin requires the possibility that there be some distinction between these constraints. Simmonds argues that the criteria of fit we should adopt will vary according to the reason why the distinction between interpretation and invention matters in a specific context.[113] This suggestion seems acceptable, and indeed in accordance with Dworkin's own views.[114] From this then, if we turn to look at the practice of law, we will see that the distinction between interpreting and inventing is important precisely because the practice of law requires that we interpret. The reason for this lies in the demands of integrity, which entail that we must maintain consistency with past decisions when making an interpretive judgement on current ones. Thus Simmonds concludes that law as integrity provides the criteria of fit for the interpretation of legal practices.[115] This seems to be a satisfactory conclusion. However, it raises a serious difficulty for Dworkin, as law as integrity also provides the substantive justification for these same practices, and thus Dworkin's distinction appears to be on the brink of collapse. We must therefore consider if there is any way in which he might challenge the initial premise of this argument that judgements of fit and substance must be kept distinct.[116] In the past, in his argument with Fish, we have seen that Dworkin has relied on the complexity of our interpretive convictions in order to ward off challenges to this distinction. However, once it becomes clear that both judgements derive from the same value, this supposed complexity starts to look somewhat simple. Here we need to be careful, as value-dependence itself does not necessarily result in simplicity. For example, in science this is not the case.[117] Nevertheless, fit is a significant constraint on science precisely because the complexity thesis still holds, and not because fit is independent. With the idea of interpretive checks and balances becoming suspect, when it turns out that everything emerges from the same evaluative judgement, ie., integrity, complexity is lost.[118] It is this and not value-dependence that undermines Dworkin's claim to complexity.

Marmor sees all this as either leading us to endorse the internal skeptics' positions, or instead to revise the theory altogether.[119] However, he fails to see the full possibilities of the incommensurability thesis, equating it with a form of internal skepticism.[120] In fact, it allows us to assert the benefits of our interpretations without making the claim that they exist in an objective sense as truths. Thus by adopting this thesis we can assert that our interpretive convictions are dependent on the practice within which we are interpreting, and that our interpretive constraints are inter-dependent, without being forced to assert that all interpretations are as good as each other. Additionally, this does not have the result that skepticism does of destroying the coherence enterprise, for each interpreter will believe in his own interpretations and thus impose a coherence within his own aesthetic theory. Therefore the insights of law as integrity are not lost to us.

Interpretation and Intention

We now turn to consider the role of authorial intention within an interpretation. In considering this, we will concentrate on Dworkin's arguments in *Law's Empire*, as here he undertakes a lengthy discussion of this question and investigates the complexities of adducing this intent. However, a preliminary investigation of his earlier work on this subject will be informative. By placing the weight of interpretation in the hands of the individual interpreter, and his particular views, Dworkin has sought to move away from a purely intention-bound form of interpretation towards a constructive variation. In 'How Law is Like Literature', Dworkin presents an early version of this thesis. Here, whilst acknowledging that no plausible theory of interpretation holds that the intention of the author is always irrelevant, Dworkin argues that it is not always necessary to know of it in order to assess the value of a particular work.[121] Dworkin also argues that theorists who seek to bind interpretation to the author's intent miss various complexities in this state of mind, which can be expressed crudely in the form that the "characters seem to have minds of their own".[122] Here Dworkin uses the example of John Fowles who in writing *The French Lieutenant's Woman* supposedly changed his mind as to how the story was to develop,[123] and indeed allegedly changed his mind about the 'point' of the novel having seen the film adaptation. Dworkin argues that the intentionalist would wish to view that as being either the result of realising a subconscious intention one had possessed all along, or instead as simply a change of intention. However, for Dworkin these new accounts are produced by confronting not his earlier self but the work he has produced.[124] What is occurring here is simply another new interpretation of his work, for an author is capable of detaching what he has written from his earlier intentions and beliefs.[125] Indeed, Dworkin argues, again using John Fowles as an example, in seeking to produce a work of art the creator's intent must include the intention to create something independent of his intentions.[126] This then provides the basis for Dworkin's theory as to the role of the author's intention, and he concludes by connecting this with the law, pointing out that in the same way that a novelist's intention can be complex and structured so can that of a legislator.

Stanley Fish has once again been critical of Dworkin's views on this issue. At the heart of Fish's comments lies the idea that "one cannot read or reread independently of intention, independently that is, of the assumption. that one is dealing with marks or sounds produced by an intentional being".[127] Intention is an interpretive fact and must be construed. Fish's point is that it is impossible not to construe it.[128] Whilst this does not indubitably follow from Fish's use of 'intention', his use of the word is not very helpful for if we see ourselves as construing intent whenever we deal with marks or sounds produced by an intentional being, we render the idea effectively useless, as all statements of the author's intent will on this basis simply be a means of re reporting an interpretation of the work. As Dworkin points out "we can read *Hamlet* in a psychodynamic way without supposing that Shakespeare either did or could have intended that we do so".[129] Fish's response to this in 'Wrong Again' is to admit that his account renders intention "methodologically useless", but that this "is precisely my thesis ...

that in whatever way one establishes an interpretation, one will at the same time be assigning an intention".[130] In reply to Dworkin's point that any author may himself reconceive his interpretation of his work, Fish responds that since intention is an interpretive fact, there is nothing to stop it being interpreted again, even by the author. With the example of Hamlet, if we are convinced that its meaning is psychodynamic, but that Shakespeare could not have intended this, then what we are doing is "attributing the meaning to an intentional agent other than Shakespeare", such as the spirit of the age.[131] Again, Fish's argument does seem to follow from his initial premise and seems satisfactory as far as textual interpretation is concerned. However, much of Dworkin's concern lies with the interpretation of texts where the intention is not derived firom that text itself. For example, if faced with the interpretation of a particular statute, the relevant intent is pre-textual, although we may be able to derive it from other texts such as the parliamentary debate preceding its implementation.[132] Given this situation Peter Brooks seems correct in asserting that "you are better off with Dworkin's attempt to insulate interpretation from intentionalism".[133]

With this background we can now turn to Dworkin's work on intention in *Law's Empire*. Here he puts forward three arguments in order to ground his own 'best light' theory of interpretation, and see off the challenge of the author's intent theory. Dworkin is confronting here the argument that interpretation involves the recovery of the author's intention and this enables us to view the object of interpretation as it really is. Dworkin counters that to do this we must apply the 'best light' strategy in any case, and that if we view the purpose of interpretation as being the retrieval of the author's intent this can only be as a result of having applied the techniques of constructive interpretation. Finally, Dworkin argues that in interpreting social practices it is essential to differentiate participants' statements from an interpretation of the practice as a whole.

Dworkins first two arguments seem to be aimed at breaking down the distinction between conversational and constructive interpretation and to show that it is more accurate to describe this practice as being constructive.[134] Dworkin begins his account with what seems to be a response to Fish's argument. He first defines intention as being a 'conscious mental state', and then goes on to assert that we must "notice Gadamer's crucial point that interpretation must *apply* an intention".[135] This then takes up Fish's point that we cannot interpret without positing an intention, and draws a distinction with Fish's definition of that intention. Here Dworkin uses the example of a contemporary production of *The Merchant of Venice* to show that an interpretation must draw together two periods of 'consciousness' by updating Shakespeare's artistic intentions for a contemporary audience. In this way 'fidelity' to Shakespeare's more discrete and concrete opinions about his characters might be "treachery to his more abstract artistic purpose".[136] This reveals that whilst we must apply an intention this can be a complex matter involving the interpreter's own artistic conventions, as we must seek to find the best means to express the artistic intentions of the author as interpreted. Dworkin adds further complexity to this by considering an argument put forward by Stanley Cavell as to the interpretation of a character in Federico Fellini's film *La Strada*. Cavell's argument is that, were we to interpret this character as a reference to the Philomel legend and then ask Fellini about this, he might reply that, although he has not heard the story before, it captures the feeling he had about that character and he would accept it. We might in these circumstances argue, as Cavell does, that this interpretation is therefore intended by Fellini. Dworkin's point in discussing this is to show how our conception of intention differs from the conscious-mental-state version that he rejects. The object of this is to show that the interpreter's convictions are again called into play here, and will often be crucial in establishing the artistic intention.[137]

Dworkin's second argument is to suggest that the debate as to the role of authorial intent within interpretation "should be seen as a particularly abstract and theoretical argument about where value lies in art".[138] Thus arguments in favour of the author's intent model must nevertheless use the constructive model to ground their claim. In other words, this must amount to making the best of the art that is being interpreted by placing the author's intent at the fore. Dworkin is therefore claiming that, whether or not the author's intent view is correct, an attempt to establish this will turn on the plausibility "of some more fundamental assumption about why works of art have the value their presentation presupposes".[139] Taking these two arguments together, Dworkin seems to be trying to show how constructive interpretation is linked to intentionalism. The first argument clearly shows that, whilst we must always apply an intention, this will often be complex and involve the interpreter's own artistic convictions. There will be an interaction between the interpreter and his interpretation of the author's intentions in a wide, artistic sense. Similarly, the second argument does not seek to remove the role of the author's intent, but instead to show that some form of constructive interpretation will always be necessary prior to this.

Before we turn to look at how Dworkin applies this to the interpretation of social practices we should first consider John Stick's criticism that this analogy will not hold, as in art we simply make the best of the work before us whereas in law the entire practice must be interpreted.[140] This criticism has intuitive appeal, but is based on a misunderstanding of Dworkin's interpretive theory. Dworkin's analogy between law and literature is based on the idea that law represents a single, coherent text analogous to a chain novel. Thus, as with a work of art, we are simply making the best of that before us.[141] Furthermore, in a case we will interpret only certain aspects of the body of law, as is the situation where we interpret only one piece of a writer's work.

Dworkin's third argument is directed at the idea that to make the best of our social practices we must interpret them constructively, not by reference to the intent of particular participants. This is because, if we seek to discover the intentions of the participants individually, then we will learn what various members think the practice requires, and not what it really requires. This is because participants in a practice will disagree as to its best interpretation. We could instead argue that we should look for the intentions of the community itself, conceived as some form of group consciousness. Again, however, we need some form of interpretive method to test this judgement. Dworkin, of course, concludes that we must therefore adopt the method of constructive interpretation in order to decide for ourselves what the practice really requires on its 'best' interpretation. This argument is convincing precisely because in this situation it is difficult to identify the author of a social practice.[142] This is why, as we noted earlier, Dworkin's argument is at its strongest where we are dealing with a situation in which it is not possible to derive any intention from the 'text'. The first two arguments, as to artistic interpretation, come closer to breaking down the distinction between constructive and intentionalist interpretation because in that situation the author's intent plays a stronger role. Thus, although in interpreting a social practice we must still imply our intention, the constructive model seems best suited to this because there is no obvious author of the practice.

Conclusion

In introducing pragmatism, Dworkin argued that it afforded greater flexibility to judges and therefore was logically superior to conventionalism. Judges acting on a pragmatist conception of law consider themselves free to decide cases in a way that they can best serve the future good, and therefore have only an attenuated doctrine of precedent. Dworkin pointed out that a sophisticated pragmatist would seek to strike a balance between this flexibility and the need for predictability. The statutes and precedents he enforced would be employed as if they were legal rights, and where the judge sought to introduce an element of flexibility he would present it as a surprising interpretation of the law. This is referred to by Dworkin as the 'noble lie' strategy. However, Dworkin argued that this account did not accord with the way we think about the law and the role of the judge within the legal system. For this reason, he argued that pragmatism lacked the necessary 'fit' as an interpretation of our practices. The argument as to whether pragmatism provided a good justification of our practices was used by him to introduce the virtue of integrity and the idea of personification entailed by that virtue. Whereas pragmatism is concerned with consistency in strategy, Dworkin argued that our practices are best viewed as reflecting a concern with consistency in principle, and that this is explained only when we interpret law as integrity. The challenge for Dworkin therefore was to show that this was the case, and he admitted that if he could not meet it then "we must reconsider the popular disdain for pragmatism".[143] Having considered Dworkin's arguments for the fit and substantive value of integrity, we have however concluded that Dworkin fails to establish it as an independent virtue. This places him in a dilemma, as his argument against pragmatism is founded in the attractiveness of the conception of law as integrity.

Steven Smith attempts to resolve this dilemma by arguing[144] that law as integrity could be subsumed *within* pragmatism because, even if Dworkin's claim that we are concerned with consistency in principle is sound, "there is no obvious reason why a legal pragmatist ... could not embrace it" whilst maintaining the belief that "we should respect the past only in so far as it is useful for promoting future good".[145] This argument seems to assume that we can embrace consistency in principle for strategic reasons. If that is so, then it is mistaken for if we decide to maintain consistency in principle only in so far as it is useful for promoting future good, we are in fact pursuing consistency in strategy. This is incompatible with law as integrity which requires consistency in principle, regardless of strategy. Whether or not we accept this, Smith maintains that Dworkin is best interpreted as a pragmatist. Much of the reason for this lies in the seemingly broad interpretation of pragmatism he puts forward. Smith understands pragmatism as asserting that we "should do what will produce the most good in the future, *using* the past but not counting it as valuable for its own sake",[146] and argues that if we accept this then the case for pragmatism seems almost overwhelming. These two propositions are taken as coming close to the status of self-evident truths, but on closer examination this does not seem to be the case. The idea that we should choose and act so as to maximise the future good is far from self-evident, and clearly antagonistic to the idea of tolerance and liberal neutrality. There would therefore be some difficulty in subsuming Dworkin within this conception. Smith seems to be edging towards a utilitarian position, and is forced to fall back on a claim that this proposition should at least apply to public officials with whom his argument is specifically concerned. Similarly, the contention that we should use the past, but not consider it valuable for its own sake, is far from being self evident.[147] Smith attempts to justify this by arguing that our present choices and acts can only affect the future, not the past, and from this he argues that "continuity with the past is valuable only in so far as it helps to promote good in the future".[148] The difficulty with this is that it does not seem to fit our current legal practices which place a greater weight on past decisions, and it seems to be bound up with the communitarian view that we should do what is best for the community's future. We will see later that that argument is far from being self-evidently true. Further, with respect to the law, it is certainly not the case that past decisions remain unaffected by decisions in future cases, for the past is constantly being re-written through new interpretations. However, this does lead us into an argument put forward by Stanley Fish, examining the status of the three conceptions of law.[149]

Fish contends that Dworkin's criticism of the alternatives he offers to law as integrity, namely conventionalism and pragmatism, are 'academic' because neither is a position that one could put into practice. By contrast, Fish argues that a judge cannot fail to put law as integrity into practice. If we look at the first of these claims, that conventionalism and pragmatism are not positions that can be put into practice, it appears that Fish misrepresents Dworkin's description of these conceptions. Fish argues that conventionalism is not a plausible position because it depends upon the assumption that explicit or literal meanings do in fact exist, when in fact where this appears to be the case the meaning actually " flows from interpretive assumptions so deeply embedded that they have become invisible".[150] However, Dworkin does recognise this, and adheres to it in his description of conventionalism. Fish's argument as to the possibility of adopting pragmatism is based on a citation of Dworkin's description of the pragmatist judge as one who does not take into account any form of consistency with the past.[151] However, Fish neglects to quote the qualifying clause: "as valuable for its own sake".[152] This appears to subtly alter the pragmatist position with respect to past decisions. Nevertheless, Fish's argument is still relevant. This is that it is impossible to cut oneself off from the history preceding one's decision, for institutional and legal histories are "not materials the legal actor thinks *about*; they are the materials with which and within which he thinks".[153] In this way his very thinking "is irremediably historical, consistent with the past in a sense that it flows from the past".[154] This seems to reveal a difficulty with Dworkin's claim that continuity with the past is valuable only in so far as it promotes future good. We cannot but have regard for the past, and hence our continuity with it cannot be broken. The claim however is a weak one, as Fish's definition of what constitutes consistency with the past will always apply. We always interpret within a particular historical context and awareness, but it seems wrong to suggest that because of this we cannot be consistent in principle without previous judgements. There will be continuity, but not necessarily consistency, in our interpretations. However, this does point us towards a more satisfactory account of Dworkin's position here.

Dworkin's argument was that a pragmatist judge need not regard consistency with the past as valuable for its own sake. Fish argues that this means that he can disregard the past, when in fact that is impossible because he interprets within an historical context. However, this can be interpreted in a different way, so that Dworkin is not committed to that position. He argues that the "great debates of constitutional method are debates within interpretation, not about its relevance",[155] and in the same way debates about Dworkin's three conceptions fall within the interpretive concept of law. Steven Smith notes that the pragmatists' satisfaction with a lesser degree of order would seem to exclude Dworkin from their ranks,[156] and in the same way the conventionalists' stricter requirements exclude him. The debate between the conceptions thus seems to centre on the standard of 'fit' that judges should and do apply. A pragmatist judge will be one who finds himself content with a relatively low degree of fit with the past, although of course he cannot ignore that history. By contrast, the conventionalist judge will possess strict standards of fit, and as such will rule out decisions that the pragmatist judge will consider. However, it should be stressed that there is no difference in their working methods. The difference is in their *subjective* notions of what is required by fit. This seems to be explicitly recognised by Dworkin in his discussion of 'the chain of law' where he draws an analogy between our differing senses of fit and a situation in which one scientist accepts stricter standards for research procedure than another.[157] Fish's argument that pragmatism is not a plausible position therefore appears to be mistaken. Additionally, we should note that differentiating between the three conceptions in this way does not require that you must adopt integrity as a distinct virtue. We can possess the sense of fit that accompanies law as integrity without accepting that particular conception.

Fish's second argument, that law as integrity is a position that one could not fail to put into practice,[158] is more persuasive. This argument is built on the notion that this must be the case simply because the other two conceptions are implausible. However, Fish proceeds to provide an independent argument for this claim. This is based on the idea that "there are no such things as 'personal preferences' if by that phrase one means preferences formed apart from contexts of principle",[159] and that as a result it is a mistake to oppose preference to principle. Instead, any conflict will be between preferences that represent different principles, for in thinking of ourselves as judges we will automatically conceive our task as being judicial and act accordingly. Fish argues that when a judge adds a new link to the chain of law, whatever shape this now has it will be a principled one, and thus law as integrity is the name of the practice naturally engaged in by "any judge whose ways of conceiving his field of action are judicial, that is, by any judge".[160] Fish claims that from the moment a judge sees a case as a case he is already in the act of fashioning "a story in which his exposition of a case exists in a seamless continuity"[161] with his exposition of the enterprise as a whole. Indeed, Dworkin himself cites the pragmatist judge Richard Posner as an example of a theorist who bases his decisions on a single 'economic' principle,[162] indicating the 'natural' truth present in law as integrity. However, we have already argued that Dworkin fails to establish integrity as a distinct virtue, and that Fish seems to apply a weak definition of what consistency entails. Nevertheless, as this argument is put forward within the wider context of Fish's opposition to theory in general, we must consider it within that context. In Fish's argument, the conjoining of preference and principle puts everything on the basis of persuasion, with principles simply being preferences that have for now gained the force of authority. This move towards seeing the importance of rhetoric appears to create a problem for Dworkin in that his project seems to go beyond simply uncovering truths about judicial practice to an examination of the underlying theory.[163]

Fish's essential argument is contained in the title of his book *Doing What Comes Naturally*,[164] which refers to "the unreflected actions that follow from being embedded in a context of practice".[165] Fish contends that where this is the case, what we think to do "will not be calculated in relation to a higher law or an overarching theory but will issue from new as naturally as breathing".[166] Fish's point is that there are no independent grounds for interpretation, and as a result no escape from rhetoric. He discusses this with specific reference to Dworkin in his article 'Dennis Martinez And The Uses Of Theory'.[167] This article is built on a journalist's question to a baseball pitcher, Dennis Martinez, as to what words of wisdom his coach had imparted to him prior to a game. Martinez's response to this is that the coach told him to "throw strikes and keep 'em off the bases", to which Martinez replied "OK", and he drives this reply home to the journalist by adding "what else could I say? What else could he say?".[168] Fish regards this as a brilliant account of what occurs "between fully situated members of a community", and a wonderful rebuke to "the outsider who assumes the posture of an analyst".[169] This leads Fish to make the claim that what Martinez is actually saying is something like this: "Look, it may be your job to characterise the game of baseball in terms of overriding theories, but it's my job to play it; and playing it has nothing to do with following words of wisdom ... and everything to do with already being someone whose sense of himself and his possible actions is inseparable from the kind of knowledge that words of wisdom would presume to impart."[170] In the same way, Fish would prefer his judges to be good at being judges. By contrast, it is Fish's claim that, for Dworkin, the better judge is the better philosopher, and that indeed "in Dworkin's view, a judge is always a philosopher",[171] bad judges simply being those whose philosophy is hidden from themselves. However, as the Dennis Martinez example illustrates, this does not appear to follow, for "no theoretical apparatus is needed to do what practice is already doing",[172] namely providing the embedded agent with a sense of what is required by his role. Fish does acknowledge that Dworkin's account of the judicial role is persuasive in one important respect, namely that of self-presentation or persuasion. For Fish "Dworkin, in short, is a rhetorician".[173] Our goal now then becomes one of seeking to cast our decisions in their best light, and as such is pragmatic in nature, as we seek to put across decisions in terms of theory, in order that they are better received in the future. If Dworkin is interpreted as seeking strategy for the presentation of decisions then Fish argues that "it might even be something you could actually use". However, if instead Dworkin's claim is understood as a method for producing judicial decisions then his claim fails, and "the best that *he* can be is a cheerleader. (C'mon, fellows, do your best.)".[174]

This argument against Dworkin is an application of Fish's more general argument against theory. For Fish, theory has no consequences,[175] and what appears to be theory is in fact a form of practice that Fish calls 'theory-talk'. On this argument, all disputes arise at the level of rhetoric, and are thus a matter of persuasion. However, for this argument to be correct, Fish is forced, as he acknowledges, to rely on a narrow definition of theory. For Fish "a theory, in short, is something a practitioner consults when he wishes to perform correctly, with the term 'correctly' here understood as a meaning independently of his preconceptions, biases, or personal preferences".[176] Thus Fish rejects 'looser' uses of the word 'theory', such as its use to refer to high-order generalisations, or descriptions of underlying assumptions. This appears to exclude our standard use of 'theory' in the law, which is to refer to just such higher-order generalisations. As Peter Brooks indicates, this is a two-way process, with theory deriving from a reflection on the general principle applied in practice before itself being fed back into that practice.[177] The result of Fish's own use of 'theory' is, as we have seen, to cast everything at the level of persuasion, and this has important repercussions for the practice of law. Whilst this move undoubtedly follows from Fish's argument, it does not seem to have the impact he believes it to. Fish's restrictive definition of theory means that all Dworkin can ever be, if he is to play a useful role, is a rhetoritician, yet this is presented by Fish as if he were damning Dworkin with faint praise.[178] Additionally, Fish seems to underestimate the role that Dworkin could play even here, for much of the controversy over matters such as judicial selection procedure and solicitors being given greater rights of advocacy lies in the ability to present a case. By being cast in the role of rhetorician Dworkin does not lose his place at the centre of the jurisprudential stage.[179] Indeed, given Fish's restrictive definition of 'theory' he might well ask along with Denis Martinez "what else could he be?". Even on Fish's restrictive terms Dworkin has a useful part to play here. Fish mocks Dworkin as simply being a cheerleader urging judges to do their best. In fact, the role of coach seems more appropriate with Dworkin instilling in its place the art of, and need for, rhetoric. Fish mentions in his footnotes the so-called 'Charley Lau objection',[180] which refers to a batting coach who consistently managed to improve the performance of those he taught. We may yet come to view Dworkin as the Charley Lau of judging.[181]

Dworkin applies Gadamer's argument that we can collapse the distinction between theory and practice. For Dworkin an interpretive theory of law is an interpretive theory of legal practice, though it may be more abstract than any particular legal practice. This breaks down Fish's distinction, for as Dworkin has argued "there is no difference, in the case of the law, between thinking in and with the practice".[182] A good judge will naturally see that "he must be in Fish's terms, a theoretician as well as, and in virtue of, occupying his role as a participant".[183] This does not mean that each time a lawyer speaks he must first construct a theory of his enterprise, but that he will recognise the argumentative nature of his views and the vulnerability of these two theoretical challenges. In this way theory and practice are joined together as each feeds on the other. In his reply to this, Fish admits that "in some practices ... the relationship between explanatory and performance skills is closer that in others", and that "judging is one such practice".[184] However, Fish maintains that even here "while theory or theory talk will often be a *component* in a performance of a practice, it will not in most cases be the driving force of the performance".[185] In other words, the introduction of theory is used to give an argument more weight, but not to determine the nature of the argument itself. This does not seem to offer an accurate picture of our legal practices. What Fish portrays as unreflective is often a result of intense controversy and debate, out of which the law ultimately evolves and develops.[186] The argument ultimately seems to hinge on Fish's unusual use of the word 'theory', which seems to prevent him from seeing its intimate relation to practice. Fish argues that if theory truly is second nature here, as Dworkin argues, then "it simply confuses matters to separate it out and give it an honorific name".[187] This reduces the debate to one of semantics, with Fish appearing to recognise the intimate nature of theory and practice, but refusing to see it as constructive.[188] However, it does seem useful to maintain the distinction, if only to indicate how they are interactive.

Much of the difficulty for Fish, then, lies in his claims about 'theory'. Fish applies a restrictive definition of the word in order to reach his conclusion that it is rhetoric that is important, and that theory has no consequences. However, as Roland Barthes has pointed out, theory is in fact a necessity, for even when purporting to simply do what comes naturally in fact there is the unacknowledged theory as an ideology.[189] The move away from grand theory in the human sciences has been a feature of recent philosophical debate. However, as Peter Brooks argues, this did not entail for Barthes, and need not entail for anyone, the claim that theory is without consequences.[190] By converting the debate into one about rhetoric, Fish seems essentially to have simply substituted practice for areas theorists traditionally regard as being covered by theory. Thus it is now practice that must highlight those situations of particular importance, frame our options, and provide our means of evaluation. Whilst this conclusion is perfectly acceptable, it seems to say little, and one is led along with Brooks to the conclusion that we "need no longer fear that Fish is a sting-ray", for force has simply become the force of reasoned persuasion.[191] Even in Fish's rhetorical world we must still make choices, and here it is to Dworkin, not Fish, that we should turn. It is ironic that in proposing the end of theory, Fish is signing his own death warrant, for he has nothing beyond his own 'theory' to fall back on.

Notes

1 Dworkin 1986 p.165.
2 Id.
3 Id. p.166.
4 Id. p.167.
5 Reaume 1989 at p.393.
6 Id. p.392.
7 Dworkin 1986 pp.404-407.
8 Id. p.406.
9 Id. p.405.
10 Reaume 1989 p.393.
11 See Dworkin 1986 pp.176-184.
12 Id. p.181.
13 Id. p.182.
14 Id.
15 Id. p.183.
16 Soper 1987 p.1181.
17 [19831 1 AC 410. See Dworkin 1986 pp.23-29 where Dworkin discusses the case, and pp.162-163 where he considers the pragmatist approach to it.
18 Soper 1987 p. I I 8 1.
19 Id.
20 Id.
21 Id.
22 See Dworkin 1986 pp.162-163.
23 See id. at p.162: "The pragmatist will pay whatever attention to the past is required by good strategy". See too Soper 1987 at p.1181: "the pragmatic decision will be that of a single author, consistently maximising justice or efficiency without worrying about past political decision except for reasons of strategy."
24 Westmoreland 1991, especially at pp.178-179.
25 Id. p.178.
26 Nozick 1974 p.28 cited id. at p.178. Dworkin acknowledges his debt to Nozick here - see Dworkin 1986 p.437 n.19.
27 Westmoreland 1991 p.179.
28 Id.
29 Id.
30 Dworkin 1986 pp.440-441 n.19 in which Dworkin affirms his fundamental agreement with Rawls.
31 Dworkin 1977 p.180. See pp.179-182 generally on this point.
32 Id. p.182.
33 Dworkin 1986 p.180.
34 Id. p.181.
35 Id.

36 This point is also made by Denise Reaume - see Reaume 1989 pp.398-399.
37 Indeed, the abortion debate in the United Kingdom often takes this form, suggesting that compromise solutions are not always contrary to our intuitions. On Dworkin's terms, the law on this issue is a checkerboard statute.
38 Westmoreland 1991 p.178.
39 Dworkin 1986 p.51.
40 Id. p.52.
41 See Dworkin 1986 (a) pp.146-166.
42 Id. p.150.
43 Id.
44 Dworkin uses the example of the re-telling of a joke, which may involve a new and original form, in order that the point of the joke is brought out more clearly. See id.
45 Id.
46 Id. p.160.
47 Id. p.159.
48 Id. p.161.
49 Id. p.162.
50 Id. p.152.
51 Id. p.153.
52 Fish 1989 Chapter Four at pp.87-102.
53 Id. p.95.
54 Dworkin 1986 (a) p.159.
55 Fish 1989 p.94.
56 Dworkin 1986 (a) p.159.
57 Fish 1989 p.93.
58 Id. p.94.
59 For example see Grossvogel 1979. Fish cites various other works - Fish 1989 p.559 n.13. He gives his own interpretation of Christie's work at pp.96-97.
60 For example, James Joyce's *Ulysses* is likely in many sections to be interpreted differently by different readers.
61 Dworkin 1986 (a) pp.149-150.
62 Id. p.150.
63 See Fish 1989 p.562 n.15.
64 This appears in Dworkin 1986 (a) Chapter Seven at pp.167-177. This essay draws on material in Dworkin 1983.
65 Dworkin 1986 (a) p.168.
66 Id.
67 Dworkin protests that there is not more constraint present in his account here than in Wittgenstein's example of the man who doubted what he read in the newspaper and bought another copy to check it (id. p.168).
68 Dworkin 1986 (a) p.151.
69 See further on this feature of Dworkin's work Fish 1989 pp.100-102.
70 Dworkin 1986 (a) p.169.

71 Id.

72 This is particularly the case in Dworkin's original reply to Fish on this point (see Dworkin 1983 pp.307-308). Here Dworkin goes so far as to claim that his views on the novels of Agatha Christie rely "on my own judgment and my expectations that almost all readers will agree" although "that is not to say that no-one will disagree" (at p.308). This certainly does not seem to be the inference in 'How Law Is Like Literature'.

73 Fish 1989 ch.5 at pp.103-119.

74 Id. p.106.

75 Fish also gives the example of the chain-novelists who were the producers of the television serial 'Dallas'. At one point in the plot the idea was introduced that one year of the serial had simply been the dreams of one of its characters. This does not seem to indicate the existence of strong constraints on the genre - see Fish 1989 pp.562-563 n.15.

76 See n.72 supra.

77 This appears at p.304, but not in the abridged version printed in Dworkin 1986 (a).

78 Dworkin 1983 p.304.

79 Id. p.294. See also Dworkin 1986 (a) pp.169-171.

80 Dworkin 1986 p.231.

81 See for example Fish 1989 p.106.

82 Dworkin 1986 p.232.

83 Indeed, Fish makes the point that "paradoxically, one can be faithful to legal history only by revising it ... in such a way as to accommodate and render manageable the issues raised by the present" (Fish 1989 p.94).

84 Dworkin 1986 p.232.

85 Id. p.233.

86 Id. p.234.

87 Fish 1989 p.89.

88 Dworkin 1986 p.238.

89 Id.

90 See in particular Dworkin 1983 pp.305-306 where Dworkin is dismissive of Fish on this point.

91 Fish 1989 p.97.

92 This section of the essay is essentially the same as Dworkin 1983 but is more clearly set out.

93 Dworkin 1986 (a) p.171.

94 Id.

95 Id. p.173.

96 Id.

97 Id. p.176.

98 Id.

99 Id. p.176.

100 Id.

101 Fish 1989 p.563 n.31.
102 Id. p.114.
103 Id.
104 In addition, Dworkin's assertion that he has "no arguments for the objectivity of interpretive judgments except interpretive arguments" (see Dworkin 1986 (a) p.171) appears to be inconsistent with his holistic theory of legal interpretation in that it implies that interpretive judgments constitute a closed system (see Marmor 1991 p.407).
105 This thesis has been recognised by, *inter alia*, Max Weber, Isaiah Berlin, Steven Lukes, Bruce Ackerman and Joseph Raz. See further Gardbaum 1991 at p.1356.
106 This seems to be the argument put by Andrei Marmor - see Marmor 1991 pp.408-409.
107 Raz 1986 p.324.
108 Dworkin 1986 pp.231-232.
109 Id. p.237.
110 Id. p.235.
111 Id.p.232.
112 Simmonds 1987 at p.478.
113 Id.
114 See for example Dworkin 1986 p.70: "That itself is an interpretive question, and the answer would depend on why the question of continuity arises."
115 Simmonds 1987 p.479.
116 This argument is influenced by one put forward by Marmor 1991 pp.410-411.
117 Id.
118 Id. p.411.
119 Id.
120 See n.106 supra.
121 Dworkin 1986 (a) p.155.
122 Id. p.156.
123 This is probably not a particularly sound example, as Fowles is renowned for his intellectual trickery - see for example *The Magus*.
124 Dworkin 1986 (a) p.157.
125 Id.
126 Id.
127 Fish 1989 p.99.
128 Id. p.100.
129 Dworkin 1983 p.310.
130 Fish 1989 p.117.
131 Id. p.119.
132 The English courts are now at liberty to refer to such material, bringing them into line with most similar jurisdictions.
133 Brooks 1990 at p.1153.
134 See Dworkin 1986 p.59 where he himself suggests that there may be "a deep

connection among all forms of interpretation".
135 Id. p.55.
136 Id. p.56. A recent example of this occurred with Sally Potter's film adaptation of Virginia Woolf's novel *Orlando*. In an interview with the *Sunday Times*, Potter asserted that "the further I got into my research, the more strongly I felt that it would be untrue to the spirit of Virginia Woolf to be overly reverent to the book".
137 This argument seems to be a version of Dworkin's thesis in 'How Law Is Like Literature' in which he showed how artistic intention could be complex.
138 Dworkin 1986 p.60.
139 Id. p.61.
140 Stick 1986 pp.387-393.
141 Stick does correctly assert that this analogy holds best with literature as opposed to other forms of art - see Stick 1986 p.393. To make the analogy clearer we might distinguish between legal systems - we are only concerned with an interpretation of one particular system.
142 Id. p.397. Whilst Stick is skeptical of Dworkin's first two arguments, he is more positive about the third.
143 Dworkin 1986 p.163.
144 Smith 1990 p.418.
145 Id.
146 Id. p.420.
147 The fact that Smith cites Anthony Kronman as disagreeing with this claim reveals it to be far from self-evident - see id. at p.423 n.70.
148 Id. p.423.
149 Fish 1989 Chapter Sixteen at pp.356-371.
150 Id. p.358.
151 Dworkin 1986 p.95 cited Fish 1986 p.360.
152 Dworkin 1986 p.95.
153 Fish 1989 p.360.
154 Id.
155 Dworkin 1986 p.360.
156 Smith 1990 p.438 n.144.
157 Dworkin 1986 p.235. This analogy is, as stated, found in Dworkin's discussion on the chain of law in Chapter Seven. However, it appears to relate to interpretation in general and not just to interpretation of law as integrity.
158 Fish 1989 p.361.
159 Id. p.366.
160 Id. p.368.
161 Id.
162 Dworkin 1986 p.276 and p.44 n.1.
163 See for example Dworkin 1986 p.79: "we hope to develop a positive theoretical account of the grounds of law, a program of adjudication we can recommend to judges and use to criticize what they do" (our italics).

164 Fish 1989.
165 At p.ix.
166 Id.
167 Id. Chapter Seventeen.
168 Id. p.372.
169 Id.
170 Id. p.373.
171 Id. p.385.
172 Id. p.388.
173 Id. p.389.
174 Id. p.392.
175 Id. p. 14.
176 Id. p.378.
177 Brooks 1990 at p.1151.
178 See Fish 1989 p.391: "Of course, Dworkin would not accept my praise of him as a rhetorician".
179 See Lee 1990 p.258. Lee generally agrees with Fish's various attacks on Dworkin, but even he is prepared to admit that here we should say "Come back Dworkin : much is forgiven".
180 Fish 1989 p.581 n.3.
181 See for example Hoffmann 1989. Hoffmann, then a Justice of the High Court, concludes that "readers who want to know what judges are supposed to be doing will do better to buy *Law's Empire*" - see p.145.
182 Dworkin 1991 p.381.
183 Id.
184 Fish 1991 p.76.
185 Id. p.77.
186 See further Dworkin 1991 p.387 n.25.
187 Fish 1991 p.79.
188 See Dworkin 1991 p.388 n.25. See also the editors' Introduction at p.6 where they state that "the gap between Fish and Dworkin seems to have narrowed considerably".
189 Barthes 1966 cited Brooks 1990 at p.1151.
190 Brooks 1990 p.1151.
191 Id. p.1152.

5 Integrity, Liberalism and Community

Integrity and the Moral Legitimacy of Law

Dworkin regards integrity as a normatively superior conception to conventionalism and pragmatism because for him it is only by linking legal argument with the idea of genuine political community that law can be said to have a proper moral content. Integrity brings together the past and the present and introduces the fraternal idea of treating members of a community as equals. Integrity assumes a deep personification of the state because it views the state as having principles that it may compromise. Therefore, in order to defend the conception from attack, Dworkin must defend the viewpoint that sees the community as a distinct moral agent. He sees this defence in the neighbourhood of fraternity,[1] or as it is more commonly known, community. His theory is that a political society that accepts integrity as a virtue will thereby become a special form of community in that its moral authority to apply coercion will be promoted. Although this is not the only argument in favour of integrity, or the only valuable consequence of it,[2] it is the most important.[3]

Dworkin examines the link between integrity and the moral authority of the law.[4] He distinguishes the problem of the legitimacy of coercive power from that of whether citizens have genuine moral obligations arising from the law. For whilst obligation is not a sufficient condition for coercion it is close to a necessary one.[5] Dworkin asserts that for a state to be legitimate it must arrange its constitutional structure and practices so as to place a general obligation on its citizens to obey those political decisions that impose duties upon them. His argument is that a state that embraces integrity as an ideal will have a better case for legitimacy than one that does not. Dworkin first considers various arguments that have been advanced in the past to legitimate the use of coercion.

Firstly, he considers the argument that we have tacitly consented to such an arrangement in that we have not chosen to emigrate. This is easily dismissed for the consent must be more free and we must have a more genuine choice if this is to hold. Furthermore, as Dworkin points out, there is no choice to be free from sovereigns altogether.[6] The second argument considered is that there is a duty to be just. On this model we have a duty to support just or nearly just institutions. However, this does not adequately explain legitimacy because it does not tie political obligations sufficiently tightly to the particular community and thus fails to show how legitimacy flows from and defines citizenship.[7] Finally, Dworkin looks at the most popular defence, which is that of 'fair play'. This argument is based on a benefits and burdens analysis. We receive benefits from a political institution and thus must bear the burdens of it, including the obligation to accept its political decisions. Dworkin puts forward two counter arguments to this analysis. Firstly, it assumes that we can incur obligations by receiving that which we do not seek, and would reject given the opportunity. This seems unreasonable. Secondly, it is crucially ambiguous, in that it is unclear what constitutes a benefit from a political institution. If we must show that we are better off than under any other possible system, then the principle is too strong, for this will never be true for all citizens. Equally, if we must show only that we are better off than if there were no system at all, then it is too weak. Thus Dworkin argues that we must seek our explanation of legitimacy elsewhere.

Robert Westmoreland rejects this conclusion.[8] He argues that Dworkin's first objection to the argument from fair play is bound up with Robert Nozick's radical libertarianism, which holds that there can be no 'positive' right that is not the product of agreement. Westmoreland however argues that, even in a pluralistic society such as our own, there are certain basic goods which it can be assumed everyone needs[9] and which only political society is likely to provide. With regard to Dworkin's second argument, Westmoreland argues that a middle way can be found between the extremes painted by Dworkin. Here law must achieve some minimum level of justice and citizens take the benefit of having a settled system.[10] In this way both of Dworkin's objections are met. Whilst this defence of the argument from fair play is persuasive, we may still not find that account of political obligation attractive. Westmoreland's account rests on a 'thin' notion of community in which political society provides the basic goods and a minimum level of justice. Does this accurately reflect the way we think of the role of the political community? Dworkin's aim is to better explain this and hence to clarify the nature of political obligation.

True Communities

We have seen that Dworkin puts forward a number of arguments to establish that law as integrity is the 'best' conception of the practice of law. Dworkin first argues that we should recognise the political virtue of integrity in order that we might explain our intuitive rejection of 'checkerboard' statutes. In its simplest form integrity represented the virtue described in the phrase that we should 'treat like cases alike'.[11] However, built into this idea is the assumption of a particularly deep personification of the community or state.[12] A political community will display the virtue of integrity when it consistently applies its best understanding of justice, fairness, and procedural due process to situations before it, despite any moral conflict that may exist within the community. Based on this argument Dworkin contends that integrity has a good 'fit' with our practices. He maintains that integrity offers an attractive description of our practices and that we should "look for our defence of integrity in the neighbourhood of fraternity or, to use its more fashionable name, community".[13] He then proceeds to argue that a political society accepting integrity thereby becomes a special form of community in that its moral authority to assume and deploy a monopoly of coercive force is promoted.[14] Another consequence of adopting integrity is the promotion of self-government. Integrity is required as "a citizen cannot treat himself as the author of a collection of laws that are inconsistent in principle", nor see that collection as "sponsored by any Rousseauian general will".[15] This leads us to the conclusion, as Paul Kahn notes, that "Dworkin's sovereignty is *the people as the state*".[16] Finally, in considering the puzzle of legitimacy we noted Dworkin argues that "a state that accepts integrity as a political ideal has a better case for legitimacy than one that does not".[17] Having drawn together these various claims, we are now in a position to examine the arguments that Dworkin puts forward to establish and ground them.

Dworkin's concern is with the legitimacy of the use by the state of coercion in order to enforce the law. It is argued that moral legitimacy is to be found in the obligations of community. Dworkin's arguments are perhaps best understood as a response to Charles Taylor's claim that western liberal democracies are undergoing a legitimation crisis. Taylor argued that this was a result of a lack of identification with the good of the common life, caused by the political culture of individual rights that liberalism engenders.[18] Dworkin's attempt to legitimate his liberal theory of law within the constructs of community may be seen as a reply to Taylor's social thesis. Dworkin's argument is then that we can be morally affected by being given that which we do not ask for or choose, where this arises as the result of an obligation of role. These are the responsibilities generated by membership of some biological or social group as determined by social practice. Dworkin chooses to refer to the obligations that arise from this membership as 'associative or communal obligations',[19] and his main contention is that political obligation numbers among these associative obligations. We must therefore consider the character of these obligations in order to discuss this claim.

Associative obligations are among the most important to us, for they include obligations to colleagues, friends and family. They are also quite complex because, although they will be determined by social practice, they are subject to interpretation and thus to controversy. This can be seen if we attempt to compose even a brief interpretation of the general practice of associative obligation. The connection between these obligations and choice is complicated: "it is a history of events and acts that *attract* obligations, and we are rarely even aware that we are entering upon any special status".[20] This is true of obligations that arise through friendship, and in particular those within a family, where membership is a matter of the least choice, but is often said to carry the greatest obligation.[21] Dworkin therefore argues that we have a duty to honour our obligations in situations where social practice attaches a special responsibility to membership of a particular group, but this natural duty holds only when certain other conditions are met.[22] Prominent among these conditions is reciprocity, but of an abstract type. Dworkin argues that the members of a group must by and large adhere to four conditions about the responsibilities they owe their fellow members for these to be considered genuine fraternal obligations.[23]

Before we examine these conditions, we should first note that Dworkin's argument here appears to be influenced by Michael Sandel's claim that fraternity is as valuable a virtue as justice, and is sometimes preferable.[24] Sandel's argument is based on a critique of Rawls's use of Hume's notion of the circumstances of justice. It is these circumstances of justice that give rise to the virtue of justice, but Sandel argues that, because these circumstances are empirical conditions, justice will only be the first virtue of those societies in which "the resolution of conflicting claims among mutually disinterested parties is the most pressing social priority".[25] Sandel therefore posits the existence of "a range of more intimate and solidaristic associations",[26] in which the values and aims of the participants are sufficiently close that the circumstances of justice rarely prevail. Citing Hume himself, Sandel uses the examples of the family and friendship.[27] He then generalises from this to a broad range of human associations in which the circumstances of justice will not predominate. Sandel's conclusions are that "as Hume's account confirms, the remedial character of justice entails another set of virtues" and that because of this we cannot state in advance whether "an increase in justice is associated with an overall moral improvement".[28] Again Sandel uses the examples of family and friendship to ground these claims.[29] This argument offers many similarities to that presented by Dworkin, for both are concerned with the virtue of fraternity and argue that we can abstract from the examples of family and friendship and see this virtue as present in the wider community. However Dworkin avoids many of the problems present in Sandel's analysis through his treatment of justice.[30] Dworkin argues that associative obligations are subject to interpretation, and here justice will play its usual role in determining for a given purpose what his associative responsibilities, properly understood, really are. Thus any apparent injustice present in an associative institution may be isolated as being mistaken once we examine the justification behind that practice. There is however no guarantee of this, and we may reach a deeply sceptical conclusion, whereby "no competent account of the institution can fail to show it as thoroughly and pervasively unjust".[31] In this circumstance we must abandon the institution, for its practices can impose no genuine obligations on us. Through this account of the interpretive role of justice in understanding the nature of associative obligations Dworkin manages to avoid the difficulties highlighted by Simon Caney in Sandel's account of justice as a 'remedial virtue'. We should however note at this point that Caney's first criticism of Sandel is that "while the relationship between family and friends *might* support his case, it is implausible to think that political society could be conceived along these lines", and this therefore betrays "Sandel's Utopian belief that society can be understood as a group of friends or a family".[32] This criticism appears to apply equally to Dworkin, and we must therefore consider Dworkin's arguments for his claim that political society is a form of associative institution.

In order to support his argument, Dworkin must first specify those qualities of a community that lead to the creation of an obligation of role. He must then show that a political community can fulfil those criteria, and finally he must be able to demonstrate that such a political community would be one that interprets law as integrity.[33] If successful in this three-stage argument, Dworkin would then be able to ground his claims for integrity. His first argument is to specify the conditions necessary for the existence of associative obligations. As we have already seen, Dworkin lays down four conditions here. He argues that the community must demonstrate a concern that is: (i) *special*, holding distinctly within the group; (ii) *personal*, running directly between each member; (iii) the responsibility should flow from a more general responsibility of *concern* for the well-being of the other members; and (iv) there should be *equal* concern for all members.[34] Dworkin argues that a community that meets these conditions may be considered a 'true community', for the responsibility it deploys are "special and individualised and display a pervasive mutual concern that fits a plausible conception of equal concern".[35]

These conditions are an attempt by Dworkin to set out a liberal theory of equality that is situated within a communitarian framework. This in turn may be seen as an attempt to utilise the embeddedness thesis proposed by Michael Sandel and Alasdair MacIntyre in order to ground his liberal theory of community.[36] We shall see that there are extensive difficulties with the embeddedness thesis. Dworkin asserts that under his conditions the roles and rules of society "are equally in the interests of all ... no-one's life is more important than anyone else's".[37] Yet, as Paul Kahn points out, whilst the first part of this, requiring an equal interest, may well be asserted by all communities, the second part, on equal value, is likely to be asserted only by some select group of communities that satisfy Dworkin's idea of equality.[38] Worse than this is the fact that Dworkin offers no evidence for his claim that these communities would be the only 'true' communities. Kahn points out that a further difficulty here is that, as we have already seen, Dworkin has argued that justice is an interpretive concept,[39] but his argument here contends that only a community that supports an interpretation of justice that accepts a particular view of individual equality can sustain its legitimacy.[40] This would require an external account of justice that is ruled out by Dworkin's own interpretive theory. In fact, Dworkin argues that the conditions for true community are achieved by interpreting law as integrity, not by applying a particular account of justice. However, it is arguable that these conditions can indeed be seen to be an aspect of justice and this is why Kahn makes this mistake. It is a requirement of justice that we treat people with equal concern, and whilst this obviously requires consistency in principle, that consistency is internal to our virtue of justice and not separate from it. We have noted that Dworkin requires that justice play "its normal interpretive role in deciding for any person what his associative responsibilities, properly understood, really are",[41] and that whilst the obligations created by a true community are prima facie genuine this will not be so where the injustice is so severe and deep that these obligations are cancelled.[42] Here then justice seems to play the critical role in ascertaining if an obligation is genuine. The true community should be based on the requirement of justice that people be treated with equal concern and respect. Instead, for Dworkin the conditions seem to turn on the community's belief that it is advocating an equal concern, subject to the interpretive constraint of justice. However, this seems to allow too much potential injustice, and additionally seems to leave

Dworkin open to the charge of relativism.[43] Once we see justice as being central to the idea of equal concern, we no longer have this difficulty.

One final point discussed by Kahn is that by singling out only one particular kind of political community as being true Dworkin seems to suggest the possibility of a 'trans-communal perspective' on community, but he is already committed to the view that there is no escape from interpretation and so none from community.[44] In moving to this external account Dworkin also calls into doubt his account of the role of interpretation, for that is built on an internal account of the law. Dworkin clearly wishes to avoid the relativism that is perceived in Walzer's theory of justice, but he does not seem to succeed in discovering the means to do so here. This then presents a problem for Dworkin in that he pursues an internal account of the law, but appears to seek external justification for it.

We have seen that Dworkin argues that his account of the structure of associative obligations allows us to express the conditions that we feel must be met before political obligations come into being. He therefore concludes that "political obligation - including an obligation to obey the law - is a form of associative obligation".[45] Whilst we have noticed a variety of reasons for doubting this argument, we should follow through Dworkin's final two arguments in his attempt to ground legitimacy in a political community devoted to fraternity and integrity. Dworkin must now show that a political community can support the criteria he has set out for the existence of associative obligations before showing that such a community will be one that accepts law as integrity. Here we are directly considering Dworkin's substantive thesis that "the best defence of political legitimacy ... is to be found not in the hard terrain of contracts or duties of justice or obligations of fair play", but instead "in the more fertile ground of fraternity, community, and their attendant obligations".[46] We must consider what form a political community would take in order to conform to the four conditions Dworkin has set down as necessary for associative obligations to arise. Dworkin sets out three possible models of community that might meet this standard. The first of these, the 'de facto' model, treats community as an accident of history and geography.[47] It is therefore not a true associative community at all and hence easily rejected.[48] The second possibility discussed is the 'rulebook' model of community. This supposes that members of a political community accept a general commitment to obey rules established in a certain way that is special to that community. Self interested but wholly honest people are competitors in a game with fixed rules or are parties to a limited and transient commercial arrangement. They obey rules they have negotiated or accepted as a matter of obligation and not merely strategy, assuming that the content of their rules exhaust their obligation. This is described as being a 'natural mate' to the conventionalist conception of law.[49] Disappointingly Dworkin does not draw the connection between this idea and the communitarian critics. Instead he simply offers the criticism that this model will leave its citizens with "no sense that the rules were negotiated out of a common commitment to underlying principles that are themselves a further source of further obligation"[50] and that as a result our grounds for opposing 'checkerboard' statutes are removed. However, we have already seen that the checkerboard statute argument is unsuccessful in grounding this commitment, and thus the argument against the rule book model is simply that it does not interpret law as integrity. This leaves Dworkin's own model, that of principle, to win seemingly by fiat. On this model, the members of the community accept that they are governed by common principles as well as rules. It will thus fulfil the four conditions Dworkin has laid down as necessary for true community, at least as well as any model could in a morally pluralistic society.[51] This model satisfies the conditions of true community better than the rulebook model, as concern will be pervasive.

Having established this, the final step in Dworkin's three-stage thesis requires him to show that a community of principle will be one that accepts law as integrity. This is easily done, for a community of principle will be one that accepts integrity since it is the virtue of integrity that explains our commitment to underlying principles. Dworkin's argument may now be run backwards: a community accepting law as integrity will be based on the model of principle, and will thus fulfil the four conditions necessary to generate associative obligations and hence to obtain moral legitimacy. This seems close to being simply the semantic claim that a community that accepts Dworkin's theory of law as integrity should be labelled a 'true' community. This is particularly worrying given the nature of Dworkin's argument for, as we have already noted, the conditions for true community are not argued for and seem to violate the idea of justice as an interpretive concept. Similarly, in his final two stages of the argument Dworkin appears to offer little in the way of justification for the thesis. The discussion of the two 'alternative' models of the community is weak, with Dworkin relying on the checkerboard statute argument that he used to argue for the existence of integrity as a virtue. We have already noted weaknesses in that argument,[52] and using it here seems to lead to the conclusion that the alternative models of community are rejected simply because they do not interpret law as integrity. Dworkin must first argue for the model of principle, and then show that it would interpret law as integrity. Instead his argument is circular, for he assumes that the true community will interpret law as integrity, before he has established that this is the case. This again seems to indicate that Dworkin's argument is merely semantic for we must take as given that which Dworkin is meant to be proving. Dworkin's claims for the model of principle would be much more convincing if he had offered arguments against real-life targets, such as Michael Walzer. Instead he gives only a brief characterisation of the alternatives he offers, and as a result gives the impression that the model of principle is a winner by fiat.

However, perhaps the most worrying aspect of this for Dworkin is that the argument once again seems to fail to ground integrity as a distinct virtue. Dworkin argues that only a model of community based on integrity can satisfy the conditions he gives for true community. But, even given the weaknesses we have noticed in that claim, it seems that the conditions are met by the virtue of justice. The idea of consistency is inherent in all our virtues, and not separate from them. The principle of equal concern necessitates consistent application and thus is not subordinate to integrity, but is one of our principles of justice.

Having noticed these weaknesses in Dworkin's theory of community as set out in *Law's Empire*, let us now turn to consider his later views on the possibility of a liberal community, in order to see if he negotiates a path through these difficulties.

Liberal Community

In his article 'Liberal Community',[53] Dworkin considers the case for the liberal doctrine of toleration with regard to personal ethics. However, he does argue for the ethical 'integration' of individuals into their community with regard to political justice. This is meant to be both consistent with the arguments in *Law's Empire*, as well as being complementary to them. Thus Dworkin concentrates on contra-communitarian aspects of his theory of community in arguing for a doctrine of toleration. However, in discussing the integration of citizens into the political sphere of their community Dworkin clarifies many of the points raised by his arguments in *Law's Empire*. Dworkin's argument in 'Liberal Community' first takes the form of a consideration of the attack made on perceived liberal assumptions by "the group of political philosophers known loosely as the communitarians".[54] He considers four attacks on liberal tolerance, each of which uses the concept of community in an increasingly more substantial and less reductive way.[55] The first of these arguments takes the form that questions as to the shape of the democratic community's ethical environment should be decided in accordance with the majority's will.[56] Dworkin rejects this, for it assumes that this shape must always be decided in a winner-take-all fashion, whereas in the economic sphere justice requires the opposite. What is required is that property be distributed in shares such that each individual has his or her fair share of influence over the economic environment.[57] Dworkin contends that we must insist that the ethical environment be treated in the same way and allowed to be the product of the choices individuals make. We should not subject these two environments to different regimes of justice "because they are not two distinct environments, but inter-dependent aspects of the same one".[58] Thus we must accept liberal tolerance on matters of ethics.

The second argument that Dworkin considers against tolerance is based on paternalism in holding that, in a genuine political community, we have responsibility for the well-being of others. It adds that people who are genuinely concerned for others take an interest in their *critical* as well as their *volitional* well-being.[59] Our critical well-being will only be increased when we have or achieve those things that we should want. This is obviously contrary to the doctrine of tolerance, for it makes assumptions about the 'right way' to live our lives, and seeks to cure those who step outside this boundary. As Dworkin points out, this will not lead to improvement in the lives of those people if this change is achieved by means that affect our ability to consider the critical merits of the change in a reflective way, and a threat of criminal charges corrupt rather than enhance critical judgement.[60] Thus any such conversion will not be 'genuine', and hence the second argument is self-defeating.

The third argument considered by Dworkin is an argument of self-interest in that it claims that tolerance makes communities less able to serve their members' various social needs.[61] This proposition is best considered in the light of intellectual needs, and represents one of the arguments put forward by Michael Sandel. This argument is that we need community not only for culture and language but for identity and self-reference.[62] The best interpretation of this seems to be that it makes a claim of phenomenological possibility. It argues that we are embedded in the shared morality of our communities and cannot detach ourselves from this in order to reflect upon it. Dworkin rejects this phenomenology as wrong, or at least over-stated, in much the same way that Amy Gutmann has rejected it. She wrote: "what follows from 'what is good for me has to be good for someone who was born female, into a first-generation American, working class Italian, Catholic family'?".[63] In other words, we can and do detach ourselves from our connections and associations. However, Dworkin argues that even if this were not the case, it would be wrong to suppose that for every member of the community the connection could not be detached. Furthermore, even if this were the case, Dworkin argues that people would always be "able to reassemble their sense of identity, built around a somewhat different and more tolerable set of conditions",[64] when the morality that they associate with their community is shaken. Dworkin also considers here Philip Selznick's argument that ethics needs an anchor and that this is found in the shared conviction of the agent's political community.[65] This is a similar argument to that of Michael Walzer, and Dworkin makes the same point here that paradoxically our firmest convention of all is that which states that ethical and moral judgements cannot be made true or false by consensus.[66]

Dworkin regards the final argument against tolerance as the most important and interesting communitarian attack.[67] This is the claim that the well-being of the community is integral to the well-being of its citizens and that, once this is recognised, citizens will necessarily be concerned for the soundness of their community's ethical health. Dworkin agrees with the most fundamental premise of this argument, that people should identify their own interest with those of their political community, but argues that liberalism supplies the best interpretation of this. The argument for integration means that in some circumstances the community is the appropriate agency for actions affecting its members. However, this can be understood either as a metaphysical claim or as one about our social practices. Whereas the metaphysical view of integration seem community as embodying all the features of human life, on the practice view the community's communal life will be more narrowly defined to include only those acts treated as collective by the practices and attitudes that create the community as a collective agent.[68] If we turn to apply this standard to the communal life of our political community, then Dworkin claims that we will view legislative, executive and judicial decisions as communal acts, but we will not regard sexual acts in the same way. Our social practices and attitudes do not regard sexual life as communal.[69] Thus, at least for our society,[70] the interest of the political community cannot be said to extend into areas governed by personal morality, for our social practices do not regard these as part of our communal life.

These then are the four arguments that Dworkin considers against liberal toleration and which he rejects. The first two arguments are relatively weak communitarian claims and are easily dismissed. The final two arguments represent the stronger communitarian thesis, and thus pose a more serious threat. Dworkin's attack on Michael Sandel in considering the third argument, that people require community for self-identity, should be seen in the context that Dworkin's theory of community in *Law's Empire* appears to draw on Sandel's embeddedness thesis for inspiration, in positing the conditions for true community. Dworkin's argument in *Law's Empire* was an example of the partially-embedded thesis that Sandel occasionally appears to advocate, but not of the wholly-embedded one that Dworkin is criticising here. This is consistent with Dworkin's liberalism, and his position is explained in his criticism of the fourth attack on tolerance. Dworkin mentions that the conditions for political obligation set out in *Law's Empire* must be met if we are to see ourselves as ethically integrated into our community.[71] In this argument Dworkin relies on a favourite device of liberal theorists, that of the separation of spheres.[72] Dworkin separates our political community from our ethical environment on the grounds that this conforms to our social practice. This enables him to advocate tolerance whilst recognising that we are members of a community in a weak sense. Philip Selznick has attacked this part of Dworkin's argument on the basis of this distinction. Whereas Dworkin proposes that "when we speak of a nation's sexual preferences and habits we speak statistically, not, as in the case of an orchestra's performance, of some collective achievement or disgrace",[73] Selznick argues firstly that the norms that govern our sex lives are collective, and secondly that the orchestra analogy has a grave limitation. An orchestra is a special-purpose institution, whereas a political community cannot be understood in that way.[74] Every sphere of social life must be open to scrutiny if we are to create a moral community, as for Selznick, "what we prize in community is not unity of any sort, but unity that preserves the integrity of persons, groups, and institutions ... it is a unity of unities".[75] Much of Dworkin's difficulty here seems to lie in the apparent conflict between his interpretive neutrality with regard to political ends, his advocation of liberal tolerance, and the role he gives community in the sphere of political justice. In order to consider this, we must first examine the nature of liberalism, before specifically looking at Dworkin's arguments in favour of the liberal community.

In order to consider the tension that appears to exist in 'Liberal Community', between the idea of the 'communal life' and Dworkin's advocation of tolerance and hence some form of neutrality, we must first consider what is required by the idea of neutrality. In his book *Legal Right and Social Democracy*[76] Neil MacCormick discusses the question of whether the law should be used for enforcement of moral values. He first states that the question is itself a question of political morality, for practical principles of right conduct are moral principles.[77] Thus the issue at stake is not "*whether* state power should be used in accordance with moral principles but *what* moral principles should be observed in the exercise of state powers".[78] Here MacCormick draws a distinction between two possible views about the exercise of state powers. We might argue that the morally proper exercise of these powers should be based on no further moral presuppositions as to the values that citizens ought to pursue. This is the principle of moral disestablishment. Alternatively, we could argue that state power should be exercised according to further such presuppositions. In considering the first of these arguments we should note that it is grounded in the idea of personal autonomy. In other words, it argues that true moral values will be those "constituted by free self-commitment to inwardly accepted standards and values".[79] It therefore requires liberty of choice, and hence can be said to be neutral with respect to conceptions of the good life. However, this idea, which lies at the heart of Mill's idea of liberty, is subject to a number of difficulties,[80] not least that it appears to excuse the wilful harming of others in the pursuit of one's own gratification. For this reason Mill, for example, developed the 'harm' principle, in order that the state could exert force in order to prevent persons from doing harm to others. Once this step is taken the idea that state power should never be used to enforce moral values seems to have been breached. Indeed, as MacCormick points out "any principle whatever which allows that the state may resort to *punishment* necessarily allows state enforcement of *some* moral values".[81]

Thus liberals have turned instead to the second option we outlined. Whilst this is commonly referred to as liberal neutrality, this is something of a misnomer given that it allows the presupposition of values that citizens ought to pursue. MacCormick instead usefully refers to this as a 'limited moral establishment', which gives a clearer idea of the character of this argument. Liberals do have positive political values, for example the respect of others' equal rights, and they also have institutions and practices that are designed to embody and promote these values. It is therefore incorrect to speak of liberal 'neutrality'. Similarly, if liberalism simply stands for toleration, then it "stands for everything, and it takes a stand for nothing".[82] Charles Larmore has argued that liberal neutrality is "not meant to be one of *outcome*, but rather one of *procedure*".[83] It therefore acts as a constraint on those factors that can be used to justify a political decision. Larmore argues that the liberal state should only impost restrictions for *extrinsic* reasons because, for example, the lives of others are threatened.[84] This 'neutrality' will thus only stand for mutual respect among those committed to a similar set of values and hence is far from being neutral. Stephen Macedo asserts that "Larmore would not have us respect everyone, but only those who are reasonable".[85] The boundaries and nature of this 'neutralitv' will thus be determined by liberal political values, and can hardly be said to be neutral with respect to conceptions of the good life. Similarly Neil MacCormick asserts that what we need is a principle of limited moral establishment.[86] He draws a distinction between those situations in which we are required to respect moral personality in ourselves and those which we must respect in others. There can thus be said to be requirements of morality as to self-respect and as to other-respect.[87] MacCormick argues that we should only seek to enforce moral requirements which are other-regarding duties of respect for persons, for to enforce duties of self-respect would be to "prima facie deny that other the opportunity of self-respect as an autonomous moral being".[88] In the same way we must intervene "when a condition of a person's self-respect are endangered by another person's respect for acting towards the former".[89] However, MacCormick would only enforce such other-regarding duties to the smallest extent necessary for securing to all the conditions of self-respect as autonomous beings.[90] MacCormick's idea of a limited moral establishment therefore seems to equate with our ideas of what is required by tolerance.[91] This then sets out a framework within which we may examine Dworkin's theory of liberal community for any signs of tension between that thesis and his advocation of tolerance and its attendant claim to liberal 'neutrality' or limited moral establishment.

Dworkin's argument is that citizens will identify with their political community once they recognise that the community has a 'communal life' and that the success of their own lives is ethically dependent on the success or failure of that communal life.[92] He argues that this provides a full, genuine and intense conception of the community, and that those that argue against liberalism only argue for a different account of what a community's collective life really is.[93] The attraction of this argument lies in Dworkin's claim that the communal life of a political community exists only in its formal political decisions, and that as a result integration offers no threat to liberal principles.[94] This seems to apply MacCormick's distinction between duties of other-respect and self-respect. The communal life of the political community will lie in the enforcement of the duties of other-respect, whilst duties of self-respect are matters of personal morality. Dworkin again ties this idea into that of equality and legitimacy in arguing that the integrated citizen will accept that the value of his life "depends on the success of his community in treating everyone with *equal concern*".[95] If everyone recognises this to be the case then we will have an important source of stability and legitimacy. Dworkin accepts that this is utopian, for "we can scarcely hope that a thoroughly integrated political society will ever be realised". However, he wishes to set out "an ideal of community we can define, defend, and perhaps even grope our way towards".[96] This then is a form of perfectionism with Dworkin setting out a utopian vision of community. In setting out the conditions for true community in *Law's Empire* we noted a similar tendency which appears contrary to his stance of interpretive neutrality. Additionally, in that discussion we noted a number of difficulties relating to his discussion of those conditions. However, here Dworkin provides a more convincing explanation of his promotion of this particular form of community. We must examine this in order to see if Dworkin can maintain his commitment to the liberal virtues of tolerance, and limited moral establishment, whilst promoting one particular type of community.

Ethical Priority

The problem of promoting a liberal society whilst maintaining a doctrine of tolerance has been tackled in various ways. We shall now look briefly at the theoretical arguments involved before examining some of the solutions that have been put forward. Liberalism is typically taken to involve the defence, on both descriptive and normative grounds, of the idea that the state should be neutral with regard to conceptions of the good life. However, as we have seen, this neutrality in fact involves the presupposition of certain conceptions, albeit in the framework that promotes tolerance. Thus, whereas it is common to portray liberalism as maintaining the view that the state cannot promote moral ideals, in contrast to communitarianism, in fact this is not the case, and the difference between the two lies in the moral ideals that they promote. There are two possible reactions to the communitarians' perfectionist account. Liberals can either put forward their own perfectionist theory based on toleration, or they can argue that liberalism is justified precisely because of the neutrality it advocates. With this latter option the claim typically may take one of two forms. It may either be a claim as to the truth of pluralism, or as to the fact of pluralism.[97] Whereas the argument from the fact of pluralism appeals to the lack of any consensus as to conceptions of the good life, and thus is essentially pragmatic, the argument as to the truth of pluralism instead appeals to the idea that it is impossible to rank these competing conceptions, for we lack any standard by which to do so. We shall examine this latter argument[98] before turning to look at Dworkin's views and contrasting them with those of Raz.

The argument as to the truth of pluralism is built on the idea of the incommensurability thesis. As we have seen, this asserts that there are some claims about which we may disagree, but that cannot be resolved because we lack any standard by which to evaluate them. The argument embraces the reality of moral conflict, and does not simply assert that all conceptions of the good life are equally valid.[99] It means that, although we may accept that there are no means of resolving our conflicts, we can nevertheless argue one position to be superior. Stephen Gardbaum asserts that at least some values must be irrational if reason is the standard by which incommensurable values are identified, and in order to differentiate it from subjectivism or relativism.[100] He argues that this means that in principle it must be sometimes possible to say that one way of life is rationally superior to another,[101] and that as a result perfectionism is possible on this model. However, this appears to seek an objective conclusion from a subjective disagreement. Although it is possible in principle that one way of life will prove to be rationally, and therefore objectively, superior, this is only a weak claim, for we cannot demonstrate this to be the case. That is the whole point of the incommensurability thesis. Individuals will prefer specific conceptions of the good life, but this is at the subjective level, and we recognise that at the objective level there are no means for resolution of this conflict. For this reason the incommensurability thesis does point us towards some version of neutrality. Gardbaum argues that any resulting neutrality will be narrow in scope in that it guarantees neither impartiality nor toleration.[102] However, whilst is does not guarantee impartiality, neither do other versions of liberal neutrality. And it is undesirable that they should do so. With regard to toleration, Gardbaum argues that the incommensurability thesis would eliminate the right to be wrong. However, the thesis is compatible with the form of toleration suggested by MacCormick and Dworkin. There appears to be general agreement that duties of other-respect, or those that arise in the political sphere, should be enforced by the community. By contrast there is disagreement as to matters of self-respect, as to whether the community or the individual is the correct agency in this regard. Similarly, there is disagreement amongst individuals as to the morality to apply here. However, this is a matter on which there is no standard by which to adjudicate, and this the incommensurability thesis will operate to promote tolerance. This allows people to pursue conceptions of the good life that, though many people feel to be wrong, they themselves feel is right. This appears to be in line with other liberal doctrines of toleration. This argument then is intended to illustrate that the incommensurability thesis can be used to support a version of liberal neutrality. This is one possible approach to this difficulty.

Joseph Raz has argued in his book *The Morality of Freedom*[103] that political neutrality is impossible, and that accordingly the state must be concerned with the moral quality of the lives led by its citizens. His liberalism is 'perfectionist' in nature. The focus of Raz's thesis lies in the idea of the autonomy of the individual, and the possibility of an autonomously led life requires that there exists within society an adequate range of options. Raz argues that valuable lives will consist in the pursuit of projects, and commitments to various 'forms of life', and that as supporting valuable ways of life is a social rather than individual matter these perfectionist ideals require public action for their viability.[104] It is thus argued that the state has an integral role in the promotion of autonomy. The state is concerned with 'perfect' forms of living, though not with particular ideals, for that would be in breach of the principle of autonomy. The state must exercise tolerance, for that is required by the moral pluralism that is a result of Raz's respect for autonomy. Raz also offers a perfectionist account of autonomy in arguing that it is only valuable if spent in the pursuit of acceptable and valuable projects and relationships.[105] This is a result of his rejection of the ideal of neutrality but it appears to lead to difficulties in that it seems to mean that there is no protection for actions that are deemed morally bad but which do not affect others. This means that the harm principle has no part to play here. However, the alternative for Raz will go against his perfectionist notion of autonomy which is required by his theory. Raz does argue that morally repugnant actions should not be punished by imprisonment, but his theory of autonomy still seems unable to support the harm principle.[106] This argument for a perfectionist view of liberalism seems to fall down on the weak ideas of tolerance, autonomy, and pluralism that it adopts, particularly in allowing that we are not required to tolerate ways of life that we find 'repugnant'.[107] We must then seek an alternative account. Raz's approach adopts what Dworkin terms a 'continuity' theory in that it sees a continuous connection between a person's personal ethics, and third person ethics. By contrast John Rawls's attempt to explain the basis of liberalism as an overlapping consensus adopts a discontinuity strategy.[108] Dworkin, with Raz, wishes to pursue a continuity theory of the foundations of liberalism. His thesis is that we can construct a bridge between personal and political ethics, such that ethics becomes part of the foundations of liberalism. Dworkin's theory is thus similar to Raz's, for both see the political perspective as being defined by our personal ethics that place great weight on the idea of autonomy. This is endorsed by the state in the form of its tolerance of the plurality of exercises of this autonomy. However, whereas Raz's perfectionist view of liberalism seems founded on an unusual view of the requirements of tolerance, Dworkin seeks to explain how the force of liberal principles can arise from personal ethics in a different way.

Dworkin bases his argument on the contention that what is required by liberal justice is the equal distribution of resources,[109] and in arguing that this converts the ethical question into that of 'what is a good life for someone entitled to the share of resources I am entitled to have?'.[110] In this way the state is able to ensure that there is a variety of options open to everyone, whilst respecting the principle of liberal neutrality in developing a procedure that is endorsable as fair by everyone in society.[111] Dworkin's argument here is founded on a distinction that he draws between our volitional and our critical well-being. Someone's volitional well-being will be improved where he has or achieves something he wants, whereas his critical well-being will be improved only by his having or achieving those things that he should want.[112] This distinction can be made both subjectively and objectively, but for Dworkin it seems that the subjective approach is the correct one to adopt, for within that lies the idea of personal autonomy.[113] For Dworkin, it is critical well-being that is important to his thesis, for the "criteria of a life good in a critical sense cannot be defined contextually", as "someone lives well when he responds appropriately to his circumstances".[114] In this way, Dworkin wishes to put forward a weak version of Plato's claim that morality and well-being are interdependent in an adequate ethics.[115] Dworkin argues that, once we draw the connection between the ethical question of how we should live and the question of distributive justice, Plato's view of critical success becomes appealing: "someone does *pro tanto* a poorer job of living ... if he acts unjustly".[116] The next step in Dworkin's argument is to seek reconciliation between two ethical ideals that are widely held. The first of these is that we feel we have particular responsibilities to those with whom we have special relationships. This seems to conflict with the second ideal which requires that the just citizen insists on equal concern for all in his political life. In order to bring about this reconciliation, Dworkin claims that, if we have secured a just distribution of resources, the resources people control are morally as well as legally theirs.[117] They can then use their resources as they desire. Dworkin is thus able to ground his liberal community with the necessary level of public support whilst maintaining his advocation of tolerance.

Dworkin's final point returns us to Plato's idea that someone who does not behave in a just way will lead a worse life in consequence.[118] Dworkin adopts this idea in relation to the critical value of a life, in order to claim that in the same way it will be diminished by ignoring the injustice in one's own political community.[119] However, even if we were to devote ourselves to reducing this injustice our lives would be at least equally diminished.[120] Therefore, someone who possesses a vivid sense of his own critical interests will be 'inevitably thwarted' where his community fails in its responsibilities of justice. This is the ethical privacy that a political community has over our individual lives.

Dworkin appears to have returned here to the arguments he advanced in *A Matter of Principle* as to the relationship between equality and liberal neutrality. Those essays tended to concentrate on the attractiveness of his theory of equality based on the distribution of resources.[121] Dworkin has now shown us how that idea fits in with the liberal virtues of neutrality and toleration, and once there is a fair distribution of resources we can do as we wish with our share. Additionally, Dworkin is able to explain how those ideals square with his advocation of a 'full' account of community. For, in accordance with MacCormick's idea of a limited moral establishment, the notion of the communal life applies only to a community's formal political life, and thus will not refer to the duties of self-respect but only to those of other-respect, as described by MacCormick's thesis. This argument is therefore consistent with the liberal virtues advocated by Dworkin, for it will not affect individual autonomy within the bounds required by liberal neutrality. The most important aspect of Dworkin's argument here is that a community must aim to treat everyone with equal concern. This idea enables us to link the question of whether we have lived a good life to that of justice, for it is this idea that links the personal and political spheres. Our ethical life will be affected by the justice of the distribution of freedoms at the political level. This establishes the continuity between these factors that Dworkin is seeking, for where there is a just distribution of resources these resources belong to us both morally and legally. Thus Dworkin argues that we should strive towards the ideal of a thoroughly integrated political society through seeking a just distribution of freedoms where everyone is treated with equal concern and respect.

This is a much more persuasive account of community than that given in *Law's Empire* in that it answers many of the questions raised by that account. Dworkin links his theory of community to his application of a liberal theory of justice in a much clearer manner. The critical factor is again justice, with the ideal of a just distribution of resources being at the centre of Dworkin's argument. The virtue of integrity appears to be redundant here. The account also seems preferable to the perfectionist theory of Raz, and seems to accord with the incommensurability thesis. It therefore seems that Dworkin's account of community here is largely successful. It also seems to be compatible with the arguments in *Law's Empire*, but goes beyond that account in its discussion of distributive justice, and in so doing is more persuasive.

We now briefly return to consider Philip Selznick's criticism of Dworkin, which we mentioned in the previous section. Selznick's argument centres on the idea that what we prize in a community is 'a unity of unities',[122] and he claims that, whilst Dworkin has done much to enrich liberal doctrine, some unnecessary and burdensome baggage remains. The argument is essentially based on the idea that Dworkin should move towards a stronger notion of community. Selznick claims that, in shifting attention "from individuals to communities, welfare liberalism must deal with collective *purposes*",[123] but that this runs counter to the idea that the political community should be neutral as to ends, for on that view "the proper locus of moral choice is the autonomous person",[124] not the collective will. Selznick views neutrality as being a "perverse limitation"[125] on attempts to defuse a common good, and thus argues that Dworkin should dispense with this aspect of his theory, in order to better bring about the reconciliation of liberal and communitarian perspectives. The problem with Selznick's thesis is that he seems to have a defective understanding of what liberal 'neutrality' requires, possibly brought about because of the confession we have noticed in that idea. In criticising Dworkin's advocation of neutrality, Selznick comments that pluralism cannot be a doctrine of 'anything goes' and that it is not a synonym for boundless variety, but of course liberals have never attempted to defuse it as if it were. Thus much of Selznick's criticism seems to falter on this point. The additional reasons supplied by Selznick for his criticisms centre on a presumed desirability of the communitarian perspective: "defence of the moral order makes sense sociologically as well as morally".[126] However, we shall see that the communitarian thesis, taken as a whole, is far from satisfactory either as a description of our existing practices or as a proposal for our future ones. Selznick's claim that Dworkin should move towards this perspective is therefore both unconvincing and, unappealing. As Dworkin points out, "If we limit a political community's communal life to its formal political decisions, integration offers no threat to liberal principles, and it seems disappointing exactly for that reason".[127] However, this does not mean that integration is of no consequence. Dworkin wishes to see citizens integrated into their communities such that they accept that the value of their lives depends on the success of the community in treating everyone equally. In this way "they will share an understanding that politics is a joint venture in a particularly strong sense". [128] Dworkin therefore offers an ideal of community that is appealing, and one that we can aim towards. Clearly, he recognises the importance of community, and offers a full account of its role.[129] For example, in his article 'Why Liberals Should Care About Equality'[130] Dworkin argues that the notion of the equality of resources appeals "to the idea that each citizen is the member of a community, and that he can find, in the fate of that community, a reason for special burdens"[131] that are imposed upon him. Treating people as equals requires a "more active" conception of community membership.

Conclusion

We have argued that Dworkin's promotion of the doctrine of liberal toleration in 'Liberal Community' offers a more compelling account of community to that proposed by the communitarian critics and perfectionist liberals. Dworkin is able to put forward this version of liberal neutrality through a consideration of a need for a limited moral establishment and a consideration of the incommensurability thesis. His account of community is appealing in that it links the question of political justice to that of personal ethics, and thus enables him to give a full account of community whilst advocating an acceptance of the liberal virtues of neutrality and tolerance. Additionally, it appears to be compatible with the central thesis of *Law's Empire* although it goes well beyond that account. Furthermore, in stressing the role of justice, integrity once again appears superfluous here. This leaves us proposing a tolerant and pluralistic society which Stephen Macedo excitedly refers to as "a smorgasbord confronting us with an exciting array of possibilities".[132] For now then Dworkin's theory of community reigns supreme in the liberal empire.

Notes

1 Dworkin 1986 p.188.
2 Id. pp.188-190.
3 Dworkin describes it as "the main argument of the book" - see id. p.190.
4 This argument is found at pp.190-195.
5 Id. p.191.
6 Id. p.193.
7 Id.
8 See Westmoreland 1991 at pp.191-192.
9 This idea is derived from Rawlsian liberalism.
10 Westmoreland points out that this was advanced by Dworkin in *Taking Rights Seriously*. See Westmoreland 1991 at p.192.
11 Dworkin 1986 p.165.

12 Id. p.167.
13 Id. p.188.
14 Id.
15 Id. p.189.
16 Kahn 1989 p.72.
17 Dworkin 1986 pp.191-192.
18 See Taylor 1985.
19 Dworkin 1986 p.196.
20 Id. p.197.
21 See id. p.437 n.20.
22 Id. p.198.
23 Id. p.199.
24 Sandel 1982 pp.28-35.
25 Id. p.30.
26 Id.
27 Id. p.31.
28 Id. p.32.
29 Id. pp.33-35.
30 Simon Caney presents fine arguments against Sandel's thesis on the circumstances of justice - for a summary of these see Caney 1991 p.517.
31 Dworkin 1986 p.203.
32 Caney 1991 p.512.
33 See Kahn 1989 p.75.
34 Dworkin 1989 pp.199-200.
35 Id. p.201.
36 In this way, Dworkin's project is similar to that of Mchael Walzer, but whereas Walzer put forward a theory of liberal neutrality, Dworkin offers a theory of liberal neutrality - see post Chapter Six.
37 Dworkin 1986 p.201.
38 Kahn 1989 p.77.
39 See Dworkin at p.203 and more generally pp.73-76.
40 Kahn 1989 p.78.
41 Dworkin 1986 p.203.
42 Id. p.204.
43 See for a similar argument Reaume 1989 at pp.400-405.
44 Kahn 1989 p.78.
45 Dworkin 1986 p.206.
46 Id.
47 Id. p.209.
48 Id.
49 Id. p.210.
50 Id.
51 Id. p.213.
52 See Chapter Four.

53 Dworkin 1989.
54 See Guest 1992 p.85.
55 Dworkin 1989 p.480.
56 Id. p.481. Dworkin presents this as the view of Justice White who gave the majority judgement in the landmark case of *Bowers v. Hardwick* (1986) 478 US 186 in which the Supreme Court refused by a majority of five to four to extend privacy protection to consensual homosexual activity. See id. p.479.
57 Id. p.481.
58 Id. p.483.
59 Id. p.484.
60 Id. p.486.
61 Id. p.487.
62 Id. p.488.
63 Gutmann 1985 p.316.
64 Dworkin 1989 p.490.
65 See Selznick 1987.
66 Dworkin 1989 p.491.
67 Id.
68 Id. p.495.
69 This conclusion is of course crucial to the specific example being discussed in the article, namely the case of *Bowers v. Hardwick* - see supra. n.56.
70 Dworkin acknowledges that it is possible that some communities could have a communal sex life, for example, a community for propogation. His point is that neither the United States nor its several constituent states are communities that do so. See Dworkin 1989 p.498.
71 The emphasis placed on these conditions seems to have weakened - see Dworkin 1989 at p.499 n.25. Dworkin refers to the conditions as requiring communities to recognise citizens as equal members, and to give them their basic human rights.
72 See for example, Walzer 1983 in which there is an extended discussion of this.
73 Dworkin 1989 p.497.
74 Selznick 1989 at p.506.
75 Id. p.507.
76 MacCormick 1982 Chapter Two.
77 Id. p.18.
78 Id. pp.18-19.
79 Id. p.22.
80 See id. pp.27-34.
81 Id. p.33.
82 Macedo 1991 p.258.
83 Larmore 1987 p.44.
84 Id. p.43.
85 Macedo 1991 p.261.
86 MacCormick 1982 p.35.

87 Id.
88 Id. p.36.
89 Id.
90 Id. p.37.
91 See here Fletcher 1983.
92 Dworkin 1989 p.500.
93 Id. See also for a similar idea Gutmann 1985 p.322 : "The worthy challenge posed by the communitarian critics is not to replace liberal justice but to improve it". Dworkin seems to have taken up the gauntlet.
94 Dworkin 1989 p.499.
95 Id. p.501 (our italics).
96 Id. p.502.
97 For this distinction, see Gardbaum 1991.
98 This discussion is based on Gardbaum 1991 pp.1358-1364.
99 It thus differs from both relativism and subjectivism.
100 Gardbaum 1991 p.1360.
101 Id.
102 Id. p.1364.
103 Raz 1986. See further Guest 1992 pp.290-291; Guest 1987; Sadurski 1990.
104 Raz 1986 p.162.
105 Id. p.417.
106 See further here Sadurski 1990 pp.131-133.
107 See Guest 1987 pp.644-645. But see also Sadurski 1990 at pp.131-132 where he argues that Raz does not reject these exercises of autonomy, but his argument is nevertheless insufficient to support the harm principle.
108 This is an argument from the fact of pluralism. See Gardbaum 1991 at pp.1364-1370.
109 See further Dworkin 1986 (a) Chapter Nine.
110 Dworkin 1989 p.503.
111 See Kymlicka 1991 p.81.
112 Id. p.484.
113 See Guest 1992 p.300.
114 Dworkin 1989 p.503.
115 See id. p.502. See also Guest 1992 p.307 n.18.
116 Dworkin 1989 p.503.
117 Id.
118 See Plato 1955 Part Five Book Four. Plato makes Socrates define justice as being a virtue in the individual.
119 Dworkin 1989 p.504.
120 Id.
121 See especially Dworkin 1986 (a), Chapters Eight and Nine.
122 Selznick 1989 p.507.
123 Id. p.509.
124 Id.

125 Id. p.510.
126 Id. p.513.
127 Dworkin 1989 p.500.
128 Id. p.501.
129 See further here Caney 1992, especially pp.282-285 where Caney argues that liberal theorists have always recognised the normative value of community.
130 Dworkin 1986 (a) Chapter Nine.
131 Id. p.210.
132 Macedo 1991 p.278.

6 Wider Contexts

In this chapter we will look at the debate between the liberals and the connnunitarians and at trends in modern theories of hermenuetics in order to consider Dworkin's position on these matters in their wider philosophical context. In so doing we shall also take aspects of Dworkin's theory and examine them in greater detail than hitherto.

Liberalism and Communitarianism

One current trend in modern liberal thought has been towards recognising the importance of the communitarian critique. Many commentators have been surprised by these moves, given what they see as the weakness of the communitarian position.[1] However, liberal theorists such as John Rawls and Charles Larmore have nevertheless felt compelled to alter their theories accordingly. Rawls, for example, now emphasises that his theory is best understood as being political and not moral, and as a result he is not concerned with metaphysical propositions.[2] Rawls distinguishes his task here from that of a comprehensive doctrine - he is concerned only with American political history, not with grand theory. Rawls's concern therefore centres on the problem of how to ensure political stability and social unity in a modern pluralistic society. What he thus seeks to provide is a theory of justice that sets out the aims and limits of a democratic constitution, and thus hopefully achieves an "overlapping consensus" of support.[3] Rawls's new position is founded "not on the revisability of each person's ends, but on the plurality of different people's ends".[4] Rawls thus now grounds his theory of justice in the principle of toleration. Similarly, Charles Larmore has defended Rawls on the basis that liberal justice imposes duties on us, not because it expresses our deepest self-understandings, but because it represents the fairest possible *modus vivendi* for a pluralistic society.[5] Finally, Joseph Raz has offered a defence of liberal duties to protect and promote pluralism.[6] However, Raz differs from other liberal theorists in appealing to perfectionist ideals which he argues are unavoidable if we are to ensure the social conditions of freedom. This then combines an acceptance of the communitarian argument that liberal neutrality is impossible to maintain with the promotion of liberal values such as toleration. In this way Raz hopes to combine communitarian insights with liberal philosophy to aim towards a 'perfect' society.

How far has Dworkin's own theory of community been affected by communitarianism? Dworkin argues that there is broad agreement in modern politics that the government must treat all its citizens with equal concern and respect.[7] This can be achieved in two fundamentally distinct ways. We may either suppose that the government must be neutral on the question of what constitutes a good life, or alternatively that the government cannot be neutral on this question because it cannot treat its citizens equally without some theory as to what human beings ought to be. A liberal is someone who holds the first theory of what equality requires.[8] This set out the basic liberal position. For liberals, the good society will provide a framework of rights and duties within which individuals may pursue their own conception of the good life. It may thus be argued that the liberal defence of our rights and liberties is designed to protect our most important interest of all, namely that of leading a good life.[9] The liberal response to our modern pluralistic society has been, therefore, to advocate toleration where possible. On this there is fundamental disagreement with the communitarian philosophers who take the view that this gives us no real kind of society. Alasdair MacIntyre, for example, has argued that three centuries of liberal discourse has resulted in the destruction of the tradition of European moral theory that once formed the foundation of our political communities.[10]

Dworkin's form of liberalism is not universally shared and, as one would expect, there are major differences between the major liberal theorists on fundamentals. Take for example John Rawls who argues that, whereas liberal theory is deontological, giving priority to the right over the good, its utilitarian forebears were teleological in that they viewed the good as prior to the right. This distinction is important for Rawls, for his argument is that it is only by giving priority to the right over the good that we can properly recognise the distinctness of persons. Rawls argues that because utilitarianism is prepared to sacrifice the good of an individual for that of society it does not furnish a satisfactory account of what it is to treat people as equals. This is because utilitarianism treats the good as being prior to the right. For Rawls, each person's good should matter equally so as to restrain the pursuit of the overall good. In this way he purports to take rights seriously. The further, but dependent, distinction that Rawls regards as important is that between 'perfectionism' and 'non-perfectionism'. A perfectionist will hold a particular view as to what constitutes human perfection and will seek to achieve this. Therefore, in a society based on perfectionism, people would not be free to pursue their own conceptions of the good life, without penalty. However, Rawls advocates a non-perfectionist outlook, in which primary goods will be distributed according to a 'thin theory of the good'. This will enable many different conceptions of the good life to be pursued within the structure of society. For Rawls, the difference between these two theories lies in the priority of the right over the good, on the basis that perfectionism is a form of teleological theory.[11] In this way Rawls advocates the liberal ideals of toleration and equality. The views of Dworkin as a fellow liberal can be contrasted with those of Rawls on this issue. In *A Matter Of Principle* Dworkin argues that both Rawls and his critics share the same 'egalitarian plateau' on which it is agreed that the interests of the members of the community matter equally. Dworkin in contrast to Rawls argues that there is an equality premise that is typically contained in the utilitarian argument. This is that the wishes of each individual member of the community count on an equal basis. Utilitarianism can no longer said to be teleological, but rather is deontological, for as Will Kymlicka points out "it is the concern with equal consideration that underlies the argument of Bentham and Sidgwick and is expressly affirmed by recent utilitarians".[12] Utilitarianism on this interpretation is still subject to strong criticism, on the basis that its scheme for enforcing equality is poor, but it may not be subject to the defect Rawls outlines.

Dworkin's main theme here has been that liberal principles of justice are aimed at achieving equality of resources. He argues that this is the correct principle of distribution for a system treating people as equals, because it requires that people be put in a position equal with others, so as to be able to allow us to be free in pursuing our conception of the good life. In this way Dworkin seeks to reconcile the twin liberal ideals of equality and liberty. In order to enable people to pursue their conceptions of the good life once resources have been distributed, the liberal state will probably choose a market economy. However, his conception of equality requires a system that "produces certain inequalities (those that reflect the true differential costs of goods and opportunities) but not others (those that follow from differences in ability, inheritance, and so on)".[13] The difficulty for the liberal is that the market produces both types of inequality, yet there is no alternative that can be relied on. As a result of this, the liberal state will add to its scheme certain individual rights which will act as trumps. In this way the market allocations will attempt to bring us closer to the allocations we would have received, but for the various differences of initial advantage, luck and inherent capacity.[14] However, we may ask why we should favour this approach as opposed to one in which there is a short-term sacrifice for some individuals in order to produce a long-term gain in welfare for all. Such an argument might draw attention both to the immediate dangers to the economy and also to the interests of future generations. Dworkin places this concept in the realm of responsibility.[15] Requiring others to forgo their share of resources in order to subsidise our choices is unfair, for we are capable of adjusting our aims and ambitions, and thus we should take account of what our choice means to others. Only if those asked to lose out in the short-term have some power to help shape the future, and will at least equally benefit from the future prosperity, can such choices be justified.[16]

Having identified Dworkin's stance within the liberal position we now turn to the communitarian attack on liberalism. In order to do this, let us focus to begin with on what the communitarian position entails. It may be useful to clarify the position by dividing its argument into three broad claims.[17] Communitarians make descriptive claims about the nature of the self, they make a meta-ethical claim about the role of moral principles, and they make normative claims about the value of society. We shall examine these claims in turn, in order to assess the strength of the communitarian threat to liberalism, and thus to set the agenda for Dworkin's recent discussion of community in *Law's Empire*, and later in 'Liberal Community'.[18] In order to best represent the current direction of the communitarian movement, its claims will be examined by reference to four of its most influential scholars, namely Michael Sandel, Alasdair MacIntyre, Charles Taylor, and Michael Walzer, who each represent a different wing of the idea. In *Liberalism And The Limits Of Justice*,[19] Michael Sandel offers a critique of Rawls's political philosophy in order to identify what is in his view wrong with liberalism in general. For Rawls, as for Nozick, the separateness of persons served as the foundational criteria from which to build a theory of justice and to reject the formerly dominant utilitarian outlook. However, this has since itself become controversial, with Sandel arguing that people are embedded within their communities and have their identities defined by this membership.[20] Sandel's starting point here is Nozick's notion of persons "thick with particular traits"[21] which leads him to the idea that the self is constituted by its relationship with other members of the community, and hence to the conclusion that our aims, values, and conceptions of the good are not the product of choice. The requirement of deontology that we imagine ourselves as "independent in the sense that our identity is never tied to our aims and attachments" is then "not to conceive an ideally free and rational agent, but to imagine a person wholly without character, without moral depth".[22] This basis of Sandel's critique is echoed by Alasdair MacIntyre, who states that "the story of my life is always embedded in the story of those communities from which I derive my identity".[23] Sandel and MacIntyre therefore put forward much the same arguments against liberalism, although one difference may be that, whilst for Sandel the problem is that liberalism has faulty foundations, for MacIntyre it is that liberalism lacks any foundations at all.[24]

Sandel and MacIntyre therefore wish to encourage a constitutive theory of the self in order that the gap between persons and their commitments be drawn more tightly, and that community boundaries may be lowered amongst persons who share the same constitutive goals and commitments. Thus in this way community becomes more central than liberalism would permit. These constitutive attachments will allow that "to some I owe more than justice requires or even permits",[25] and this means that "justice finds its limits in those forms of community having gauged the identity as well as the interests of the participants".[26] Communal aims and values will not simply be affirmed by members of the community, but they will also define their identity, for "community describes not just what they *have* as fellow citizens but also what they *are*, not a relationship they choose but an attachment they discover, not merely an attribute but a constituent of their identity".[27] It is thus liberalism's requirement of reflective detachment that Sandel sees as its defect. Stephen Macedo points out that this is the same criticism that Bernard Williams directs to utilitarianism, for Williams denies that we can or should admit the pervasive reach of any impartial morality.[28] The constitutive relationship that the communitarians wish to establish between the self and its ends is however an ambiguous one. It may be given both a strong and weak interpretation, with communitarians seeming to oscillate between the two.[29]

Communitarians need to endorse strongly constitutive attachments if they are to provide an alternative to liberalism.[30] A strong interpretation would provide such an alternative, for it denies the possibility of establishing any reflective difference between "the moral subject and its deep, defining 'constitutive' goals and commitments".[31] This seems to be the interpretation that Sandel and MacIntyre wish to put forward when they argue, for example, that "the relevant question is not what ends to choose, for my problem is exactly that the answer to this question is already given",[32] or that I cannot "put in question ... social features of my existence".[33] However, this does not seem to accord with the way that we think of ourselves, for no matter how deeply we feel ourselves to be embedded within a practice we still feel able to question the value of that practice. As Michael Mosher points out, that an individual member of a constitutive community "must still say, and indeed *can* say, 'I acknowledge' these attachments"[34] seems to indicate the failure of the strong account. Sandel and MacIntyre claim that the good is to be found by a process of self-discovery, yet it is they who appear to contradict our deepest self-understandings.[35] Strong constitutive attachments do not appear to fit our modern pluralistic cultures, and instead seem to nostalgically yearn for a former time. To allow that one's external commitments can be strongly constitutive of one's identity is to place them beyond the reach of critical reflection, so that there will be no requirement of respect of the equal rights of others. Macedo gives the examples here of loyal Nazis who may have been deeply constitutive by their commitment to being "good Germans".[36] Similarly, Amy Gutmann argues that "the communitarian critics want us to live in Salem, but not to believe in witches. Or human rights".[37] Michael McDonald has argued against these criticisms, with specific reference to the argument that the communitarians themselves violate our deepest self-understandings.[38] He argues that to take the view that there are limits to self-examination does not in and of itself commit the communitarians to repressive, inhumane, or otherwise obnoxious political arrangements.[39] McDonald suggests that there exists a "powerful sense" in which people may well find givens that are beyond questioning for them.[40] However, this does not preclude re-evaluation entirely, and thus McDonald appears to be offering only a 'weak' defence. The critical point here is that, although one can clearly identify with one's community, this does not mean that our context defines who we are. For example, Jeremy Waldron points out that he is a New Zealander trained at Oxford who now writes for the California Law Review, and asks if there is some sort of common culture that makes this possible.[41] This then leads us into a consideration of the weaker interpretation of the communitarian notion of the self.

We have seen that Sandel and MacIntyre often seem to affirm the radically situated conception of the self. However, they also often seem to endorse only a partially embedded thesis.[42] Sandel, for example, refers to the subject as being able "to play a role in shaping the contours of its identity" provided it has "certain faculty of reflection".[43] Although agency consists "less in summoning the will than in seeking self-understanding",[44] Sandel allows that this may never be finally fixed and thus that re-description is possible.[45] Similarly, MacIntyre argues that the fact we are embedded in communal practices "does not entail that the self has to accept the moral *limitations* of the particularity of these forms of community".[46] MacIntyre admits that we have no readily available account of the good life, and goes as far as to concede that the "good life for man is the life spent in seeking for the good life for man".[47] It becomes hard to see how far MacIntyre's views differ in a fundamental way from those of liberalism. As

Kymlicka indicates, once MacIntyre allows for such questioning his argument against the liberal view collapses.[48] Sandel can be similarly criticised here. Whilst there will be apparent differences between his revised position and that of liberalism, for Kymlicka this hides "a more fundamental identity: both accept that the *person* is prior to her ends".[49] Although they disagree over where to draw the boundaries of the self within the person, once Sandel admits that the self can re-examine its ends his project to reveal the failing of the liberal notion of the self must itself fail. The reason for this may be that the communitarian scholars often state the wish to replace Kantian *Moralitat* with Hegelian *Sittichkeit*. However, it is far from clear that Hegel would have supported this, for he did not wish to replace *Moralitat*, but rather to give it some content. In other words Hegel did not wish to stop people asking what type of life they should lead, but instead he wished to give them "genuine reasons for answering that question in a way that harmonised with the existing traditions and practices of the community".[50] The communitarians seem to overlook this, as well as Hegel's point that we have lost the naive faith necessary if we are to consciously let the community set our goals. As Mosher puts it, the communitarians seem to "lack the master's institutional affirmation of modernity and overlook his claim that institutions must express both commitment *and* reflexivity".[51]

Therefore criticisms of the liberal notion of the self as being subject to equal concern and respect seem doomed to failure once it is admitted that the person can re-examine his ends. We now turn to consider the corollary claim to this, that the pro-responsibility account of what follows from treating people equally ignores the role played by society. This criticism of liberalism attacks the individualistic means that liberals adopt to promote the interest of the self. It is therefore the second strand of the communitarian attack on the liberal idea of the self, and is most persuasively examined by Charles Taylor, who argues that liberals promote choice at the expense of the social preconditions necessary to allow that choice. This thesis contrasts with the atomistic view that individuals can be self-sufficient outside the context of society. Taylor's basic claim is that people only develop their characteristically human capacities in society.[52] One problem for this is that most liberals are not atomist in Taylor's sense of the term, although it is true that he does not claim that they are.[53] He is instead led to argue that full acceptance of the social thesis would necessitate the abandonment of a central liberal tenet, that of the primacy of rights. However, as Kymlicka states, it is far from clear that contemporary liberal theories are best understood in this way.[54] Nevertheless, this does not end the debate for

Taylor still claims that liberals fail to recognise some duties, and pay too much attention to certain rights, as a result of their inadequate social thesis. The real difference arises here because of the differing ways in which communitarians and liberals view the common good. The communitarian pursuit of shared ends will not, of course, be constrained by any requirement of equal concern. In order to show a link between this political view and the social thesis, Taylor offers a conceptual and an empirical argument.

The conceptual argument is that liberals are committed to maintaining a particular type of society, namely one governed by a politics of mutual concern, and that once they admit to this then they have already accepted a politics of the common good. However, this is too wide, for the common good pursued by liberal society is designed to enable individual choice in conceptions of the good life. Thus Taylor requires more than this to establish that acceptance of the social thesis leads us to a communitarian viewpoint. He therefore argues that the social thesis casts doubt on the empirical possibilities of the liberal politics of equal concern. This is because of the liberal dependence on a 'culture of freedom' which means that there must be a duty to sustain that culture, for our liberty will depend upon it. Yet, as Wesley Cragg argues, any collective attempt by a liberal state to protect pluralism will itself be in breach of liberal principles of justice.[55] The difficulty with this argument is that it is accepted by liberals that there is just such a positive duty. For example, Dworkin speaks in favour of protection from "structural debasement or decay" so as to enable a greater rather than a lesser choice.[56] Dworkin further argues that our cultural pluralism "provides the spectacles through which we identify experiences as valuable" and thus it cannot be sensibly measured as one of the experiences it identifies to be weighed against others and found more or less valuable than they.[57] Thus the importance of cultural pluralism for liberalism lies prior to the value attached to it in any conceptions which may exist in society, and so the possibility of neutrality is not undermined. Taylor however goes further here. He argues that a society governed by liberal principles of neutrality would be empirically incapable of maintaining legitimacy. He identifies two difficulties with the effects of neutrality on legitimacy. Firstly, there is the possibility that some ways of life must be discouraged in order to ensure that the political culture will support and defend the value of individual liberty. Secondly, there is the possibility that Western liberal democracies are undergoing a 'legitimisation crisis'[58] brought on by the lack of identification with a common form of life. With individuals free to choose their own conceptions of the good life there is no longer an identification with the state, and thus its demands are not accepted as legitimate. At the heart of this lies the claim that the stability of adjustable community requires some recognition of principles of the good life.[59] The main difficulty with Taylor's argument seems to be that it relies on an unusual idea of liberalism. We have already noticed that liberalism is compatible with the discouragement of the incompatible ways of life, for "liberal autonomy is not neutral with regard to the value of all ways of life" and liberal society will encourage the development of a similar set of reflective capacities to those of the ideal of liberal autonomy.[60] Further, Taylor's argument that the demise in participation that he identifies has been caused by an increase in bureaucratisation and centralisation does not adequately establish that these are the result of liberalism. Even if we accept that this lack of participation is the result of the lack of a politics of the common good, Taylor does not seem to establish that legitimacy is directly related to communitarianism. The main difficulty here seems to be that the communitarians do not give any substantive picture of the common ideals from which they would build its foundations. This is perhaps unsurprising given that any plausible sense of community will refer to such a large number of people that it is "vanishingly improbable that they all hold the same moral views on any topic".[61] Further, the communitarian solution seems much worse than the liberal alternative, for if we were to find the shared ends in our historical practices, is this not "the mainstream of our tradition that excluded women and minorities, and repressed most significant deviations from white, Protestant morality in the name of the common good"?[62] This sort of attempt to promote our shared ends seems in the end to lead to a reduced level of legitimacy with marginal groups even further excluded. As Hirsch comments "the true lesson of the American Constitution is that community could not be sustained".[63]

To sum up, the social thesis offers a detailed and incisive critique of the liberal account of what is required if we are to treat people equally. Particularly in its account of the 'legitimisation crisis' it offers strong arguments against liberal neutrality, but the thesis flounders because the communitarians' own account of society is ultimately too thin.[64] However, we now turn to the contention, put forward by Michael Walzer and others, that correct moral principles will be those that best reflect the shared understandings of communities. For Walzer a society will be considered just "if its substantive life is lived in a certain way - that is, in a way faithful to the shared understandings of the members".[65] Any attempt to ignore those understandings "is (always) to act unjustly".[66] Walzer's argument therefore is based on the view that we should not look for universal principles of justice, but should turn inwards to look at our own practices.

What differentiates Walzer's arguments from those of the other communitarian critics is that Walzer wishes to defend a complex form of equality as indicated in the subtitle of *Spheres of Justice*, which asserts that the book is 'A Defense of Pluralism and Equality'. His arguments are thus constructed on decidedly liberal foundations.

Walzer's claim is based on the notion that we assign different goods and resources to different 'spheres' of justice, each of which will be governed by its own principles of fairness. These spheres must be kept separate, so that success in one sphere must not be allowed to lead to domination in another. This is the case because the different social goods constitute separate spheres of justice, each with distinct criteria of distribution. Thus someone who achieves success in the financial sector should not be allowed to use this to buy into political office. In this way Walzer argues that he is reflecting our shared understanding. Similarly, where there is disagreement as to the meaning of social goods, justice requires that the society be faithful to the disagreements.[67] Because of this reliance on the idea of shared understandings, Walzer's theory has widely been taken to be relativist, and has been criticised on this basis. However, although his claims are sweeping, his relativism is in fact "quite constrained", for his theory is actually presented as "a transcontextual metatheory, structurally valid for all communities".[68] This is put forward not as an interpretation of our practices but instead as a universal truth, with Walzer prepared to discuss not only our own society but also that of the fifth-century BC Athenians. For this reason Brian Barry argues that Walzer's position is actually best described not as relativism but as conventionalism,[69] for as the meaning of goods is socially defined, what is just becomes a matter of convention. Similarly Dworkin argues that Walzer's theory requires us to "look to social conventions to discover the appropriate principles of distribution of particular goods".[70] William Galston also notes the strains of universalism that run through Walzer's work,[71] and this is perhaps best seen in Walzer's advocation of the toleration thesis. Walzer argues that to override the shared understandings of the community is (always) to act unjustly,[72] which leads us to the conclusion that there exists a non-relative principle of toleration. It seems to follow from this that those communities that respect the understandings of their fellow communities will be superior to those that do not. A further point here is that on occasion following the shared values of one community will necessarily entail overriding the shared values of another community,[73] yet as we have seen this is to act unjustly. Here then Walzer appears to be caught in a paradox.

However, perhaps the main difficulty with Walzer's theory is that it itself violates our deepest shared understandings and hence is self-defeating. Dworkin argues that if justice is simply a matter of following our shared understandings, then where people disagree about social needs it must show that there is no shared social meaning to disagree about.[74] This does not seem to fit a society such as our own where such questions regarding justice are constantly being debated. Further, Dworkin argues that Walzer neglects the social meaning of the tradition much more fundamental than those he respects, for "it is part of our common political life, if anything is, that *justice is our critic not our mirror*".[75] Walzer is thus faithless to "the single most important social practice we have: the practice of worrying about what justice really is".[76] Justice is independent of what we currently believe it to represent; it "isn't some function or compilation of the competing claims about justice being made, it is rather what each of the competing claims claims to be".[77] Waldron points out that even if what Walzer claims is true, this is to describe from the outside, rather than participate in, the social understandings in question.[78] Thus the truth in Walzer's position does not prevent us from making serious and universal claims about justice in relation to a particular good or practice, for to do so is to "evince our subscription to the meanings that the good or practice has for us. In making the claim we are *living* it".[79] What we do not do is to simply regard our moral rules as "something we happen to do around here".[80]

Lyle Downing and Robert Thigpen have attempted to defend Walzer from these attacks on the basis that Walzer's position contains an implicit standard that "points beyond the shared conventions of particular societies, thus providing a critical perspective on shared understandings".[81] This standard, they argue, is implicit in Walzer's conception of the 'common life', which is used to refer to people's shared meanings and common interpretations of events. Downing and Thigpen argue that, although this may initially appear to be a "merely descriptive concept" Walzer "indirectly acknowledges that a given common life may deserve more or less respect",[82] based on any enquiry into the level of sharing involved in creating the social meanings. In this way societies in which there is greater participation in developing shared meanings should be considered to be more just than societies in which there is less.[83] The concept of the common life can "constitute a standard for judging shared values" and hence transcend conventionalism by pointing beyond shared understandings.[84]

However Walzer's theory does not seem to be amenable to this interpretation. Downing and Thigpen cite Walzer as characterising the 'attitude of mind' that underlies the theory of justice as one of respect for "those deeper opinions that are the reflections in individual minds, shaped also by individual thought, of the social meanings that constitute our common life".[85] They argue from this that the phrase 'shaped also by individual thought' implies that for a 'genuinely common life' to exist the citizen must share in creating the social meanings.[86] But this does not seem necessarily to follow. In the passage in question, on the penultimate page in *Spheres of Justice*, Walzer is elucidating what he means by the shared understandings of society. He states that it is "not the opinions of this or that individual, which may well deserve a brusque response",[87] and then goes on to set out the requirements we have examined. That Walzer does not appear to posit some sort of 'common life' standard is clear from his statement on the following page that "the citizens cannot be guaranteed a 'turn' everywhere. I suppose, in fact, that they cannot be guaranteed a 'turn' anywhere".[88] This hardly points to the existence of a standard whereby societies should seek to encourage greater participation in order to be considered more just. Walzer's commitment to some form of relativism is also confirmed in this section of *Spheres of Justice*, when he states that "we do justice to actual men and women by respecting their particular creations",[89] even where this is the ancient Indian cast system. Similarly, he later states that "when philosophers ... write out of respect for the understandings they share with their fellow citizens, they pursue justice justly".[90] Indeed, the only situation that Walzer admits of as not constituting a life of shared meanings is the Hegelian situation of slaves and masters, for here the two groups "are simply at war".[91]

Considered on its own, the standard of the 'common life' seems somewhat vague and severe. For instance, if we apply this standard to an example discussed by Downing and Thigpen that of the distribution of hard work, then it must be presumed that a society with full employment is more just than one with some unemployment. Thus the old USSR would be considered a more just society on this basis than those of the Western democracies, despite the existence of obvious reasons to think otherwise. We can also apply this criticism to Downing and Thigpen's preference for the collective holiday over the more individualistic vacation, on the basis that holidays answer the "felt human need for communal celebration".[92] This does not seem to be a satisfactory reason of justice for preferring holidays to vacations, the communal to the individual. In the end this argument seems to simply reflect the authors' preference for a strong notion of community over the liberal ideal of individual rights. It also seems to violate one of Walzer's guiding tenets, that there are no external or universal principles of justice for every account is a local one.[93]

Law and Hermeneutics

The Gadamer-Habermas Debate Within recent hermeneutic theory there has arisen a debate between two groups of philosophers, represented by Hans-Georg Gadamer and Jurgen Habermas. Gadamer is a hermeneutic philosopher seeking to ascertain the ontological preconditions of understanding, whereas Habermas proposes a critical hermeneutics which takes the form of a critique of systematically distorted communication.[94] By emphasising the tradition within which any interpreter must interpret, Gadamer's work has signalled a move away from the idea that interpretation can be objective, and towards a recognition of the prejudices and preconceptions we inevitably bring to such a task. For Gadamer, the best we can do is to seek a fusion of horizons between our present world and that which we are seeking to interpret. This injection of scepticism into the interpretive debate has led some theorists such as Jacques Derrida to take hermeneutical philosophy to its logical limits by claiming that texts are ultimately illegible.[95] Habermas, on the other hand, criticises Gadamer from a Marxist perspective for being too ready to accept authority and tradition, whilst not being sufficiently critical of society.[96] In addition, Habermas casts doubt on the hermeneutic claim to universality by seeking to ground a theory of communicative competence in an interpretation of psychoanalysis. This then is the basic theoretical framework within which Dworkin's theory of legal interpretation is located. Dworkin aligns himself with Gadamer "whose account of interpretation as recognising, while struggling against the constraints of history strikes the right note",[97] but he also refers to Habermas as making the "crucial observation ... that interpretation supposes that the author could learn from the interpreter".[98] Dworkin's position is therefore complicated, although he is dismissive of Derrida's thesis which amounts to internal scepticism.

At the centre of Gadamer's hermeneutic philosophy[99] lies the idea of interpretation as a holistic process operating within a hermeneutic circle, whereby we constantly alternate between specific parts of a 'text' and our conception of it as a whole. Interpretation is thus viewed on this model as a complicated process of encounter and response. Gadamer's work is highly complex, and hence any discussion of it will involve some form of simplification and isolation. However, as Gadamer himself argues, this is inevitable in any interpretation. We must therefore highlight those aspects of his work with particular relevance to Dworkin, and to the law.

Gadamer's starting point in *Truth and Method*, as expressed in his Foreword to the second edition, is "to discover what is common to all modes of understanding and to show that understanding is never subjective behaviour towards a given 'object', but towards its effective history".[100] Gadamer's wish is to focus attention on the practical concerns of legal or theological interpretations, where the outcome "is not just a better understanding of a text but its actual incorporation into our lives".[101] Whereas traditional hermeneutic theory postulates a subject approaching the object of interpretation without preconceptions, Gadamer instead argues that without these preconceptions or prejudices we are unable to understand. In order to establish this ontological aspect of understanding, Gadamer emphasises the role that tradition plays within the hermeneutic circle. For Gadamer, the idea of absolute Reason misses the fact that Reason can only actualise itself in historical conditions, and that therefore even the most neutral applications of scientific methods will be affected by our embeddedness within a tradition. In short, the interpreter will always come to the text with certain expectations of it derived from his past experience. Gadamer describes this situation as the 'horizon' of interpretation, which reflects the idea of a "range of vision that includes everything that can be seen from a particular vantage point".[102] Thus, by stressing the idea that this 'horizon' is shaped by our particular prejudices or preunderstandings, Gadamer clearly moves away from the objective school of hermeneutics.

However, this does not mean that he sees interpretation as being a purely subjective process, for Gadamer moves away from the objective-subjective dichotomy through his discussion of the role of tradition. It is here that Gadamer's radical reappraisal of the situation of the interpreter is apparent.[103] Tradition is crucial because it defines the horizon within which the interpreter operates. In this way, understanding becomes the placing of oneself within a tradition in which past and present are constantly fused. The tradition within which the interpreter operates thus not only supplies the necessary prejudices for interpretation, but also affects the way we view the 'text'. This dual historicity of text and interpreter[104] is crucial because it not only provides the possibility of interpretation and understanding, but also gives us the framework within which it occurs. The role of tradition within interpretation is called the work of 'effective-history' (*Wirkungsgeschichte*) by Gadamer, and consists of a variety of elements. Initially the interpreter's effective-history will predispose him to prejudge the possible meaning of the text.[105] As we proceed to appraise the text, this preliminary account will be altered, and new interpretations considered. Thus, as we progress through the text, our prejudices are challenged, and will either have to prove adequate to the subject or otherwise be modified. This means that 'legitimate' prejudices will be filtered out, and thus "those prejudices that are of a particular and limited nature die away".[106] It is clear then that this is a productive endeavour, with our interpretive horizon constantly being altered. For understanding to occur we must widen our interpretive horizons so as to encompass that of the text. Once this occurs there will be a 'fusion of horizons' as the understanding and meaning of the object is reached. For Gadamer then our prejudices represent the interpretive horizons of a particular present, but this is not a fixed set of opinions for the horizon of the present is being continually formed in that we have constantly to test all our prejudices and understanding is always the fusion of these horizons.

For truly scientific work to develop it is necessary that we are conscious of the role of effective-history. This requires a recognition of the hermeneutic situation which will, of course, itself be limited by historicality. Once we reach effective-historical consciousness, it becomes easier to achieve the controlled fusion of horizons, for "a hermeneutically trained mind must be, from the start, sensitive to the text's quality of newness".[107] We can never eliminate our prejudices, once we are aware of them "the text may present itself in all its newness and thus be able assert its own truth against one's own fore-meanings".[108] This then leads to the recognition that the practice of interpretation is analogous to a dialogue between the interpreter and the object of which the text speaks.[109] In interpreting a text we are seeking to discover the question to which the text holds the answer, and hence to understand the text is to understand the question. However, at the same time the text only becomes an object of interpretation by presenting the interpreter with a question.[110] Therefore in order to understand the question posed by the text, we must first ourselves have posed questions to that text and hence opened up the possibilities of meaning. From this, Gadamer proceeds to develop a theory of the universality of language. Briefly, this asserts that the purpose of hermeneutic philosophy is to understand existence itself in terms of the language that addresses us from inside it.[111] It is this linguisticality that mediates between past and present in our interpretations, and thus "the linguisticality of understanding is the concretion of effective-historical conscience".[112] This then asserts the universality of hermeneutics, for on this basis all understanding is linguistic.[113]

What are the consequences of this analysis for social theory? Gadamer's investigation into hermeneutics aims to yield a better conception of the process of understanding, and to displace the formerly influential theory in hermeneutics of objectivity, exemplified by Emilio Betti. Betti represents the view that hermeneutics is tied to interpretation based on the author's intention, and is thus in fundamental disagreement with Gadamer who is not restricted to this methodical approach. Similarly, Betti's concern to salvage a 'relative objectivity' for his interpretations through the application of a set of canons is rejected by Gadamer. Here it is vital to keep in mind Gadamer's principle of the universality of hermeneutics, on the basis that "understanding is *not* a special feature of the human sciences, but the fundamental way in which human beings exist in the world".[114] Gadamer links science with method, and points out that its introduction into the hermaneutical process "can only lead to the objectification of the 'object' and the subject's mastery over it".[115] The result of this concern with method, and hence 'objectivity', is to give rise to the distinction between interpretation and application, or theory and practice.[116] Gadamer seeks to collapse this distinction, by arguing that "the text is created anew in an interpretation which is guided by an horizon of interpretation that itself changes in the course of its activity".[117] The past is thus constantly being reinterpreted, or understood differently. This collapses the interpretation, understanding and application of the text into a 'unitary phenomenon'.[118] Thus Gadamer shows the bridge between the world of science and that of our lives, by making explicit the presuppositions present in science, its abstractions and most importantly its use of method as a guiding conception. Gadamer argues that it is important that the social sciences be conscious of the hermeneutic process, and the conditions which apply. In order for genuine understanding to occur we must achieve effective-historical consciousness, and recognise the dialogical dimension to the hermeneutical process. Whereas Betti argues that in terms of interpretation in jurisdiction we proceed from a dogmatic point of view, Gadamer argues that it is impossible to distinguish clearly between dogmatism and historical interpretation. We approach a legal text from the standpoint of the present legal situation and consider its relevance from there by mediating between past and present. Gadamer's argument is that by recognising the role our prejudices play within this we will achieve greater understanding of our interpretive practices.

We noted earlier that Dworkin appeals to Gadamer "whose account of interpretation as recognising, while struggling against, the constraints of history strikes the right note".[119] We are now in a position to consider the similarities between Dworkin and Gadamer and assess the strength of Dworkin's appeal. We have seen that, as with Gadamer, Dworkin's account of interpretation grows out of a rejection of an intentionalist account, and indeed it is in this context that Dworkin cites Gadamer with approval. There are obvious similarities between Dworkin and Gadamer in that both are seeking an account of interpretation which, whilst recognising the constraints placed on the interpreter, at the same time gives the interpreter a creative role. Dworkin seeks this in his account of the interaction of the interpretive dimensions of fit and substance, whereas Gadamer uses the idea of the interpreter's prejudices and his embeddedness within a tradition in order to achieve this. Whilst both theorists put forward a holistic account of interpretation, it is hard to resist the conclusion that Gadamer's account is more persuasive. We have already noticed the difficulties present in Dworkin's distinction between fit and substance,[120] whilst Gadamer clearly establishes his holism within the idea of the hermeneutic circle, and his notion of effective-history. In this way Gadamer clearly shows the idea of a return to the original understanding is inevitably erroneous. Dworkin strives for a similar effect with his interpretive judgements of substance, but Gadamer's notion of prejudice or pre-understanding seems to capture this idea more clearly, and links in with the notion of tradition to form a holistic framework of interpretation. Dworkin is never able to achieve this clarity, and hence his holism appears less successful. By appealing to Gadamer, Dworkin wishes to invoke this clarity. However, he does not entirely succeed in capturing it. Gadamer's point that we should aim for an effective-historical consciousness also seems to have been taken up by Dworkin, but he seems to endorse Habermas's criticisms of Gadamer as to his "too passive view that the direction of communication is one way".[121] Dworkin endorses Habermas's observation that "interpretation presupposes that the author could learn from the interpreter".[122] In order to consider this we now turn to Habermas's critique of Gadamer.

Paul Ricoeur distinguishes hermeneutic philosophy, which attempts the mediation of the past in order to determine its applicability to the present, from critical hermeneutics, which is directed at the future, and at changing the present rather than simply interpreting it.[123] Whilst Gadamer stands in the former group, Habermas puts forward a theory of critical hermeneutics. His starting point is to note Gadamer's reluctance to engage in any methodological arguments, which is tied into the ontological nature of Gadamer's discussion of tradition. For Habermas, Gadamer is too willing to accept tradition and authority, and by regarding language as the 'transcendental absolute'[124] he lacks objectivity. Habermas argues that a more adequate framework of interpretation would account for the systems of labour and domination which, in conjunction with language, constitute an objective context from which to interpret social actions. This reflects Habermas's view that a 'critically enlightened hermeneutic' will differentiate between insight and decision, and will incorporate "the meta-hermeneutic awareness of the conditions for the possibility of systematically distorted communication".[125] In this way, it will connect the "process of understanding to the principle of rational discourse", according to which truth could only be guaranteed by a consensus achieved under idealised conditions of unlimited communication free from domination.[126] Thus, Habermas's point is that hermeneutics has trouble in explaining what he terms 'systematically distorted communication', and this can only be accounted for once we recognise the theory of societal evolution. Habermas uses the example of psychoanalysis to reveal how we "repress socially unacceptable motives and channel them into acceptable forms of expression".[127] Psychoanalysis helps us to determine the events behind this 'distorted communication', and thus to fill the gaps in our self-understanding. In the same way, a general interpretation of a social system may be able to do so as well. Therefore, the point Habermas is making is that "hermeneutic consciousness remains incomplete as long as it does not include a reflection upon the limits of hermeneutic understanding".[128] The problem for hermeneutic theory is not simply the possibility of systematically distorted communication, but also that linguistic communication is itself part of more general social processes. Gadamer, in proposing a hermeneutic universality, thus appears to commit the epistemic fallacy.[129] However, despite this, Gadamer's influence remains powerful, as Habermas himself accepts in identifying four aspects in which a philosophical hermeneutic is relevant to the sciences and their interpretation.[130] Before we examine the significance of this for the law, and specifically Dworkin's own theory, we shall discuss a third view of interpretation, in order to complete our basic overview of the current debates in hermaneutical theory.

Jacques Derrida, with Gadamer and Dworkin, argues against the view that the author's intention can operate as a constraint on the way in which texts can be read. However, Derrida's application of this idea is much more extreme than that of Gadamer and Dworkin. Derrida argues from the inherent subjectivity of interpretation to the view that as a consequence we can never hope to interpret with any kind of certainty. This leads him to conclude that the hermeneutic enterprise is erroneous, for what we actually require is 'dissemination' whereby we would point to the ultimate illegibility of texts. However, despite the fact that Derrida is often critical of the practice of hermeneutics, his own theory is perhaps best understood as a variant of hermeneutic philosophy, as he seems to take hermeneutics to its logical conclusions, and possibly even beyond them.[131] Derrida is in agreement with the hermeneutic critique of epistemology.

However, he moves away from traditional hermeneutic philosophy by arguing that it does not go far enough. Thus, whilst Derrida is in agreement with the hermeneutic argument that interpretations are reliant on the self-understandings of the interpreter as well as the context in which the interpretation is made, he goes beyond hermeneutics by arguing that the process of interpretive change, and thus also of self-interpretation, is not one that points inevitably towards rationality but instead is one of chance. No interpretation can claim to be definitive and the practice of deconstruction leads to a multitude of interpretations. Whilst theorists such as Dworkin seek to show an ultimate coherence within a text, Derrida's project is instead aimed at showing the complexity and duplicity of text. For example, Derrida's discussion of the Declaration of Independence centres on the idea that the signature on the Declaration authorises its signing, and thus that a paradox arises here.[132] This approach, which occurs in Derrida's more recent work, makes it clear that his thesis is much more radical than that of hermeneutics. By giving a critical reading to texts, Derrida brings out their unperceived and hidden contradictions, and thus seeks to undermine their coherence and sense. Whilst hermeneutics seeks to reconstruct the text, Derrida instead pursues dissemination, which aims to reveal the futility of the hermeneutic exercise by illustrating the essential 'undecidability' of textual meaning. Derrida locates this undecidability at the syntactical, as opposed to the semantic, level in claiming that words have "a double-contradictory, undecidable value that always derives from their syntax".[133] Dissemination is the practice of exploring these contradictions, without the need to worry about the semantic dimension of reference and truth-value.[134] By viewing the work of writers as standing within speech-marks,[135] Derrida reveals text with no decidable meaning, leading to the need for dissemination. Indeed, Derrida applies this analysis to his own work, and admits that it also lacks any decidable meaning. This argument appears to be a variant on one associated with fictional claims "as being neither true nor false because they do not even attempt to refer to reality".[136] By viewing the text as standing in quotation marks, Derrida is able to make this connection. This debate leads us into an unavoidable one as to the politics of interpretation. We have already noted Habermas's critique of Gadamer for being too respectful of tradition and authority. Derrida is also critical of the hermeneutic view of the authority of the text. However, whereas Habermas argues that authority is valid if conceived in an ideal speech situation, Derrida would argue that even in such a situation the truth-claims of philosophy are undecidable.[137] Thus, whilst agreeing with Habermas in his critique on Gadamer, Derrida stands apart from him in the form that his attack takes. Indeed, Habermas labels Derrida a conservative as he seems to offer little in the way of practical defence against authority.

A Constructive and Coherent Theory

We now turn to consider Dworkin's theory in relation to the Gadamer-Habermas debate within whose boundaries it lies. Derrida's deconstructive theory offers a considerable threat to Dworkin's constructive, coherent account of the law, and so we must also consider the effects of his critique on hermeneutic theory. Finally, we must look ahead, to see if we can provide a theory of interpretation that is appropriate to the practice of law.

We have already noted the similarities between Gadamer's and Dworkin's theories and concluded that whilst Gadamer's holistic theory seems more successful than Dworkin's, they both seem to be aiming and striking a similar balance between the past and present. It is therefore somewhat surprising that Dworkin should endorse Habermas's critique of Gadamer on the basis that Gadamer offers a "too-passive view that the direction of.coccunication is one way".[138] For Dworkin, the interpretation on Gadamer's model interprets on the assumption that "he is subordinate to its author", whereas Habermas makes the "crucial observation" that interpretation supposes that the author could learn from the interpreter.[139] This view of Gadamer does not seem to cohere with Dworkin's other references to his work, nor does it seem to accurately reflect the debate between Gadarner and Habermas. Dworkin describes Gadamer's hermeneutics as "recognising, while struggling against, the constraints of history" as we have seen, and, he states that this strikes the right note.[140] This does not seem consistent with his endorsement in the Notes in *Law's Empire* of Habermas's critique, which is after all aimed at undermining Gadamer's discussion of the constraints of history. Additionally, the claim that Gadamer views the process as one-way, with the interpreter subordinate to the author of the text, seems to completely misinterpret Gadamer, whose theory was designed as a denial of the intentionalist view of interpretation, and instead sought to show the essential role in interpretation of the interpreter's own prejudices and tradition. To imply that Gadamer misses the point that the author could learn from the interpreter is erroneous, as this is exactly the point that Gadamer himself is making.

Habermas's critique, as we have seen, focuses on Gadainer's willingness to accept tradition and authority, and his resultant failure to explain situations of systematically distorted communication. This critique does indeed call into question Gadamer's claim to universality. However, as Habermas himself accepts, Gadamer's hermeneutics still retain their relevance for the social sciences. What seems particularly important to notice here is that the disagreement as to the role of tradition largely turns on the politics of the interpreter. Habermas, as a Marxist commentator, is thus particularly keen to stress the domination that can lead to distorted communication. Gadamer, by contrast, argues that this is simply utopian, and as such does not affect the realities of interpretation. Within the law it would seem that Gadamer's model is the more appropriate, as there the emphasis on keeping in line with tradition is particularly acute.[141] Hence it is suggested that, whilst Habermas's critique creates problems in adopting Gadamer's hermeneutics universally, in terms of the law Gadamer appears to offer an appropriate theoretical model. As William Outhwaite notes, social theory is "both value-impregnated and value-generating", and as a consequence "Gadamer's notion of dialogue has a peculiar poignancy here".[142] Gadamer's model of interpretation seems particularly appropriate to the law because of the general perception that 'method' is at work.[143] In terms of legal interpretation, most practitioners are far from achieving effective-historical consciousness, and thus Gadamer's theory is particularly important in identifying the role that our effective-history plays in interpretation, so that we can move towards the conditions of genuine interpretation.[144] It is surprising then in the light of this that Dworkin appears to be critical of Gadamer for being too one-sided in his hermeneutic account, for Gadamer's theory seems to fit the law particularly well. Of course, by accepting Gadamer's hermeneutic philosophy on this point, the question is begged as to how this can be defended against the deconstructive theory posed by Derrida.

Perhaps the main difficulty with Derrida's theory of deconstruction, is that it proposes no reconstruction, and thus seems to leave us with no way forward once we recognise its insights. For this reason, as we have seen, Habermas has charged Derrida with conservatism in that his approach is so radical that it is unlikely to have any effect on practice, for Derrida seems to lack any norms by which to sustain a move towards a society based on criticism. Derrida, like Fish,[145] locates dispute at the level of rhetoric, which still leaves us with a reasoned decision to make. This simply seems to relocate the debate. However, Derrida's account does lead us towards a more helpful solution. The first point to note here is that Derrida's ideas on deconstruction and dissemination must presuppose that it is possible to construct a prior version of the text's sense, for otherwise there would be nothing to take apart. This seems to lead us towards the conclusion that, even should dissemination subsequently disrupt the shape of this prior understanding of the text, it does not necessarily lead to the conclusion that it cannot be reconstructed. For that there are "difficult interpretive decisions in practice does not entail undecidability or the impossibility of understanding in principle".[146] Indeed, the possibility of the unity of a text in a sense depends on the possibility of deconstruction and dissemination, for we can only ever see these inconsistencies in the text against the wider backdrop of the text's unity.[147] Thus, in order to protect our interpretations from collapsing, we may well have to exploit these differences rather than seek to avoid them. In this way, Derrida's views move towards a reconciliation with those of Gadamer. Perhaps Derrida's main insight for us here is that it is not always possible to establish commensurability in seeking to reconcile differences.[148] This points us towards the application of the incommensurability thesis in interpretive disputes.

We now examine how these issues affect Dworkin's constructive, coherent account of legal interpretation. We first consider whether Dworkin can maintain his constructive account of interpretation, whereby we seek to make the best of that being interpreted. David Hoy claims that it is possible to interpret without necessarily conforming to Dworkin's constructive account.[149] As an example, Hoy uses the example of understanding and interpreting a person, and argues that when we try to understand that person we "do not generally try to make that person into the best sort of person anyone could be".[150] After all, not everyone is a moral saint, and there is no reason to interpret anyone as being one. A similar point has been made by Steven Knapp who argues that if Dworkin were correct, then on being approached on the street by a mugger we would interpret the ensuing conversation into the best instance possible of street communication, only removing any inexplicable error in the conversational.[151] These views are clearly mistaken as to the details of constructive interpretation on Dworkin's model. Dworkin's argument is that constructive interpretation "strives to make an object the best it can be as an instance of some assumed enterprise",[152] and not the best that anything can be. Thus, on Hoy's example, we do not have to interpret everyone as being a moral saint. We simply interpret a person as the best person that that person could be, not the best sort of person anyone could be.[153] Interestingly, Hoy seems to have realised this error, as it is he, rather than Dworkin, who replies to Knapp's comments.[154] Hoy concludes that "Dworkin's word 'best' can mean 'best given the circumstances' or 'best for practical purposes'".[155] Hoy notes that Dworkin's point is "perhaps a thin one".[156] Interpreters are simply doing what comes naturally by putting forward their 'best' interpretation on this model, as if they did not believe this to be the case they would not put forward that interpretation.

Hoy has also argued against Dworkin's description of the application of theory within interpretive practice. He argues that Dworkin's theory of interpretation requires that to understand a literary work "I must be interpreting it so that it conforms with my conception of what art is".[157] Hoy asserts that this goes against his theory of what literary critics do, on the basis that "understanding is not just the relation of subsuming a particular under a more general concept".[158] Rather, our conception of aesthetic value can be adjusted through our encounters with new works. Hoy's argument here seems to be based on a rejection of Dworkin's distinction between the interpretive constraints of fit and substance. We have already noted difficulties with Dworkin's use of these constraints, and Hoy makes a similar point. However, for Hoy the difficulty seems to be that he regards the constraint of substance as being superfluous, as he does not agree with Dworkin that we are generally confronted with more than one interpretation, each of which fits equally well.[159] Hoy thus concludes "that 'best fit' is a necessary goal of interpretation, but not 'best liked', which seems neither sufficient or necessary".[160] Again, this seems to rest on a misreading of Dworkin's theory, such that Hoy and Dworkin are in fact largely in agreement here. Dworkin does not appear to be committed to the view that an interpreter must stick rigidly to his aesthetic theory and simply subsume new interpretations within this. If this were the case, then Dworkin would indeed be committed to the view that best fit is the sole constraint on interpretation, but clearly he is not. Dworkin must allow for changes in our aesthetic theories, and this would appear to occur in the post-interpretive stage of interpretation.[161] Indeed, given that one of Dworkin's reasons for writing *Law's Empire* seems to be to encourage judges to interpret law as integrity, much of this would be lost if they were unable to alter their substantive theories. The reason for Hoy's error seems to derive from his discussion of the fit-substance distinction. Much of this itself comes from Dworkin's somewhat confused discussion of this, where he seems at times to say that the two are not really distinct, and then appears to separate them. Much of this confusion may be eradicated if we were to view the distinction as intended to reflect Gadamer's discussion of tradition and prejudice. In this way we can see that Hoy's suggestion that we simply require the best fit requirement is shown to be mistaken as, whilst we do indeed interpret within tradition, we can only interpret that tradition in the light of our prejudices or preconceptions (the 'best light' requirement). By looking at the distinction this way, the inter-related nature of interpretive constraints is made much clearer, and this seems to achieve that which Dworkin is aiming for. Thus it seems that Dworkin can at least maintain his constructive attitude towards legal interpretation.

Dworkin's argument that our interpretations can form a coherent whole based on the virtue of integrity is challenged by deconstructionist theory. Some legal theorists will point to the existence of irreconcilable contradictions within the law,[162] whilst others will argue that judges should interpret the law so as to subvert the existing institutions[163] and thus in the short term bring about incoherence within the law. Hoy argues that such critical judges are still interpreting, as the "best interpretation is not necessarily one that sees the particular text or object in the best or most favourable light".[164] However, this again seems to miss the point. Dworkin's argument is that to deliberately make something the worst it can be is either to be incoherent or deceptive.[165] This does not mean that the best reading is necessarily going to be particularly attractive, simply that it is more attractive to the interpreter than any alternative. Thus one can reconcile a critical approach to the law with Dworkin's constructive account of interpretation. Interestingly, Hoy himself makes this point in replying to an argument put forward by Steven Knapp against Dworkin.[166] Thus, once again, Hoy seems to have recognised the weakness of his earlier argument, and moved towards the position held by Dworkin. Nevertheless, this still leaves Dworkin with some difficulties in establishing the possibility of coherence.

In order to consider this we must briefly examine the requirements placed on judges by Dworkin's account of integrity. Dworkin readily admits that Hercules knows that the law is far from perfectly consistent in principle overall and that legislative supremacy gives force to some statutes that are inconsistent in principle with others, but despite this he assumes that these contradictions are not so pervasive and intractable that his task is impossible.[167] The recognition of these inconsistencies leads Dworkin to a distinction between inclusive and pure integrity,[168] where inclusive integrity represents the adjudicative principle that governs our current law. The coherence of our current law as represented by inclusive integrity will thus be required to take account of all the component virtues, and will therefore reflect, so far as possible, coherent principles of political fairness, substantive justice, and procedural process.[169] Pure integrity by contrast represents an abstraction from these various constraints, and shows the law as it would be, were judges free to pursue coherence in the principles of justice that flow through and unite different departments of law.[170] Where we achieve coherence, current law gropes optimistically towards this ideal of purity. The difficulty with this is that, as Hoy points out, only Hercules can know that this single scheme and therefore this ideal will obtain.[171] For the rest of us it remains only a metaphysical postulate that cannot be proven. It is for this reason that Critical scholars have argued that we need not share this view, based as it is on Dworkin's optimistic outlook. Dworkin's response to this has been to shift the burden across to the Critical Legal Studies movement which he feels must show that the flawed and contradictory account is the only one available if it is to succeed.[172] Given that Dworkin admits that contradiction is common within our legal system, this seems to be an unsatisfactory response.[173] Here the debate seems to be situated at the level of the politics of interpretation, with Dworkin putting forward an optimistic appraisal, and Critical scholars a more pessimistic one.

Conclusion

We noted earlier that many of the difficulties with Dworkin's theory of interpretation were avoided once we recognised the claims of the incommensurability thesis. This enabled him to maintain the main tenets of his theory, although certain specifics were altered. We have argued in this chapter that Gadamer's hermeneutic philosophy is particularly appropriate to an analysis of the law, given its emphasis on the role of tradition and the influence of the interpreter's prejudices. In describing the interaction of these factors, Gadamer gives us an holistic framework that goes beyond Dworkin's somewhat confused version.[174] However, it has been pointed out that this is nevertheless consistent with Dworkin's interpretive approach, and indeed Dworkin himself cites Gadamer as an influence. In contrast to Gadamer's view on the role of tradition, Habermas has argued for a 'universal pragmatics'[175] whereby the force of tradition would be subject to criticism, based on the idea that much communication occurs under situations of domination and is as a result systematically distorted. Oddly, Dworkin appears to endorse Habermas's critique,[176] but this is an error contrary to Dworkin's theory. In the same way, Dworkin and Gadamer both argue against the conventional intentionalism of theorists such as Betti, and in favour of giving the interpreter a wider role.

In examining the deconstructive philosophy of Jacques Derrida, we noted how this can be reconciled with the hermeneutic philosophy of Gadamer. Gadamer argues that the ideal interpreter must presuppose the unity and consistency of the text. This obviously appears to be threatened by Derrida with his stress on the contradictory nature of texts. However, we noted that this is not necessarily the case as contradiction can only ever be identified against a backdrop of unity, and that as a result, a precondition of unity is necessary for the possibility of deconstruction. Put briefly, this means that Derrida must presume a construction in order for him to have something to deconstruct. It is in their attitudes to this analysis that it appears that Dworkin and Gadamer differ. Despite the recognition of these contradictions, Dworkin argues that the interpreter should nevertheless seek to apply an inclusive integrity to the text. Dworkin thus chooses to adopt a holistic coherent approach to the law.[177] Nevertheless, in doing so he refuses to consider the possible claims of a Critical approach whereby we would make the lack of inclusive integrity apparent in order to more quickly bring about the justice of pure integrity. Dworkin seems to be deliberately blinding his interpreters from reality and the politics of interpretation that arise here.[178]

However, it is possible to apply an analysis that draws on themes in Gadamer's work, and which seems to offer a more satisfactory account of interpretation. Gadamer proposes that, in order to understand hermeneutically, interpreters must be 'open' to the text, and thus willing to challenge their prejudices as highlighted by the text. If we apply this analysis here, although we will start with the presupposition of the unity of the text, by opening ourselves to the newness of the text we may come to see that it does indeed contain certain contradictions. In recognising this incommensurability, an interpreter on this model would not seek to construct some form of inclusive integrity ignoring these contradictions. Instead, by being open to the text, and prepared to challenge his prejudices, he would acknowledge them and include them as part of his interpretation of the text. By bringing these contradictions into the open we are better able to progress towards an understanding of the text as a whole. Concealment is ultimately self-defeating as it will eventually prevent such progress. By bringing a contradiction into the open it is also more likely in the case of the law that means might be found to put this right, and thus move us closer towards the ideal of pure integrity. For example, to point out that two statutes are contradictory, rather than to seek to hide this through some form of inclusive integrity, will possibly lead to the repeal of one of the statutes and hence the progression of the law. Thus in applying Gadamer's hermeneutics in this way we can recognise the force of deconstruction without having to adopt a thorough-going Critical perspective. In this way we come to the recognition that a good reading "aims at balancing the complexity of the text against its sense".[179]

Having reached this conclusion, we must now see how this fits into a general hermeneutic theory. One of the significant features of Dworkin's theory of interpretation is that it seeks to incorporate both contestability and correctness within the same framework. We have argued that, through the application of the incommensurability thesis, it is indeed possible to accept that there is genuine disagreement as to which interpretation is the 'correct' one, and at the same time put forward one's own interpretation as the best.[180] This is also consistent with Gadamer's philosophical hermeneutics. However, Hoy feels that Dworkin and Gadamer part ways as to the question of whether we need the "strong requirement that there be ultimately one right interpretation".[181] As we have seen before, this applies a common misreading of Dworkin's position as to the possibility of right answers. Dworkin has more recently further clarified his position, pointing out that his original point was "a very weak and commonsensical legal claim".[182] In fact, the argument is one against skepticism and in favour of the incommensurability thesis, in that it states that we can argue that our interpretations of hard cases are the best on the facts.[183] Additionally, it accords with Gadamer's notion that the ideal interpreter must presuppose the unity of the text by arguing that from an internal perspective we will often act as if there were one right answer. However, the claim is weak and certainly does not go so far as to state that there is ultimately only one right interpretation.[184] Thus, Gadamer and Dworkin appear to be in agreement. Following on from this, the idea of the hermeneutic circle comes into play. Through this our pre-understanding of the text, and our prejudices, are placed before the text and a circular, dialogical, process begins until understanding is reached through the fusion of the horizons of the interpreter and the text. In this way, understanding involves "the interplay of the movement of tradition and the movement of the interpreter".[185] This process will be on-going whenever we interpret a text. Because of this, it is often compared with John Rawls's notion of 'reflective equilibrium',[186] which also involves a dialogue between our pre-understanding of the issue, and the conceptual articulation of this. This again is attractive, as Dworkin supports the idea of reflective equilibrium in relation to his conception of justice, and thus this links in well with his theory of interpretation.[187] However, in the same way that Rawls is unclear as to whether reflective equilibrium can ever be achieved,[188] it must be extremely doubtful that law could ever work itself pure through the means of the hermeneutic circle. As with reflective equilibrium, purity can only ever be anticipated, for even if one account appears to have attained it the next account is likely to lose it, and seek to re-establish it through different means. The only way we are ever likely to come to a halt is where we recognise the ultimate undecidability of the text, and hence its unintelligibility.[189] As Hoy says, this is an impractical endpoint to interpretation, and can only be reached by ideal interpreters such as Hercules.[190] Instead, we should stress the critical elements of hermeneutic philosophy, such as the autonomy of the text and the interpreter's role in opening up to his message.[191] In this way we will see the historicity that governs our interpretive practices and better accept the existence of critical pluralism within those practices. By doing so we will avoid relativism and naturally move towards a toleration of others' interpretations. Thus our theory of community will link in with our theory of interpretation, with both expressing the virtue of toleration.[192]

This appears to be a view of law as hermeneutics that combines the insights of Gadamer's hermeneutic philosophy with those of Dworkin's interpretive legal theory. Whilst Dworkin does not recognise aspects of this thesis, and is in disagreement with others, notably in his requirement of inclusive integrity, nevertheless it seems to fit in with his broader theoretical intentions. This is indicated by the application of Gadamer's theory which Dworkin himself appeals to. We suggest that this offers a more convincing account of law as hermeneutics, and one that coheres with much of Dworkin's theory.

Notes

1 See for example Kymlicka 1989 p.58: "Given the weakness of the communitarian critique, the recent changes in Rawls's views are somewhat surprising". The same point is made by Kukathas and Pettit 1990 at p.133: "in some ways it is surprising that Rawls should feel the need to deal with such charges".
2 See Rawls 1985.
3 See Rawls 1987.
4 Kymlicka 1989 p.59.
5 Larmore 1984.
6 See Raz 1986.
7 Dworkin 1986(a) p.191.
8 Id. p.192.
9 See Kukathas and Pettit 1990 at p.94 with reference to Will Kymlicka.
10 See the reference here id. p.96.
11 See Kymlicka 1989 pp.34-35 for a critique of this. Kymlicka argues that Rawls and the perfectionists do not disagree over the priority of the right and the good, but instead about how best to define and promote people's good. Rawls is therefore mistaken to claim that perfectionist theories are teleological.

12 Id. p.25.
13 Dworkin 1986 (a) pp.195-196.
14 Id. p.207.
15 See Kymlicka 1989 pp.38-39. Kymlicka argues that, whereas Rawls views this conflict again as being one over the relative priority of the right and the good, Dworkin is correct instead to identify it as being one of responsibility.
16 See Dworkin 1986 (a) p.211.
17 This categorisation is used to helpful effect by Simon Caney in his article, Caney 1992.
18 Dworkin 1989.
19 Sande 1982.
20 Derek Parfit has similarly attacked Rawls here, but with the argument that the person is not necessarily a coherent entity over time and that there is thus separation and distance within the self as well as outside it - see Parfit 1984.
21 Nozick 1974 p.228.
22 Sandel 1982 pp.163 and 179.
23 Maclntyre 1981 p.205. A similar claim is made by a number of other scholars - see Caney 1992 at p.274 n.3 for a list of these.
24 See Gutmann 1985 at p.309. H N Hirsch argues that Maclntyre's complaint is "more specific" than Sandel's in that his concern is with the failure of liberal society to educate modern man to cultivate the classical virtues - see Hirsch 1986 at p.427.
25 Sandel 1982 p.179.
26 Id. p.182.
27 Id. p.150.
28 Macedo 1991 p.243.
29 Caney 1992 p.275.
30 See here Cochran 1989. Cochran argues that the theories of the self are themselves too thin.
31 Macedo 1991 p.244.
32 Sandel 1982 p.59.
33 Maclntyre 1981 p.220.
34 Mosher 1991 p.295.
35 See Kymlicka 1989 p.53.
36 Macedo 1991 p.245.
37 Gutmann 1985 p.319.
38 McDonald 1992.
39 Id. p.12 1.
40 Id. p.120.
41 Waldron 1989 p.582.
42 Cochran argues that "no theorist of community ... believes that persons seek their goods 'totally' within unchanging social roles" - see Cochran 1989 p.432.
43 Sandel 1982 p.152.
44 Id. p.153.

45 Id.
46 MacIntyre 1981 p.205.
47 Id. p.204.
48 Kymlicka 1989 p.57.
49 Id. p.55.
50 Id. p.54.
51 Mosher 1991 p.297.
52 Taylor 1985 p.190.
53 See Kymlicka 1989 p.75; Caney 1992 pp.279-280 where Caney sets out why liberalism is compatible with the social thesis.
54 Kymlicka 1989 p.75.
55 Cragg 1986 at p.47.
56 Dworkin 1986(a) p.230. See Kymlicka 1989 pp.79-81 for a similar discussion of Rawls and Raz.
57 Dworkin 1986(a) p.228.
58 Kymlicka 1989 p.82.
59 For example, Raz has argued that an appeal to perfectionist ideals is unavoidable for liberal society to work - see Kymlicka 1989 pp.80-81.
60 Macedo 1991 p.251.
61 Waldron 1989 p.582.
62 Gutmann 1985 p.319.
63 Hirsch 1986 p.439.
64 See here Cochran 1989 pp.432-435.
65 Walzer 1983 p.313.
66 Id. p.314.
67 Id. p.313.
68 See Galston 1989 p.122.
69 Barry 1984 at p.807.
70 Dworkin 1986(a) p.216.
71 Galston 1989 pp.123-124.
72 Walzer 1983 p.314.
73 Caney 1992 p.288.
74 Dworkin 1986(a) p.217.
75 Id. p.219.
76 Id.
77 Kymlicka 1989 p.232 paraphrasing Dworkin's argument in *Taking Rights Seriously* - see Dworkin 1977 pp.128-129.
78 Waldron 1989 p.579.
79 Id.
80 Id. See further pp.574-578.
81 Downing and Thigpen 1986 p.456.
82 Id. p.457.
83 Id.
84 Id. p.470.

85 Walzer 1983 p.320 cited by Downing and Thigpen at p.457.
86 Downing and Thigpen 1986 p.457.
87 Walzer 1983 p.320.
88 Id. p.321.
89 Id. p.314.
90 Id. p.320.
91 Id. p.250 fn.
92 Downing and Thigpen 1986 p.469. This does not seem to suggest the defence of pluralism that is central to Walzer's work.
93 Walzer 1983 p.314.
94 These definitions reflect those in the glossary in Bleicher 1980.
95 David Hoy suggests that Derrida's thought is best read as a variant of hermeneutics - see Hoy 1985 pp.43-64.
96 Habermas has an unusual relation to Marx. He is critical of the more mechanistic aspects of Marxism, preferring instead a humanistic approach. See further Skinner 1985 p.17 and Giddens 1985 pp.121-139.
97 Dworkin 1986 p.62.
98 Id. p.420 n.2.
99 See Gadamer 1975 and Gadamer 1980 at pp.128-140. See too Bleicher 1980 Chapters Five and Six, Henley 1990, Hoy 1987, Outhwaite 1985 and Sherman 1988.
100 Gadamer 1989 p.xix.
101 Outhwaite 1985 p.25.
102 Gadamer 1989 p.261.
103 See Bleicher 1980 p.109.
104 Sherman 1988 p.390.
105 Gadamer 1989 p.273.
106 Id. p.263.
107 Id. p.238.
108 Id.
109 Id. p.341.
110 Bleicher 1980 p.114.
111 Id. p.115.
112 Gadamer 1989 p.351.
113 See further Gadamer 1980 pp.136-140 where Gadamer sets out his thesis that "misunderstanding is language bound" (p.139).
114 Outhwaite 1985 p.29.
115 Bleicher 1980 p.125.
116 Betti has accused Gadamer of offering a mere descriptive phenomenology. This is a result of Betti's concern with offering a methodology of hermeneutics, and thus Gadamer seeks to show that it is Betti who is deficient in this respect.
117 Bleicher 1980 p.125.
118 Id. p.124.

119 Dworkin 1986 p.62.
120 See Chapter Two supra.
121 Dworkin 1986 p.420 n.2.
122 Id.
123 Ricoeur 1970.
124 Bleicher 1980 p.155.
125 Habermas 1980 p.205.
126 Id.
127 Bleicher 1980 p.156.
128 Habermas 1980 p.190.
129 See further Outhwaite 1985 p.37.
130 See Habermas 1980 pp.186-187.
131 This suggestion is put forward by David Hoy in Hoy 1985 p.50. This discussion is based on Hoy 1985, Hoy 1987 and Culler 1979.
132 See Hoy 1987 pp.336-339 and Kramer 1988 for a discussion of the 'paradox of the signature'.
133 Derrida 1981 p.221.
134 Hoy 1985 p.55.
135 For the sense of this claim see Hoy p.56.
136 Id. p.57.
137 Id. p.62.
138 Dworkin 1986 p.420 n.2.
139 Id.
140 Id. p.62.
141 But see Donato 1988 pp.1538-1541. Donato argues that Dworkin "makes the past a speaker of too much authority" (p.1541). This debate seems to parallel that as to which conception of law is 'best' on the constructive model.
142 Outhwaite 1985 p.38.
143 See further here, Sherman 1988 at pp.396-402. Sherman concludes that interpretation in the law is the application of 'legal-method'. However, he seems to fail to see that this still entails an unconscious application of effective-history. Nevertheless, he seems to reach the correct conclusion in arguing that lawyers need to "open their prejudices to challenge, and the ability to reflect upon the force of tradition" (at p.401).
144 See Joseph 1989 where Philip Joseph argues that Gadamer's philosophical hermeneutics accounts for "the rationality of constitutional change" (p.123) and points out that the Antipodean judiciary are confronting their prejudices to challenge the sovereign text. He concludes that hopefully "the waiting may not be long" (p.123) for our judiciary to follow suit.
145 Derrida is one of the main influences on Fish, and there are many similarities in their positions.
146 Hoy 1985 p.63.
147 See Sherman 1988 p.394.
148 This point is also made by Hoy - see Hoy 1987 p.337.

149 Id. pp.337-339.
150 Id. p.338.
151 Knapp 1991 pp.327-328. Knapp seems to be referring to Dworkin 1986 p.53.
152 Dworkin 1986 p.53 (our italics).
153 Hoy 1987 p.338.
154 Hoy 1991 p.353.
155 Id.
156 Id.
157 Hoy 1987 p.340.
158 Id.
159 Id. p.342.
160 Id. p.344.
161 See Dworkin 1986 p.66.
162 This view is most associated with the Critical Legal Studies movement.
163 This seems to be Roberto Unger's view - see Unger 1983.
164 Hoy 1987 p.346.
165 See Dworkin 1986. p.421 n.12.
166 See Hoy 1991 p.354. See Knapp p.328.
167 Dworkin 1986 p.268.
168 Id. p.404-407.
169 Id. p.405.
170 Id. p.406.
171 Hoy 1991 pp.347-348.
172 Dworkin 1986 p.274.
173 Hoy is in agreement here. He points out that as Dworkin's account of interpretation results in inevitable controversy, no one account can ever be said to be definitive - see Hoy 1991 p.349.
174 Andrei Marmor gives an account of this confusion - see Marfnor 1991 pp.405-412.
175 Bleicher 1980 p.235.
176 Dworkin 1986 p.420 n.2.
177 Hohim does not necessarily lead to the adoption of a coherence theory - see Marmor 1991 pp.405-406 for a discussion of this in relation to Dworkin.
178 See further Hoy 1991 p.350.
179 Hoy 1985 p.64.
180 This appears to be the conclusion that Hoy draws - see Hoy 1987 p.354, However, he does not mention the revisions to Dworkin's interpretive theory that are necessary for this conclusion.
181 Hoy 1991 p.355.
182 Dworkin 1991 p.365. Dworkin describes the misunderstanding of this claim as the 'right answer farrago'.
183 See further here Guest 1992 p.160 n.18.
184 Dworkin has pointed out that some critics, such as Brian Barry and Joseph Raz have suggested that he has changed the character and importance of the

one-right-answer claim. Dworkin states that he has not. He does however seem to be down-playing its role compared with *Taking Rights Seriously*. There appears to have been a change of emphasis, if not importance - see Dworkin 1991 p.382 n.1.

185 Gadamer 1989 p.261.

186 See for example, Hoy 1987 at pp.332 and 353 and Henley 1990 p.21.

187 Dworkin also mentions this connection - see Dworkin 1986 p.424 n. 17.

188 See Rawls 1971 pp.47-50.

189 See Hoy 1985 p.64.

190 Hoy 1991 pp.356-357.

191 See further Bleicher 1980 p.234.

192 James Donato comes close to a similar conclusion, although he sides with Habermas in attacking Gadamer for putting too much stress on tradition and as a result is critical of Dworkin's theory of interpretation - see Donato 1988 pp.1540-1541. He states that "Dworkin's subjectivism clearly suggests ... the model of an open society". (p.1541)

Bibliography

I Books and Articles Cited

Alexander, L, (1987), 'Striking Back at the Empire: A Brief Survey of Problems in Dworkin's Theory of Law', 6 Law and Philosophy 419.

Altman, A, (1986), 'Legal Realism, Critical Legal Studies, and Dworkin', 15 Philosophy and Public Affairs 205.

Balkin, J.M., (1993), 'Understanding Legal Understanding: The Legal Subject and the Problem of Legal Coherence', 103 Yale, L.J. 105.

Barry, B, (1984), 'Imitations of Justice', a review of Michael Walzer, *Spheres of Justice*, 84 Columbia Editions du Seuil Law Rev. 806.

Barthes, R, (1966), *Critique et Verite, Editions du Seuil.*

Bix, B, (1993), *Law, Language and Legal Determinancy*, Clarendon Press.

Bleicher, J, (1980), *Contemporary Hermeneutics*, Routledge and Kegan Paul.

Brooks, P, (1990), 'Bouillabaisse', a review of Stanley Fish, *Doing What Comes Naturally*, 99 Yale L.J. 1147.

Caney, S, (1991), 'Sandel's Critique of the Primacy of Justice: A Liberal Rejoinder', 21 British Journal of Political Science 511.

Caney, S, (1992), 'Liberalism and Communitarianism: A Misconceived Debate', 40 Political Studies 273.

Christie, G, (1986), 'Dworkin's "Empire"' a review of Ronald Dworkin, *Law's Empire*, Duke L.J. 157.

Cochran, C, (1989), 'The Thin Theory of Community: The Communitarians and their Critics', 37 Political Studies 422.

Coleman, J, (1984), 'Negative and Positive Positivism', in Cohen (ed.), *Ronald Dworkin and Contemporary Jurisprudence*, Duckworth, at pp.28-48.

Cragg, W, (1986), 'Two Concepts of Community or Moral Theory and Canadian Culture', 25 Dialogue 31.

Culler, J, (1979), 'Jacques Derrida', in Sturrock (ed.) *Structuralism and Since*, Oxford University Press, at pp.154-180.

Dalrymple, J, (13.06.1993), 'Judges in the Dock', The Sunday Times, Section Two, p.1.

Derrida, J, (1981), *Dissemination*, Athlone Press.

Donato, J, (1988), 'Dworkin and Subjectivity in Legal Interpretation', 40 Stanford Law Rev. 1517.

Downing, R, and Thigpen, L, (1986), 'Beyond Shared Understandings', 14 Political Theory 451.

Dworkin, R, (1977), *Taking Rights Seriously*, Duckworth.

Dworkin, R, (1977(a)), 'No Right Answer?', in Hacker and Raz (eds.), *Law, Morality and Society: Essays in Honour of H.L.A.Hart*, Oxford, at pp.58-84.

Dworkin, R, (1983), 'A Reply by Ronald Dworkin', in Cohen (ed.), *Ronald Dworkin and contemporary Jurisprudence*, Duckworth, at pp.247-300. 'My Reply to Stanley Fish (and Walter Benn Michaels): Please Don't Talk About Objectivity Any More', in Mitchell (ed.), *The Politics of Interpretation*, Chicago, at pp.287-313.

Dworkin, R, (1986), *Law's Empire*, Fontana.

Dworkin, R, (1986(a)), *A Matter of Principle*, Oxford University Press.

Dworkin, R, (1987), 'The Bork Nomination', 34 New York Review of Books 3.

Dworkin, R, (1989), 'Liberal Community', 77 California Law Rev. 479.

Dworkin, R, (1991), 'Pragmatism, Right Answers, and True Banality', in Brint and Weaver (eds.), *Pragmatism in Law and Society*, Westview, at pp.359-388.

Finnis, J, (1980), *Natural Law and Natural Rights*, Oxford University Press.

Fish, S, (1989), *Doing what Comes Naturally: Change, Rhetoric, and the Practice of Theory in Literary and Legal Studies*, Oxford University Press.

Fletcher, G, (1983), 'The Watchdog of Neutrality', a review of Bruce Ackerman, *Social Justice in the Liberal Stage*, 83 Columbia Law Rev. 2099.

Fuller, L, (1969), *The Morality of Law*, Yale University Press.

Gadamer, H-G, (1989), *Truth and Method*, Sheed and Ward, 2nd revd. edn.

Gadamer, H-G, (1980), 'The Universality of the Hermeneutical Problem', in Josef Bleicher, *Contemporary Hermeneutics*, Routledge and Kegan Paul, at pp.128-140.

Gallie, (1965), 'Essentially Contested Concepts', 56 Proceedings of the Aristotelian Society 167.

Galston, W, (1989), 'Community, Democracy, Philosophy (The Political Thought of Michael Walzer)', 17 Political Theory 119.

Gardbaum, S, (1991), 'Why the Liberal State Can Promote Moral Ideals After All', 104 Harv. Law Rev. 1350.

Giddens, A, (1985), 'Jurgen Habermas', in Skinner (ed.), *The Return of Grand Theory in the Human Sciences*, Cambridge University Press, at pp.121-139.

Guest, S, (1987), 'Review of Joseph Raz, *The Morality of Freedom*', 103 LQR 642.

Guest, S, (1992), *Ronald Dworkin*, Edinburgh University Press.

Gutmann, A, (1985), 'Communitarian Critics of Liberalism', 14 Philosophy and Public Affairs 308.

Haakonssen, K, (1981), 'The Limits of Reason and the Infinity of Argument', 67 Archiv fur Rechts-und Sozialphilosophie 491.

Habermas, J, (1980), 'The Hermeneutic Claim to Universality' in Josef Bleicher, *Contemporary Hermeneutics*, Routledge and Kegan Paul, at pp.181-211.

Hart, H.L.A., (1961), *The Concept of Law*, Clarendon Press, 2nd ed., 1994 ed. Raz.

Hart, H.L.A., (1983) *Essays in Jurisprudence and Philosophy* , Oxford University Press.

Henley, K, (1990), 'Protestant Hermeneutics and the Rule of Law: Gadamer and Dworkin', 3 Ratio Juris 14.

Hirsch, H.N., (1986), 'The Threnody of Liberalism', 14 Political Theory 423.
Hoffman, L.H., (1989), 'Review of Simon Lee, *Judging Judges*', 105 LQR 140.
Hoy, D, (1985), 'Jacques Derrida', in Skinner (ed.), *The Return of Grand Theory in the Human Sciences*, Cambridge University Press, at pp.43-64.
Hoy, D, (1987), 'Dworkin's Constructive Optimism v. Deconstructive Legal Nihilism', 6 Law and Philosophy 321.
Hoy, D, (1991), 'Is Legal Originalism Compatible with Philosophical Pragmatism?', in Brint and Weaver (eds.) *Pragmatism in Law and Society*, Westview, at pp.343-358.
Hume, D, (1739), *A Treatise of Human Nature*.
Hutchinson, A, (1987), 'Indiana Dworkin and Law's Empire', a review of Ronald Dworkin. *Law's Empire*, 96 Yale, L.J., 637.
Joseph, P, (1989), 'Beyond Parliamentary Sovereignty', 18 Anglo-American Law Rev. 91.
Kahn, P, (1989), 'Community in Contemporary Constitutional Theory', 99 Yale L.J., 1.
Knapp, S, (1991), 'Practice, Purpose, and Interpretive Controversy', in Brint and Weaver (eds.), *Pragmatism in Law and Society*, Westview, at pp.323-342.
Kramer, M, (1988), 'The Rule of Misrecognition in the Hart of Jurisprudence', 8 OJLS 401.
Kukathas, C, and Pettit, P, (1990), *A Theory of Justice and its Critics*, Polity.
Kymlicka, W, (1989), *Liberalism, Community, and Culture*, Oxford University Press.
Larmore, C, (1984), 'Review of Michael Sandel, *Liberalism and the Limits of Justice*', 81 The Journal of Philosophy 338.
Larmore, C, (1987), *Patterns of Moral Complexity*, Cambridge University Press.
Lee, S, (1990), 'Law and Literature: Goodbye Austin, Hello Austen', 10 OJLS 252.
Lyons, D, (1977), 'Review: Principles, Positivism, and Legal Theory', 87 Yale L.J. 415.
McDonald, M, (1992), 'Liberalism, Community, and Culture', a review of Will Kymlicka, *Liberalism, Community, and Culture*, 42 University of Toronto L.J. 113.
MacCormick, N, (1978), *Legal Reasoning and Legal Theory*, Oxford University Press.
MacCormick, N, (1981), 'The Limits of Reason: A Reply to Dr. Knud Haakonssen', 67 Archiv fur Rechts-und Sozialphilosophie 504.
MacCormick, N, (1982), *Legal Right and Social Democracy*, Oxford University Press.
Macedo, S, (1991), *Liberal Virtues*, Oxford University Press.
MacIntyre, A, (1981), *After Virtue*, Notre Dame.
Marmor, A, (1991), 'Coherence, Holism, and Interpretation: The Epistemic Foundations of Dworkin's Legal Theory', 10 Law and Philosophy 383.
Marmor, A, (1995), *Law and Interpretation*, Clarendon Press.
Marmor, A, (1992), *Interpretation and Legal Theory*, Clarendon Press.

Moore, M, (1995), 'Interpreting Interpretation' in *Law and Interpretation*, ed. Andrei Marmor, Ch. 1, Clarendon Press.
Mosher, M, (1991), 'Boundary Revisions: The Deconstruction of Moral Personality in Rawls, Nozick, Sandel, and Parfit', 39 Political Studies 287.
Nozick, R, (1974), *Anarchy, State, and Utopia*, Basic Books.
Olivier, L, (1982), *Confessions of an Actor*, Wiedenfeld and Nicolson Ltd.
Outhwaite, W, (1985), 'Hans-Georg Gadamer', in Skinner (ed.), *The Return of Grand Theory in the Human Sciences*, Cambridge University Press, at pp.21-39.
Parfit, D, (1984), *Reasons and Persons*, Oxford University Press.
Plato, (1955), *The Republic*, trans. Lee, Penguin.
Rawls, J, (1971), *A Theory of Justice*, Oxford University Press.
Rawls, J, (1985), 'Justice as Fairness: Political not Metaphysical', 14 Philosophy and Public Affairs 223.
Rawls, J, (1987), 'The Idea of an Overlapping Consensus', 7 OJLS 1.
Raz, J, (1972), 'Legal Principles and the Limits of Law', 81 Yale L.J. 823.
Raz, J, (1983), 'A Postscript', in Cohen (ed.), *Ronald Dworkin and Contemporary Jurisprudence*, Duckworth, at pp.81-86.
Raz, J, (1986), *The Morality of Freedom*, Oxford University Press.
Reaume, D, (1989), 'Is Integrity a Virtue? Dworkin's Theory of Legal Obligation', 39 University of Toronto L.J. 380.
Ricoeur, P, (1970), *Freud and Psychology: An Essay on Interpretation*, Yale.
Sadurski, W, (1990), 'Joseph Raz on Liberal Neutrality and the Harm Principle', 10 OJLS 122.
Sandel, M, (1982), *Liberalism and the Limits of Justice*, Cambridge University Press.
Selznick, P, (1987), 'The Idea of a Communitarian Morality', 75 California Law Rev. 445.
Selznick, P, (1989), 'Dworkin's Unfinished Task', 77 California Law Rev. 505.
Sherman, B, (1988), 'Hermeneutics in Law', 51 MLR 386.
Silver, C, (1987), 'Elmer's Case: A Legal Positivist Replies to Dworkin', 6 Law and Philosophy 381.
Simmonds, N, (1987), 'Imperial Visions and Mundane Practices', Cambridge L.J. 465.
Simmonds, N, (1990), 'Why Conventionalism Does Not Collapse Into Pragmatism', Cambridge L.J. 63.
Skinner, Q, (1985), 'Introduction', in Skinner (ed.), *The Return of Grand Theory in the Human Sciences*, Cambridge University Press.
Smith, S, (1990), 'The Pursuit of Pragmatism', 100 Yale L.J. 409.
Soper, P, (1983), 'Legal Theory and the Obligation of a Judge: The Hart/Dworkin Dispute', in Cohen (ed.), *Ronald Dworkin and Contemporary Jurisprudence*, Duckworth, at pp.3-27.
Soper, P, (1987), 'Dworkin's Domain', a review of Ronald Dworkin, *Law's Empire*, 100 Harv. Law Rev. 1166.

Stick, J, (1986), 'Literary Imperialism: Assessing the results of Dworkin's Interpretive Turn in *Law's Empire*', 34 UCLA Law Rev. 371.

Taylor, C, (1985), *Philosophical Papers: Volume Two*, Cambridge University Press.

Unger, R, (1983), 'The Critical Legal Studies Movement', Harv. Law Rev. 584.

Waldron, J, (1989), 'Particular Values and Critical Morality' 77 California Law Rev. 561.

Waldron, J, (1995), 'Legislators' Intentions and International Legislation', in *Law and Interpretation*, ed. Andrei Marmor, Ch.9, Clarendon.

Walzer, M, (1983), *Spheres of Justice*, Basic Books.

Westmoreland, R, (1991), 'Dworkin and Legal Pragmatism', 11 OJLS 174.

II Cases Cited

Anisminic Ltd v. Foreign Compensation Commission [1969] 2 A.C. 147.

Bowers v. Hardwick, (1986) 478 U.S. 186.

Henningsen v. Bloomfield Motors Inc. 32 N.J. 358, 161 A.2d 69 (1960).

McLoughlin v. O'Brian [1983] 1 A.C. 410.

Riggs v. Palmer 115 N.Y. 506, 22 N.E. 188 (1889).

Steelworkers v. Weber (1979) 443 U.S. 193.

III Other Works of Relevance

Allen, T.R.S., (1993), 'Justice and Fairness in Law's Empire', Cambridge L.J. 64.

Balkin, J, (1987), 'Deconstructive Practice and Legal Theory', 96 Yale L.J. 921.

Bell, D, (1971), 'Hard Cases and the Need for Principles', 81 Yale L.J. 921.

Betti, E, (1980), 'Hermeneutics as the General Methodology of the *Geisteswissenschaften*', in Josef Bleicher, *Contemporary Hermeneutics*, Routledge and Kegan Paul, at pp.51-94.

Beyleveld, D, and Brownsword, R, (1987), 'Practice made Perfect', 50MLR 662.

Brewer, S, (1988), 'Figuring the Law: Holism and Tropological Inference in Legal Interpretation', 97 Yale L.J. 823.

Bruns, G, (1983), 'Law as Hermeneutics: A Response to Ronald Dworkin', in Mitchell (ed.), *The Politics of Interpretation*, Chicago University Press, at pp.315-320.

Cotterrell, R, (1987), 'Liberalism's Empire: Reflections on Ronald Dworkin's Liberal Philosophy', American Bar Foundation Research Journal 507.

De Marneffe, P, (1990), 'Liberalism, Liberty, and Neutrality', 19 Philosophy and Public Affairs 253.

Duncanson, I, (1989), 'Power, Interpretation, and Ronald Dworkin', 9 University of Tasmania Law Rev. 278.

Fallon, R, (1987), 'A Constructivist Coherence Theory of Constitutional Interpretation', 100 Harv. Law Rev. 1189.
Finnis, J, (1987), 'On Reason and Authority in Law's Empire', 6 Law and Philosophy 357.
Fuller, S, (1988), 'Playing Without a Full Deck: Scientific Realism and the Cognitive Limits of Legal Theory', 97 Yale L.J. 549.
Guest, S, (1986), 'Review of Philip Soper, *A Theory of Law*', 102 LQR 332.
Kress, K, (1987), 'The Interpretive Turn', 97 Ethics 834.
Kymlicka, W, (1991), *Contemporary Political Philosophy*, Oxford University Press.
Lee, S, (1988), 'Law's British Empire', 8 OJLS 278.
Lee, S, (1988), *Judging Judges*, Faber and Faber.
Leonard, S, (1989), 'How Not to Write About Political Theory (A Response to Wallach)', 17 Political Theory 101.
Levinson, S, (1982), 'Law as Literature', 60 Texas Law Rev. 373.
Lyons, D, (1983), 'Moral Aspects of Legal Theory', in Cohen (ed.), *Ronald Dworkin and Contemporary Jurisprudence*, Duckworth, at pp.49-69.
Lyons, D, (1987), 'Reconstructing Legal Theory', a review of Ronald Dworkin, *Law's Empire*, 16 Philosophy and Public Affairs 379.
Michaels, W.B., (1983), 'Is There a Politics of Interpretation?', in Mitchell (ed.), *The Politics of Interpretation*, Chicago University Press, at pp.335-345.
Posner, R, (1988), *Law and Literature: A Misunderstood Relation*, Harvard University Press.
Postema, G, (1987), "Protestant" Interpretation and Social Practices', 6 Law and Philosophy 283.
Rakowski, E, (1991), 'Posner's Pragmatism', 104 Harv. Law Rev. 1681.
Raz, J, (1986), 'Dworkin: A New Link on the Chain', a review of Ronald Dworkin, *A Matter of Principle*, 74 California Law Rev. 1103.
Ricoeur, P, (1980), 'Existence and Hermeneutics', in Josef Bleicher, *Contemporary Hermeneutics*, Routledge and Kegan Paul, at pp.236-256.
Sagoff, M, (1983), 'The Limits of Justice', a review of Michael Sandel, *Liberalism and the Limits of Justics*, 92 Yale L.J. 1065.
Sandel, M, (1989), 'Moral Argument and Liberal Toleration: Abortion and Homosexuality', 77 California Law Rev. 521.
Simmonds, N, (1986), *Central Issues in Jurisprudence*, Sweet and Maxwell.
Smith, S, (1990), 'The Restoration of Tolerance', 78 California Law Rev. 305.
Soper, P, (1989), 'Legal Theory and the Claim of Authority', 18 Philosophy and Public Affairs 209.
Stick, J, (1986), 'Can Nihilism be Pragmatic?', 100 Harv. Law Rev. 332.
Wallach, J, (1987), 'Liberals, Communitarians, and the Tasks of Political Theory', 15 Political Theory 581.
Williams, B, (1989), 'Dworkin on Community and Critical Interests', 77 California Law Rev. 515.

Index

acceptance and validity 14
aesthetics 20, 76-7, 80, 85, 152
Alexander, L. 64
Altman, A. 61-2
art and literature 29-30
authorial intention within
interpretation 87-91

Balkin, J. M. 32
Barry, B. 139
Barthes, R. 98
Bentham, J. 132
best light requirement 152
Betti, E. 144-5, 154
Bix, B. 40, 41
Brennan, J. 64
Brooks, P. 89, 97, 98

Caney, S. 109
Cavell, S. 90
chain of law 94-5
integrity and 75-87
chain novelists 81-2
Chandler, R. 76
Charley Lau objection 97
checkerboard statutes 70-1, 73-5,
112
Christie, A. 76, 79, 80, 82
Christie, G. 40
citizenship 105-6
Coleman, J. 15, 18, 22-3, 44, 51, 52
common life 140-1
communitarianism 113, 124
and liberalism 113-16, 119, 130-41
communities
models preconditional for
associative obligations 111-12
true 106-13
as unities of unities 124
well-being of 115
compromises 74-5
concepts and conceptions
distinguished 47-51
constitutive theory of the self 134-5
continuity theory of ethics 121
conventionalism 48, 49, 51, 56-7, 93,
94
arguments against 58-61
'bilateral' 59
Dworkin's arguments against 55-61
pragmatism and interpretation 47-68
strict and soft 15, 18, 51-4, 58
two-stage defence of 59
unilateral 59
conventions, explicit and
implicit extensions of 52-3
convictions 56-7
Cragg, W. 137

deconstructionist theory 148, 150-1,
153, 154-5
Derrida, J. 142, 147-9, 150-1
154
Dickens, C. 81, 82
disagreements, legal, in particular
cases 33-4
discretion
senses as depending on context 5-6
see also judicial discretion
dissemination 147. 148
distorted communication 147
Downing, L. 140-1
Dworkin, R.
change of methodology 43-4
early views and critics 1-28
methodological change 43

three conceptions of law 48
Dworkin, R: writings
'Hard Cases' 12, 16
'How Law is Like Literature' 76-8, 80, 83, 87-8
Law's Empire 1, 29, 32, 33, 37-40, 42, 43, 47, 52, 62, 74, 83, 84, 86, 87, 89, 113, 116, 119, 123, 125, 133, 152
'Liberal Community' 113, 116, 125, 133
A Matter of Principle 64, 123, 132
'My Reply to Stanley Fish (and Walter Benn Michaels)' 81
'No Right Answer?' 21
'On Interpretation and Objectivity' 80, 83
Taking Rights Seriously 1, 23, 29, 33, 40, 43, 51, 61-2
'The Bork Nomination' 64
'The Model of Rules I' 1, 3, 13, 22, 43
'Why Liberals Should Care About Equality' 124-5

effective-history (*Wirkungsgeschichte*) 143-4, 150
embeddedness thesis 95, 110, 116, 133-5, 143
equality of resources, achieving 132
ethical environment, and will of majority 113-4
ethical ideals, reconciling 122
ethics 115, 116, 118
and priority 119-25

fairness and fair play 70-1, 74, 106
Fellini, Federico 90
fictional texts, interpreting 30
fidelity towards law 34
Finnis, J, 20
Fish, S. 58, 66, 76-9, 80-5, 87-9, 93-5, 145
fit
criteria to be adopted 86-7
interpretation as according with requirements of 55-8
force, collective 49-50
Fowles, J. 88
fraternity *see* communities
Fuller, L. 60

Gadamer, H-G. 89, 97, 142-9, 152 154-7
compared with Dworkin 142, 145-6
Gadamer-Habermas debate 142-9
Dworkin and 149-54
Gallie, W.B. 47
Galston, W. 139
Gardbaum, S. 120
good life, the 131
grounds of law 33-4
Guest, S. 50, 51, 61
Gutmann, A. 114, 135

Haakonssen, K. 19-21, 34
Habermas, J. 142, 146-50, 154
see also Gadamer-Habermas debate
Hamlet 79-80, 88-9
hard cases 3, 19, 21, 33, 40, 77
Dworkin on 12, 16
Hart, H.L.A. 1, 7, 23, 39, 60
on acceptance/validity distinction 14-15
concept of law 50-1
on criterion of identity 11-12
Dworkin on 6, 23
on rules 10
The Concept of Law 2-3
Hayek, F. 60
Hegel, G. W. F. 136, 141
Hercules 12, 40, 41, 73, 74, 153-4 157
hermeneutics, law and 142-54, 155, 156

Hirsch, E. D. 138
How, D. 151-7
Hume, D. 108
Hutchinson, A. 49-50

identity, criterion of 11-12
identity and self-reference, community and 114-16
incommensurability thesis 119-20, 151, 154, 155, 156
individual autonomy 121
individuation 8
integrity
and chain of law 75-87
and interpretation 69-104
and the moral legitimacy of law 105-6
pure and inclusive 70
as a virtue 69-75
see also law as integrity
intention
definition 89
and interpretation 31-2, 87-91
see also authorial intention
interpretation 58
constructive and creative 75
definition 29
and intention 31-2, 87-91
as uncertain enterprise 147-8
see also hermeneutics
interpretive constraints, nature of 78-83
interpretive convictions as checks on one another 80-1, 86
interpretive judgements, and subjectivity 83-7
interpretive theory 29-46

judges
ideal *see* Hercules
as philosophers 96
judicial conclusions, differing 40-1
judicial custom 11-12
judicial discretion 10-13, 18-19
and defences of legal positivism 5-6
as weak 21-2
justice
aims of liberal principles of 132
maximin view 75
as a virtue 108-9

Kahn, P. 107, 110, 111
Kant, I. 73, 136
Knapp, S. 151
Kymlicka, W. 132, 135-6

Larmore, C. 117, 130
law
as hard facts 22-3
as integrity 48, 53-4, 92, 93, 155
as social convention 23
core and penumbral uses of term 35-7, 39
legal disagreement, nature of 32-4
legal positivism 1-3
Dworkin's critique 3-24
first defence of 6-13
as interpretive idea 78-9
second defence of 13-24
legal rights 62, 63
legitimacy *see* moral legitimacy
legitimisation crisis 137-8
liberal community 113-19
liberal neutrality *see* moral establishment, limited
liberal state, restrictions imposable by 117-18
liberalism
and communitarianism 113-16, 119, 130-41
definition 119
linguisticality 144
literature *see* art and literature

MacCormick, N. 15-22, 34, 116-18, 120, 123

McDonald, M. 135
Macedo, S. 117, 125, 134, 135
MacIntyre, A. 110, 131, 133-6
market, liberalism and the 132
Marmor, A. 32, 87
maximin view of justice 75
meaning 29-30
method, science linked with 145
Mill, J. S. 117
Milton, J. 81
moral establishment, limited 117
moral judgements 42
moral legitimacy of law, and
  integrity 105-6
moral values, law as means of
  enforcing 116-17
morality, as distinguished from law 51
Mosher, M. 134, 136

negative positivism 22
no-right-answer thesis 29, 39-40
noble lie 62, 63, 64, 92
Nozick, R. 73, 106, 133

obligations, associative or communal
  107-11
Olivier, L. 30
one-right-answer thesis 18-21, 39-42,
  43
Outhwaite, W. 150

paradox of the signature 148
paternalism 114
perfectionism and non-perfectionism
  131-2
personal morality 115, 116
Plato 122
pluralism 137
  'truth of' 119-20
political community, citizens'
  identification with 118-19
positivism *see* legal positivism;
  negative positivism
Posner, R. 95
pragmatics, universal 154
pragmatism 48-9, 61-5, 71-3, 92-4
  see also conventionalism,
    pragmatism and interpretation
principles
  consistency 55
  defined 12
  of discretion 10-11
  distinguished from rules 4, 8, 9,
    15-16
  role of, in legal reasoning 3-4,
    17-18
  weight dimension 15-16
protected expectations 52

Rawls, J. 47, 74, 75, 108, 121,
  130-2, 133, 156
Raz, J. 7, 13, 52, 85, 120-1, 123, 130
Reaume, D. 70
reflective equilibrium 156
respect for self and others 117-18,
  120, 123
rhetoric 96, 98
Ricoeur, P. 146
rules
  defining 10
  distinguished from principles 4, 8,
    9, 15-16
  primary and secondary 2

Sandel, M. 108, 110, 114, 115-6,
  133-6
self
  constitutive theory of 134-5
  respect for 117-18, 120, 123
Selznick, P. 115, 116, 124
semantic theories of law 35-7, 49
sexual life 115,116

Shakespeare, W. 30, 79-80, 88-90
Sidgwick, H. 132
Simmonds, N. 38, 39, 48-50, 54-
skepticism, internal and external 42, 84, 87
slavery 83-4
Smith, S 92-3, 94
social sciences 150
Soper, P. 36-7, 39, 49, 51, 53, 54, 71-3
sources test 7
Stick, J. 90-1
strategy, consistency 55
subjectivity, imterpretive judgements and 83-7
substance, judgements of 86-7
surprise 59

Taylor, C. 107, 133, 136-8
theory, Fish on 96-8
Thigpen, R. 140-1
tolerance
  attacks on liberal 113-15
  doctrine of, and liberal society 37-9, 119-20

unitary phenomenon 145
utilitatianism 132
  and justice 73

validity, and acceptance 14
values, incommensurability of 85-6
virtue, justice as a 108-9

Waldron, J. 32, 135, 140
Walzer, M. 111, 113, 115, 133, 138-41
well-being, volitional and critical 122
Westmoreland, R. 73-5, 106
Williams, B. 134
Wirkungsgeschichte ('effective history') 143-4, 150

For Product Safety Concerns and Information please contact our EU representative GPSR@taylorandfrancis.com Taylor & Francis Verlag GmbH, Kaufingerstraße 24, 80331 München, Germany

Batch number: 10725923

Printed by Printforce, the Netherlands